Improving
Adolescent Literacy

Content Area Strategies at Work

Improving Adolescent Literacy

Content Area Strategies at Work

Douglas Fisher
San Diego State University

Nancy Frey
San Diego State University

PEARSON
Merrill
Prentice Hall

Upper Saddle River, New Jersey
Columbus, Ohio

Library of Congress Cataloging-in-Publication Data

Fisher, Douglas
  Improving adolescent literacy : content area strategies at work / Douglas Fisher,
Nancy Frey.
    p. cm.
  ISBN 0-13-111348-8
  1. Reading (Secondary) 2. Content area reading. I. Frey, Nancy.
II. Title
  LB 1632.F57 2004
  428.4'·071'2—dc21   2003013775

Vice President and Executive Publisher: Jeffery W. Johnston
Senior Editor: Linda Ashe Montgomery
Editorial Assistant: Laura Weaver
Production Editor: Mary Harlan
Production Coordinator: Carlisle Publishers Services
Design Coordinator: Diane C. Lorenzo
Cover Design: Jeff Vanik
Cover Image: Corbis
Text Design and Illustrations: Carlisle Publishers Services
Production Manager: Pamela D. Bennett
Director of Marketing: Ann Castel Davis
Marketing Manager: Darcy Betts Prybella
Marketing Coordinator: Tyra Poole

This book was set in Souvenir by Carlisle Communications, Ltd. It was printed and bound by Courier Kendallville, Inc. The cover was printed by Phoenix Color Corp.

Pearson Education Ltd.
Pearson Education Singapore Pte. Ltd.
Pearson Education Canada, Ltd.
Pearson Education–Japan
Pearson Education Australia Pty. Limited
Pearson Education North Asia Ltd.
Pearson Educación de Mexico, S.A. de C.V.
Pearson Education Malaysia Pte. Ltd.

10 9 8 7 6 5
ISBN: 0-13-111348-8

Preface

We believe that teachers matter. We believe that students can learn when taught well. We believe that an interesting curriculum and quality instruction are critical ingredients for student success. We believe that literacy is the foundation for learning. And we believe that literacy instruction can be infused into all content areas. Now that you understand our perspective on teaching and learning, we invite you to examine the research-based strategies that we have found to be especially useful in secondary classrooms.

In this book, we present a number of instructional strategies with examples across traditional content areas. These strategies include:

- Anticipatory activities
- Read-alouds and shared reading
- Questioning
- Notetaking and note making
- Graphic organizers
- Vocabulary instruction
- Writing to learn
- Reciprocal teaching

The purpose of each of these instructional strategies is to enhance students' comprehension of the content—the ultimate goal of all educators. Together we can help adolescents improve their understanding of the world and their role in it.

Text Organization

This book is organized into ten chapters. In chapter 1, we present a number of common questions that teachers ask about content area literacy instruction. Chapters 2 through 9 each discuss one of the instructional strategies identified above. In each of these chapters, we first present a scenario of a teacher using the strategy. We then provide a rationale for this strategy as well as the research base that supports its use. We end each of these chapters with an example of the strategy being used in an English, science, social studies, mathematics, and elective class. The final chapter of the book provides information about test preparation that can be infused into all content areas. We also use a number of margin notes to provide readers with additional information including web sites, definitions, examples, further readings, and reflective questions.

Acknowledgments

We have had the opportunity to learn alongside a number of skilled teachers as they delivered their content in ways that have increased their students' literacy learning. We thank all of the teachers who invited us in and provided us with detailed information about their practice.

In addition, we need to acknowledge that this book would not have been completed without the support, assistance, and encouragement of several key individuals in the City Heights Educational Collaborative. Rita ElWardi, Tom Fehrenbacher, Christine Johnson, and Lee Mongrue have been with us every step of the way. Their contributions have been invaluable. Doug Williams, the principal of Hoover High School, has been an inspiring leader, mentor, and friend throughout this project. Dr. Ian Pumpian's vision of schools in which all students are respected and valued learners has been a constant force in our writing. And finally, our editor Linda Montgomery's belief in this project and her skill in guiding us from concept through production have resulted in this book that you are reading.

We would also like to thank the reviewers who offered their thoughtful comments as this work progressed. Their feedback made this a better book and we thank them. These reviewers include: Thomas W. Bean, University of Nevada, Las Vegas; Carole L. Bond, The University of Memphis; Jeannine S. Hirtle, University of Texas at Arlington; William Kist, Kent State University, Stark Campus; Jay A. Monson, Utah State University; Gregory P. Risner, University of North Alabama; and Mary M. Witte, Baylor University.

Douglas Fisher & Nancy Frey

Contents

Chapter 6

Picture This: Graphic Organizers in the Classroom   103

Chapter 7

Word for Word: Vocabulary Development Across the Curriculum   121

Educator Learning Center:
An Invaluable Online Resource

Merrill Education and the Association for Supervision and Curriculum Development (ASCD) invite you to take advantage of a new online resource, one that provides access to the top research and proven strategies associated with ASCD and Merrill—the Educator Learning Center. At **www. EducatorLearningCenter.com** you will find resources that will enhance your students' understanding of course topics and of current educational issues, in addition to being invaluable for further research.

How the Educator Learning Center Will Help Your Students Become Better Teachers

With the combined resources of Merrill Education and ASCD, you and your students will find a wealth of tools and materials to better prepare them for the classroom.

Research

- More than 600 articles from the ASCD journal *Educational Leadership* discuss everyday issues faced by practicing teachers.
- A direct link on the site to Research Navigator™ gives students access to many of the leading education journals, as well as extensive content detailing the research process.
- Excerpts from Merrill Education texts give your students insights on important topics of instructional methods, diverse populations, assessment, classroom management, technology, and refining classroom practice.

Classroom Practice

- Hundreds of lesson plans and teaching strategies are categorized by content area and age range.
- Case studies and classroom video footage provide virtual field experience for student reflection.
- Computer simulations and other electronic tools keep your students abreast of today's classrooms and current technologies.

Look Into the Value of Educator Learning Center Yourself

Preview the value of this educational environment by visiting **www.EducatorLearningCenter.com** and clicking on "Demo." For a free 4-month subscription to the Educator Learning Center in conjunction with this text, simply contact your Merrill/Prentice Hall sales representative.

Chapter 1

Teachers Matter and What They Do Matters Most: Using Literacy Strategies, Grouping, and Texts to Promote Learning

NANCY FREY AND DOUGLAS FISHER

The figures on adult literacy are alarming. *USA Today* recently reported that one in five high school graduates cannot read their diploma and 21 million Americans cannot read at all ("Illiteracy Still a Problem," 2000). The National Adult Literacy Survey (NALS), a study of 14,000 adults ages 16 and over, revealed that 44 million adults could not read well enough to read the label on a food can (National Institute for Literacy, 2002). By some estimates, lost productivity due to low levels of literacy approaches $225 billion dollars a year (National Jewish Coalition for Literacy, 2002). Low literacy achievement appears to take its toll in human costs as well—70% of those arrested in the United States have literacy skills in the lowest two levels on the NALS (NJCL, 2002).

Reports on young adults entering post-secondary schools and the job market indicate that many do not possess the necessary literacy skills (Martin, 1998; Pitts, White, & Harrison, 1999). This has recently spotlighted the need for adolescent literacy instruction in secondary schools (e.g., Moore, Bean, Birdyshaw, & Rycik, 1999). This is all the more challenging because the varied types of reading require multiple literacies.

Multiple literacies acknowledge that the skills students use at home, school, and work differ.

Having said that, it is important to note that the reading achievement of high school youth is profoundly influenced by quality instruction. In fact, several researchers (e.g., Allington & Johnston, 2000; Darling-Hammond, 1999; Joyce & Showers, 1995) suggest that the professional development of teachers is critically linked to student achievement and literacy levels of students.

See *http://www.reading.org/focus/adolescent.html* for the International Reading Association's position statement on adolescent literacy.

We maintain that literacy must become the responsibility of the whole school. While we do not suggest that every content teacher must become a "reading teacher," we believe that every secondary school teacher can assist in the literacy development of adolescents. As literacy becomes a schoolwide practice, the following questions are those that we hear most often when teachers are beginning to incorporate new ways of thinking and acting in their classrooms.

- Why can't English teachers take care of the literacy needs of students?
- How do we know that literacy instruction in all content areas matter?
- What do you mean by content areas?
- What are the differences in texts and text structures and why does that matter?
- If students can't read, what should I do?
- How can I group students to maximize their learning?
- How do I ensure that I'm offering an enriching, safe, and motivating classroom environment?
- Where does classroom management fit in?
- Are some instructional strategies only good for specific content areas?
- Why should teachers help students apply what they learn?
- What do you mean by "reflective teaching"?

Our responses are based on our experiences spending time in a wide range of classrooms. While answering these questions, we often think of students like:

- Dimetra, who has read every book you can name. She is known on campus as a very bright kid. However, she gets bored in class easily, especially when she finds the task not challenging.
- Dinuba, who is a recent immigrant from Somalia. She is learning English as a third language and wants to get an education in America. She struggles with the English language and the social aspects of schooling.
- Dylan, who reads several grade levels below his peers. He has been progressing through school without strong reading or writing skills. As a defense, he often tells the teacher that he was too busy surfing or listening to music to do his homework.

Why Can't English Teachers Take Care of the Literacy Needs of Students?

For more information on standards-based lesson planning, see Fisher & Frey, 2001. *Responsive curriculum design in secondary schools: Meeting the diverse needs of students.* Lanham, MD: Scarecrow.

More information on text structures will appear later in this chapter.

The short answer is that student achievement is the responsibility of all educators regardless of their specific content area. Additionally, literacy levels of secondary students are directly correlated to their academic achievement across the curriculum.

English teachers get one period like every other teacher. Certainly English teachers play an important role in the literacy development of students—especially in terms of literary response, understanding genres, and expository writing. However, English teachers also have content that must be delivered and standards that must be addressed. Furthermore, the text structures differ greatly between narrative and non-narrative texts. In fact, texts differ greatly across subject areas. For instance, mathematics textbooks are organized differently than social studies texts. It would be an artificial and futile exercise for English teachers to attempt to duplicate the structures of each content area text, than to teach related literacy skills that are detached from conceptual understanding.

The longer answer has to do with defining literacy itself. How do students learn content in any class? Let's take history for example. It seems to us that they have to read, listen, and watch. How do students demonstrate their knowledge and understanding of history? They must speak and write clearly. These skills—reading, writing, speaking, listening, and viewing—are the core areas of language arts. As you can see, they are critical skills in *every* classroom. Each teacher in the school helps students increase their literacy skills through the content area with specific instructional approaches. As Elizabeth Moje (1996) suggested, we have to think of ourselves as teaching *students* not *subjects*. That means we have to understand students' current performance and know how to improve it—regardless of how well they currently read or write. This book focuses on several specific instructional approaches that have been researched and reviewed by teachers across the curriculum, from science to math to physical education.

How Do We Know That Literacy Instruction in All Content Areas Matters?

The evidence is mounting. A study by Fisher (2001) suggested that a schoolwide focus on literacy instruction could impact schoolwide achievement. In fact, this book grew out of the desire of teachers across content areas to share their successes in instruction.

Further evidence can be found in Reeves' (2000) study of highly effective schools. Schools described as 90/90/90 (90% free/reduced lunch, 90% of students are ethnic minorities, and 90% at or above mastery level on standardized achievement tests) were analyzed for common factors. The results are encouraging for schools everywhere. Shared characteristics included a schoolwide focus on achievement, agreed upon curriculum choices, and an emphasis on writing (Reeves, 2000). It is possible that many schools who have not achieved the same levels of success as the 90/90/90 schools share these same characteristics. However, we believe that the key to success lies in another part of the report. All of these high achieving schools shared another important element—they stick with their plans. These schools "are not lurching from one fad to another. . . they are consistent" (p. 193).

We concur with this approach and see the evidence in our own school experiences. We believe that it takes time and collegial conversations to develop a shared vocabulary of teaching and learning, and these conversations spring from a habit of reflective teaching. In other words, it is not a program, a set of books, or a box of materials that creates a high achieving school. It is always teachers who matter, and what they do that matters most.

Students appreciate this level of consistency as well. Keep this in mind as you introduce literacy strategies to your classroom.

Current news about what teachers and administrators around the nation are doing is published weekly in *Education Week* at *www.edweek.org*.

What Do You Mean by Content Areas?

We use the term, "content areas" to refer to specific disciplines within the secondary school. Traditionally, this included English, social studies, science, and math. All other courses were considered "electives" or non-core classes. However, we use the term "content area" to convey the notion that there are academic standards designed by local, state, and national groups for specific classes.

Thus, we recognize as content areas any class for which there is a scope and sequence of the curriculum. We do not use the antiquated terms "core" and "non-core" to create a hierarchy within the schools.

See Figure 1.1 for a list of content area organizations and their accompanying web sites.

Figure 1.1   Professional Organizations for Teachers

Professional Organizations

American Alliance for Health, Physical Education, Recreation and Dance
1900 Association Drive
Reston, VA 20191-9527
www.aahperd.org

Association for Supervision and Curriculum Development
1703 North Beauregard Street
Alexandria, VA 22311-1714
www.ascd.org

International Reading Association
800 Barksdale Rd.
PO Box 8139
Newark, DE 19714-8139
www.reading.org

National Art Education Association
1916 Association Drive
Reston, VA 20191-1590
www.naea-reston.org

National Association for Bilingual Education
1030 15th Street NW, Suite 470
Washington, DC 20005-1503
www.nabe.org

National Association for Music Education
1806 Robert Fulton Drive
Reston, VA 20191
www.menc.org

National Council for the Social Studies
8555 16th Street, Suite 500
Silver Spring, Maryland 20910
www.ncss.org

National Council of Teachers of English
111 W. Kenyon Road
Urbana, IL 61801-1096
www.ncte.org

National Council of Teachers of Mathematics
1906 Association Drive
Reston, VA 20191-1502
www.nctm.org

National Science Teachers Association
PO Box 90214
Washington, DC 20090-0214
www.nsta.org

PEAK Parent Center–Education of students with disabilities
611 North Weber, Suite 200
Colorado Springs, CO 80903
www.peakparent.org

TASH–Education of students with disabilities
29 W. Susquehanna Blvd., Suite 210
Baltimore, MD 21204
www.tash.org

What Are the Differences in Texts and Text Structures, and Why Does That Matter?

The answer to this question also has two parts. The first part focuses on textbooks as they are used in many secondary classes. Each content area utilizes common text structures and styles to convey information. The second part involves the *instruction* of the text structures and styles. We believe that students should be explicitly taught the structures and styles used in their textbooks. We have seen students approach expository (informational) text as if it is narrative, looking for the familiar story structure of characters, setting, plot, and the like. Unfortunately, knowledge of narrative structures is unlikely to be of much help in a calculus textbook. However, explicit instruction in the types of structures found in their textbooks and the signal words associated with them will sustain and improve their comprehension of the course readings.

Common Expository Text Structures

The most common types of text structures include:

1. exemplification (concept/definition),
2. compare/contrast,
3. cause/effect,
4. problem/solution, and
5. sequential.

Exemplification text describes people, places, or phenomena. Nearly all content area textbooks have passages that are descriptive. Signal words for exemplification text structures include descriptive adjectives, adverbs, and phrases. For instance, the mummy isn't merely old, it is

> wrapped in discolored linen bandages wound tightly around the entire body, lying undisturbed for thousands of years deep in the cool, dark mudbrick pyramid.

Compare/contrast text structures also rely on descriptive text, but instead explain how two or more people, places, or phenomena are similar or different. Like exemplification, most textbooks contain some compare/contrast passages as well. Signal words like *although, yet, while, however, same/different, like/unlike* and other words that show opposites are likely to appear.

> Although the first mummies were probably accidental, mummification became an art in ancient Egypt. While members of the noble classes were mummified, poor people usually were not.

Cause and effect text structures, which show the causal relationships between phenomena, can be deceptively similar to compare/contrast, but their signal words give them away. Words like *since, because, as a result,* and *if. . . then* statements are frequently seen in these passages.

> Because the Incas lived in the high Andes, they created ice mummies that were preserved in the thin, frigid mountain air.

Another text structure is *problem/solution*. Seen frequently in mathematics textbooks, they contain signal words like *question, answer, thus, accordingly,* and *decide.* A challenge of problem/solution text is that it is more subtle than some of the others, and may develop over the course of several sentences or paragraphs.

> Theft and the desert climate have taken their toll on Egyptian mummies. Accordingly, the government has taken steps to preserve the remaining mummies by installing climate controlled displays and sophisticated security devices.

More easy to detect is our final text structure, the *sequential* or *temporal* (time-based) passage. These signal words jump out of the text for most readers and include words like *first, next, last, before, afterwards, another,* and *finally.*

(If you were paying attention to the structure of this sequential paragraph, you knew we were coming to the end by the use of the word *final*).

Signal words are also helpful to students who are taking standardized tests. See chapter 10 for a discussion on test-taking skills.

The <u>first</u> step in the mummification process was to remove all the internal organs. <u>Next</u>, the embalmer drained the body of fluids. <u>Finally</u>, the body was wrapped in linens.

Common Text Styles

In addition to these text structures, each content area uses some common styles that students should understand. In English, for example, fiction is the most frequent text students encounter. Teachers can help students understand fiction by providing them with ideas about how this genre is structured. For example, students should understand plot, character development, setting, denouement, and climax, for this is the language of that content area.

As you can imagine, this categorization system does not work for a science book. Science textbooks are often organized using introductory thesis paragraphs, followed by supporting details in subsequent paragraphs. Vocabulary is essential to the field of science and is frequently introduced through a bolded word and an example.

However, students may find this format frustrating because an explicit definition may not be found in the body of the text. Pictures and charts, not surprisingly, are used to illustrate phenomena. Although many text structures may be utilized throughout the science book, cause and effect is the most common.

On the other hand, social studies textbooks use a more journalistic style. Narrative text may be embedded, particularly in sidebar features about interesting people or events. Readers can expect that the chapters and headings will be organized by concepts, and this may prove confusing at times. For instance, a chapter entitled "America's Dark Days" is more ambiguous than one that reads "Poverty and Economic Depression in the 1930s." Prior knowledge is critical—and often assumed—in many social studies textbooks, and gaps in a student's experience or prior knowledge may derail their ability to comprehend the passage. Unlike diagrams in science books that are usually conceptual in nature, photographs are more frequently used in social studies materials to illustrate important people, places, and events. These can be enlightening for students because they are more concrete. Like all textbooks, social studies books rely on a variety of text structures, although cause and effect is dominant within a chronologically arranged format.

Mathematics textbooks are distinctly different from those encountered in other content areas. Each chapter follows a predictable pattern, usually an introduction of a concept or algorithm, followed by an explanation, an example, and then a problem. The main idea appears in the chapter title or headings and features comparatively little extended text passages. Instead, extensive amounts of symbols and numbers communicate complex concepts. In addition, unique technical vocabulary like *rhombus* and *integers* are used. Students, particularly those who are English language learners, are likely to be confused by mathematical words with multiple meanings such as *set, prime,* and *radicals.* The text structure is almost always sequential.

Although elective courses like physical education, health, art, music and vocational courses like auto shop and welding rely less on traditional textbooks as a source of information, they do exist. Students' use of these texts may be complicated by the amount of prior knowledge necessary, as well as the amount of content-specific vocabulary needed. A positive is that these content areas tend to use a great deal of primary source information, including newspaper and magazine articles, film, slides,

Chapter 6 contains extensive discussion about vocabulary instruction.

The PBS Teacher Source website at *www.pbs.org/teachersource* contains links to lesson plans, activities, resource guides, and materials across many subject areas.

and CD-ROMs and other electronic media. Using these materials requires a great deal of visual literacy, although this type of literacy mirrors the changing modes of information retrieval and interpretation in our society (Bruce, 1997).

If the Students Can't Read the Text, What Should I Do?

When students cannot read the textbook, the teacher must mediate for them. However, in our experience it is not just the student who cannot read the textbook who should cause the teacher concern. What about students who choose not to read? We must counter—what is the teacher doing to communicate the importance of reading in his or her class? As Rieck pointed out in 1977, teachers can "telegraph messages against readers" (p. 646) when they do not discuss the assigned readings in class, test students on the required readings, or fail to demonstrate their love of reading in front of students. The importance of Rieck's findings cannot be underestimated—her study of 300 secondary students who had been identified by their teachers as disliking reading yielded surprising results. In contrast to the teacher reports, she found that more than half of them reported that they enjoyed reading. Instead, she found that the teachers who had identified these students engaged in counterproductive instructional practices that the students interpreted to mean that reading was unnecessary for success in the class. Specifically, these teachers did not discuss assigned readings or test on the content of the readings. Furthermore, for these content areas teachers assigned the readings by the number of pages, not the purpose of the reading. Most disturbing of all, these same students either did not know or didn't believe that their teacher liked to read, despite having spent 200 instructional hours in the class. Clearly, the role of the content area teacher as a model and motivator for readers is essential.

> Students gain greater understanding of the content when multiple information sources are used.

Having said that, we do not believe that the textbook should be the only source of content information for students.

It is unlikely that any one textbook would suffice, year after year, to meet the needs of every student who enters your classroom. Another concern is the explosion of information in content areas, especially history, geography, and the sciences. Content teachers who remain current in their field of study continually augment their curriculum to reflect new knowledge, typically in the form of outside readings.

Evidence suggests that all teachers should read to their students for two reasons—to build background knowledge and to teach efficient methods for comprehending the content. Considering the textbook as only one resource encourages teachers to incorporate a wide range of instructional materials into their classrooms.

> See chapter 3 for more information on read alouds and shared reading.

Consider the perspective offered by a textbook: it serves as a summary of the *textbook author's* knowledge of the content. While valuable, it is several degrees removed from the primary source information used by the authors in developing the textbook. When all the events and historical figures of World War II may occupy a few pages in the World History textbook, there is little room for the details. Since textbooks can only rarely provide a comprehensive picture of the period of study, instruction often becomes focused on memorizing the facts and chronology of events. History textbooks, while presenting correct factual information, often provide a narrow, singular perspective (Tunnell & Ammon, 1996), and are often criticized for avoiding controversial topics (Perlmutter, 1997). With the widespread attention being given to the integration of literacy across the curriculum, many teachers who use a history textbook as a resource, supplement it with literature selections (Johnson & Ebert, 1992; Moss, 1991).

Use a Variety of Materials

Carol Hurst's children's literature web site offers information and lesson ideas on award-winning books at *www.carolhurst.com.*

In addition to textbooks, we suggest that teachers use young adult literature, music, videos, web sites, poetry, newspaper articles, magazines, biographies and autobiographies, authentic sources such as diaries and letters, and guest speakers to engage students in topics of study.

Throughout this book we provide examples of multiple sources of information that can be used to ensure that students understand and remember content information. As you can imagine, Dimetra would be as challenging to many teachers as Dylan because of her advanced reading ability!

How Can I Group Students to Maximize Their Learning?

What should be the criteria for admission into a specific class? Should reading skill be the determinant? Should prerequisite completion play a role? Do teacher recommendations matter? What about English language learners and students with reading disabilities—which classes should they take? These questions are gripping high schools all over the country. Most likely the school administration has created policies on each of these issues. However, we support the practice of heterogeneous grouping in which students of diverse abilities and skills are educated together. This contrasts with past practices of ability grouping and tracking, and responds to the research evidence that tracking is harmful to students' emotional well-being (Oakes, 1985). It's interesting to look at the success of high schools that have de-tracked. Typically, when the low-level and remedial classes are eliminated, achievement increases (Oakes & Wells, 1998).

Effective grouping strategies like reciprocal teaching are discussed later in the book.

Placing students in fixed and static groups for the purpose of instruction, with little likelihood of working with a wide range of students, constitutes tracking. Instead, we advocate the use of flexible grouping arrangements in mixed ability classrooms. As the use of these cooperative learning groups increases in secondary school classrooms, we must state some cautions about grouping. First, we believe that students should be grouped and regrouped for different activities and for different purposes. Fixed groups, especially based on ability, run counter to all the wise practices that our best teachers are implementing (Lapp, Fisher, & Flood, 1999). Many instructional strategies are available to today's teachers that can enable the learning of academic skills in heterogeneous groups.

Think about someone like Dylan. Can you imagine his confusion when he participates in lessons designed to increase community and appreciation of diversity, but then never gets to interact with some of his peers because they are always in another group? This is not to say that a teacher would *never* group students together who are struggling to understand a particular concept. When organizing academic units, teachers often bring specific students together to provide explicit instruction based on their needs. After receiving instruction from the teacher, they return to their heterogeneous groups. The important point here is that class groups are not permanent, and that teachers group students in such combinations that *everyone* has a chance to demonstrate their best skills in a particular setting.

Second, as you will read, we encourage the use of cooperative groups. We know from experience that this dynamic is very powerful! But students don't know instinctively how to work cooperatively (Johnson & Johnson, 1998). They need to practice cooperative learning and see it modeled, not just hear about it. And imagine both

Dimetra's and Dinuba's concern when they never see examples of their teachers co-operating as partners, or worse, watch their teachers behave in ways that indicate they are not as accepting of differences as they might otherwise admit. Actions speak louder than words!

How Do I Ensure That I'm Offering an Enriching, Safe, and Motivating Classroom Environment?

The most effective teachers we know have lots of books and resource materials in their classrooms and encourage students to read and investigate all the time. These resources should reflect the diversity in a community. Dinuba would be really surprised if she never saw anyone who looked like her in the classroom books she encounters. While quantity is good where books are concerned, quality is even better. Books and other instructional materials (including audio and videotapes, computer programs, periodicals, etc.) must reflect different types of families, non-traditional gender roles, cultural uniqueness, as well as a variety of languages and accessible formats. In addition, books that address sensitive issues should be available so that students know it's acceptable to discuss these topics. Displaying these kinds of books helps to create a safe environment and comfort level where students feel free to ask tough questions.

Introduce Classroom Materials

As many teachers know, it is not enough to display materials. Students may be reluctant or unaware of the array of books available in the classroom. Much like a guest who has arrived at a party, these books need to be introduced to the class. One of the strategies that we use is "read, write, pair, share." Particularly when introducing a new book or topic, teachers find this four-step approach helpful.

Step 1:   *Read:* Students either read silently, or follow along as the teacher reads aloud.

Step 2:   *Write:* Students quickly write their impressions or reactions to the text, or answer a specific question.

Step 3:   *Pair:* Students turn to a partner and talk about what they've written.

Step 4:   *Share:* Large group sharing, which is much less intimidating after having just shared with a partner.

In order for all students to participate in this activity, the teacher should provide appropriate accommodations or modifications for students who need them. The teacher may need to model creative interaction strategies for eliciting discussion from students who are shy, who have difficulty speaking the language, or who are unable to express themselves verbally.

More ideas for infusing issues of tolerance and diversity in your classroom are available at *www.tolerance.org/101_tools/index.html.*

Where Does Classroom Management Fit In?

A smooth running classroom is the goal of every teacher, but sometimes it may feel like an elusive dream. This seems to be particularly true during the first years of teaching, when the complexities of curriculum, procedures, logistics, and instructional

For more ideas on classroom management, see "Personalizing the Secondary Classroom" at *www.teachersvision.com/lesson-plans/lesson:6711.html*.

savvy converge. And ineffective classroom management can interfere significantly with your ability to teach and your students' capacity to learn. One way to effect classroom management is to set classroom procedures, record-keeping processes, and clearly defined rules and expectations (Wong, 1991).

Having said that, all the procedures, processes and rules amount to a whole lot of nothing if they are not attached to engaging curriculum and dynamic instruction. A classroom management plan is analogous to the poles of a tent—without them, the structure is a formless mass. The tent poles are there to support something. In your classroom, that "something" is your curriculum and instruction. What students learn, and how they learn it, is an important element of a smooth running classroom. When student engagement and interest is up, behavior issues tend to decline.

No classroom is ever completely devoid of discipline problems, but if you notice a pattern of recurring difficulties, then a closer look at the academic atmosphere may be in order. For example, does classroom chatter seem to be a constant source of trouble? Check to see how often students have an opportunity to interact with one another during instruction. Do some students refuse to participate in activities that require reading? Perhaps the text level and the student are mismatched. Are student notes disorganized or non-existent? Specific instruction on note-taking strategies, and attention to lesson organization and presentation on the teacher's part may encourage students to take better notes. While instructional strategies alone cannot resolve all management dilemmas, they can prevent or minimize many low-level troubles that create undue stress for both the teacher and the students.

Are Some Instructional Strategies Only Good for Specific Content Areas?

While we know that some instructional strategies were designed for specific areas of instruction, most are simply ways of delivering information (Moss, 2003). For example, Cognitively Guided Instruction (CGI) is used as an approach to teach students mathematics (Warfield, 2001). However, the strategies that we focus on in this book have been used successfully across content areas. In fact, examples of the actual implementation of these strategies in each content area are provided within each chapter. For example, chapter 7 is devoted to vocabulary development and provides examples of vocabulary instruction in English, social studies, math, science, and music.

Internet-based inquiries called Webquests for all content areas and grade levels are available at *http://webquest.sdsu.edu*.

It should be noted and emphasized here that specific types of vocabulary instruction are highlighted in each of the content areas. That does not mean that the strategy would not work in another content area. For example, word sorts are highlighted in a biology class. Of course, U.S. history, 3-D art, British literature, and geometry teachers also use word sorts to teach vocabulary. This holds true for all of the major strategy chapters—the specific examples in this book are not tied to a specific content area.

The strategies outlined in this book are designed to fit easily into the school day. While we identify them as "literacy strategies," most could really be called "content area instructional approaches." The strategies in this book have a research base and a practical foundation for ensuring that students understand the content that they are being taught. Your students, like ours, need guidance through content areas, not simply an assignment to "read pages 34-46 tonight." We like to think of these literacy strategies as being transportable across content areas. What we mean is that each is elastic enough to be applied to a variety of learning situations.

For example, a strategy is transportable for a student when she uses vocabulary skills learned in English to determine what "palette" means in art.

As teachers, we are thrilled when we hear students murmur in recognition when we speak of Cornell notetaking or reciprocal teaching. It tells us that our colleagues have done a great job in creating a common vocabulary across the campus. It also means that when we collectively teach these strategies, we end up spending less time mired in the mechanics of getting the lesson underway. Setting up Cornell notes becomes an instruction that takes seconds, rather than half the period. In other words, it allows us to use an instructional shorthand that gives us more time to actually teach the content. Ultimately, we hope that these strategies are transportable across the students' learning lives both in and out of school.

Why Should Teachers Help Students Apply What They've Learned?

As you have probably guessed by now, we support the idea that experiential lessons are very important for real learning (e.g., Tantraporn, 2000). Sure, we could lecture Dimetra, Dylan, Dinuba, and their peers about something like the importance of getting along and treating everyone with respect, but how much of that information would they really remember and apply at the appropriate times? The activities and discussion questions in this book provide "real-life" opportunities for students to practice what they learn in the classroom in situations that come up on campus, after school, and at home. Students also need to learn the vocabulary of tolerance, acceptance, and understanding. They should be provided with skills to reflect on their own values, and to begin distinguishing their beliefs from those of their families and friends. Secondary school students often struggle with identity issues, particularly in establishing the confidence to challenge the status quo. They require a learning atmosphere in which they can be assured they will not be judged for their thoughts, while developing an understanding that they will be judged for their actions.

A word or two might also be included about homework. We believe that homework should look different than schoolwork. Assignments to be completed at home should involve interacting with family, friends, neighbors, or professionals in the student's life, and should incorporate unique cultures, traditions, languages, and lifestyles. We have not found homework that is merely a repeat of class work to be particularly motivating for students to complete or for us to grade (Kralovec & Buell, 2001). We prefer to look at homework that tells us things we didn't know about our students. We view our students' lives in the community as a natural extension of their school lives. Our goal as educators is not to replicate a facsimile of school in the home, but rather to create opportunities for them to apply what they have learned in their own lives.

Teachers need a variety of ways to assess learning. The Eisenhower National Clearinghouse offers a useful array of assessment information at *www.enc.org/topics/ assessment.*

What Do We Mean by "Reflective Teaching"?

When we use the term reflective teaching, we are speaking of the habits of mind of effective educators who practice a recursive cycle of self-questioning and self-assessment to improve teaching and learning. Reflective teachers take the time to stand back from the fray and ask:

- How effective was I today?
- What can I learn about my teaching by looking at today's lesson?
- How can I improve my teaching?

Teaching is both an art and a science, and each of these perspectives requires that we take a step back from what we have been doing to analyze the efficacy of our practice. At best, teaching is inexact because the context keeps changing—student needs never remain static and always demand shifts in how we create meaningful learning opportunities for them. Therefore, it's impossible to replicate the same lesson exactly. You need only look to your own variation in teaching the same lesson content in two different periods. As a reflective teacher, you make adjustments and improvements to suit the needs of your students. We often hear teachers remark that they taught a lesson more effectively during second period that they did during first. This is reflective teaching in action, because they are self-questioning and self-assessing. This applies across units and entire courses as well, and we believe that a strong repertoire of strategies for your instructional toolkit can help you arrive at solutions to these reflective questions.

Two organizations committed to the teaching profession are the American Federation of Teachers at *www.aft.org* and the National Education Association at *www.nea.org.*

Teachers Never Stop Learning

The point is a simple one, but often overlooked in the busy world of a teacher: to enjoy and flourish in your job, you can never stop learning.

It is ironic that those of us in the business of learning may forget the importance of our own learning. We may be caught up in the delivery of information and the orchestration of the classroom, with little time left to engage in our own learning. After all, the teacher is the oldest in the room and by tradition's unspoken and timeless decree, the one who is supposed to know what he or she is doing.

We believe that teachers learn from one another. In this book, we have utilized a traditional approach in educational writing—define a practice, discuss its origins, and cite research-based evidence of the strategy's effectiveness in secondary classrooms. However, the majority of each chapter is filled with extended examples of real teachers instructing real students. These teachers work in every content area, and range in experience from their first year to their thirtieth. It is our hope that this book moves you beyond the definitional level of a strategy to the implementation phase, and that this transition is best accomplished by watching other teachers apply these to their own practice.

We recognize that other resources are essential, too. For that reason, we have included a list of professional organizations, web sites, and publications for you to access in your efforts to refine your practice. They can be located in Figure 1.1 in this book.

The ERIC Education Information database is a comprehensive source of research on all aspects of teaching and learning at *www.ask.eric.org.*

A Professional Invitation

The remainder of this book focuses on instructional strategies and planning tools that you will find useful in ensuring that your students can access the content of your class.

We provide examples across the content areas for the following strategies:

- anticipatory activities (chapter 2)

- read alouds and shared reading (chapter 3)

- questioning (chapter 4)

- notetaking and note making (chapter 5)

- graphic organizers (chapter 6)

- vocabulary instruction (chapter 7)

- writing to learn (chapter 8)

- reciprocal teaching (chapter 9)

In addition, we provide information on preparing students for standardized tests in chapter 10. In particular, we will discuss how these schoolwide literacy practices better prepare students for such tests. As most people know, these tests are used to determine the success of schools as well as the ability of students to attend college.

We invite you then to consider the flexibility and applicability of these research-based literacy strategies in a variety of content areas. We also urge you to consider the experiences of Dimetra, Dinuba, and Dylan. Students like them traverse the landscape of the American high school *every* day and they bring unique perspectives to the classroom. Their presence in your classroom will inspire you to apply these strategies in ways we have never considered. Because you, the teacher, matter most.

References

Allington, R. L., & Johnston, P. H. (2000). *What do we know about effective fourth-grade teachers and their classrooms?* (Report Series 13010). Albany, NY: National Research Center on English Learning and Achievement.

Bruce, B. C. (1997). Current issues and future directions. In J. Flood, S. B. Heath, & D. Lapp (Eds.), *Research on teaching literacy through the communicative and visual arts* (pp. 875–884). Newark, DE: International Reading Association.

Darling-Hammond, L. (1999). Target time toward teachers. *Journal of Staff Development, 20*(2), 31–36.

Fisher, D. (2001). We're moving on up: Creating a schoolwide literacy effort in an urban high school. *Journal of Adolescent and Adult Literacy, 45,* 92–101.

Illiteracy still a problem. (2000, November 29). *USA Today,* p. A1.

Johnson, D. T., & Johnson, R. T. (1998). *Learning together and alone: Cooperative, competitive, and individualistic learning* (5th ed.). Boston: Allyn & Bacon.

Johnson, N. M., & Ebert, M. J. (1992). Time travel is possible: Historical fiction and biography—Passport to the past. *The Reading Teacher, 45,* 488–495.

Joyce, B. R., & Showers, B. (1995). *Student achievement through staff development: Fundamentals of school renewal* (2nd ed.). New York: Longman.

Kralovec, E., & Buell, J. (2001). *The end of homework: How homework disrupts families, overburdens children, and limits learning.* Boston: Beacon Press.

Lapp, D., Fisher, D., & Flood, J. (1999). Does it matter how you're grouped for instruction? Yes! Flexible grouping patterns promote student learning. *The California Reader, 33*(1), 28–32.

Martin, J. (1998). As a blue-collar worker, does Johnny need to read? *Adult Basic Education, 8,* 139–156.

Moje, E. B. (1996). "I teach subjects, not students:" Teacher-student relationships as contexts for secondary literacy. *Reading Research Quarterly, 31,* 172–195.

Moore, D. W., Bean, T. W., Birdyshaw, D., & Rycik, J. A. (1999). Adolescent literacy: A position statement. *Journal of Adolescent & Adult Literacy, 43,* 97–112.

Moss, B. (1991). Children's nonfiction trade books: A complement to content area texts. *The Reading Teacher, 45,* 26–32.

Moss, B. (2003). *25 strategies for guiding readers through informational texts.* San Diego: Academic Professional Development.

National Jewish Coalition for Literacy. (2002). *Some facts about literacy.* Retrieved April 14, 2002 from www.njcl.net/NCJLStats.html

National Institute for Literacy. (2002). *Frequently asked questions.* Retrieved June 3, 2002 from www.nifl.gov/nifl/faqs.html

Oakes, J. (1985). *Keeping track: How schools structure inequality.* New Haven: Yale University Press.

Oakes, J., & Wells, A. S. (1998). Detracking for high student achievement. *Educational Leadership, 55*(6), 38–41.

Perlmutter, D. D. (1997). Manufacturing visions of society and history in textbooks. *Journal of Communication, 47*(3), 68–81.

Pitts, J. M., White, W, G., Jr., & Harrison, A. B. (1999). Student academic underpreparedness: Effects on faculty. *Review of Higher Education, 22,* 343–365.

Reeves, D. B. (2000). *Accountability in action: A blueprint for learning organizations.* Denver, CO: Advanced Learning.

Rieck, B. J. (1977). How content teachers telegraph messages against readers. *Journal of Reading, 20,* 646–648.

Tantraporn, W. (2000). Hands-on activities in science and mathematics education. *Science Education International, 11,* 8–10.

Tunnell, M. O., & Ammon, R. (1996). The story of ourselves: Fostering multiple historical perspectives. *Social Education, 57,* 224–225.

Warfield, J. (2001). Teaching kindergarten children to solve word problems. *Early Childhood Education Journal, 28,* 161–167.

Wong, H. (1991). *The first days of school.* Mountain View, CA: Wong Productions.

Chapter 2

Attention Getters: Using Anticipatory Activities to Inspire Learning

NANCY FREY, DOUGLAS FISHER, RITA ELWARDI, AND LEE MONGRUE

Je Quan arrives at the doorway of his 11th-grade American literature class and stops abruptly. Yellow and black crime scene tape is strung around the classroom and an outline of a body marked off in white medical tape occupies the center of the classroom floor. "Don't touch anything! You'll disturb the evidence!" Je Quan looks up in surprise to see his teacher wearing a trench coat and brown fedora. The students quickly take their seats, intrigued by what might happen next. The teacher, now transformed into a hard-boiled detective, begins. "Welcome to our study of American mystery novels. My name is Phillip Marlowe." Over the next four weeks, Je Quan's class will explore the writings of California mystery novelists Raymond Chandler and Dashiell Hammett.

One of the most influential contributions to twentieth century educational theory was the development of the field of cognitive science. Before the advent of cognitive studies, the prevailing learning theory was behaviorism, which concentrated on the role of outside stimulus as a mechanism for learning. The publication of *A Study of Thinking* (Bruner, Goodnow, & Austin, 1956) led the way for exploration of what happens inside the minds of learners and how they organize and utilize information. Over the course of the next 50 years scientists, psychologists, and educators have examined memory, emotion, schema, and experience as essential components of learning. In fact, the influence of cognitive science is so profound that it now may be difficult to conceptualize how the process of learning was perceived in the first half of the century. This book, for instance, is replete with learning approaches that reflect our profession's roots in cognitive science—scaffolding, metacognition, accessing background knowledge, and transfer of learning—to name a few.

These concepts will be further explored in chapters 6 (graphic organizers), 8 (writing to learn), and 4 (questioning).

Types of Anticipatory Activities

One aspect of learning theory that has received a great deal of attention is (please pardon us now) "attention." Anyone who has ever faced the task of teaching a group of people can appreciate the importance of attention as a factor in learning. After all, if students aren't paying attention, how can they process new information?

When we speak of attention we are not referring to behavior management, but rather to practices that elicit curiosity, provoke questions, and evoke recall of newly learned information. In addition, attention also means activating students' background knowledge about the topic. This is really the very beginning of the learning process, although it is not bound in time to the beginning of a course, class, or lesson. Good and Brophy (2002) remind us that effective teachers create memorable events throughout their lessons to capture student attention, not unlike the teacher in the opening vignette for this chapter. It is essential to note that gaining attention through anticipatory activities is not intended to provide entertainment for students, but rather to scaffold learning so that the responsibility for learning shifts to the student. A primary goal of classroom instruction is to move from teacher-directed instruction to student-centered learning. Anticipatory activities can ground new learning in meaning-based inquiry because the student's attention has been gained through an event connected to the purpose for studying the topic.

These memorable events may also utilize drama, humor, movement, or emotion to make an impression on learning.

Eggen and Kauchak (2001) suggest four instructional strategies for gaining student attention:

1. demonstrations,
2. discrepant events,
3. visual displays, and
4. thought-provoking questions (p. 271).

We will discuss each of these in detail and then take a look inside classrooms to see how teachers across the content areas are using these "attention-getters" to stimulate curiosity and promote learning.

Demonstrations

Classroom demonstrations are typically performed to display a theory, concept, or phenomenon. A demonstration of gravity is likely to involve dropping objects from a height; a demonstration of fractions and decimals might include several apples sliced into equal parts. The use of demonstrations is critical in the field of mathematics (Lee, 2000) and is associated with higher levels of learning in science (Beasley, 1982). Don't overlook the availability of technology to enhance demonstrations of complex phenomena (Brooks & Brooks, 1996). We particularly like web sites that portray scientific concepts. For instance, students can manipulate variables such as humidity and wind speed to watch a hurricane being formed (*www.discovery.com/stories/science/hurricanes/create/html*). Syracuse University offers an applet on the phases of the moon (*http://suhep.phy.syr.edu/courses/java/mc_html/phase.html*). These and many other web sites offer interesting ways for teachers to display a variety of science concepts. The use of demonstrations to illustrate and augment lecture and readings is par-

What helps you to remember? Do you remember more when your emotions are involved?

An applet is a small program automatically downloaded from the Internet.

ticularly effective for students with disabilities (Janney & Snell, 2000) and English language learners because it is enhanced by physical and kinesthetic involvement.

Demonstrations should be used judiciously in order to prevent confusion. In particular, a demonstration is likely to fail if it is not grounded in the theoretical framework (Roth, McRobbie, & Lucas, 1997). In other words, an interesting demonstration does not replace the need for deep exploration of concepts. Also, don't overlook the importance of telling students that the demonstration is important to remember, and why. These simple statements of emphasis have been shown to be effective when coupled with demonstrations (Eggen & Kauchak, 2001; Larsen, 1991).

Discrepant Events

Discrepant events are those demonstrations that involve a surprising or startling occurrence designed to command the students' attention. A performance may be staged—for instance, another teacher may be recruited to rush in to the classroom to hand the social studies teacher a copy of a newspaper dated December 7, 1941. The vignette at the beginning of this chapter, with the teacher dressed as a 1940's *film noir* detective, is a discrepant event. Hurst (2001) suggests that attention-grabbing events are a key element to content area lesson planning, along with mini-lessons and comprehension instruction. She and others (e.g. Anderson & Pearson, 1984; Smith, 1998) remind us that attention is directly related to schema, the knowledge structure utilized to comprehend. Je Quan both activated and added to his schema of "whodunit" story structures when he entered the classroom and saw the crime tape, body outline, and detective. Events such as these can assist students in organizing new information, integrating it with prior knowledge, and increasing their ability to retrieve it later (Landauer, 1975).

Many useful lesson plans are available at *http://teachers.net/lessons.*

Discrepant events also access a powerful aid to memory—emotional connection. As humans, we have a tendency to remember episodes connected to our emotional memories, such as a favorite birthday party or a first kiss. The associations may be negative as well—most readers will recall where they were when they found out about the terrorist attack on America in 2001. While discrepant events in the classroom are unlikely to be connected to such intense emotions as these, it is important to recognize that they tap into the same neural pathways (Sylwester, 1995). Music, art, and dramatic play can provide a means for accessing students' emotional memory and increase their ability to retrieve the information at a later time (Sprenger, 1999). Jorgensen (1998) calls these events "grabbers" because they command student attention and capture the imagination.

Integrated arts allows teachers to utilize visual and performing arts to teach content knowledge.

Visual Displays

While visual displays such as graphic organizers are more thoroughly presented in chapter 6, we will confine our discussion to what Hyerle refers to as "visual tools for constructing knowledge" (1996, p. 1). The rise of information technology in the last quarter of the twentieth century has fundamentally changed the way information is generated and shared. These same technologies—computers, CD-ROMs, web-based resources, and digital cameras, to name a few—are becoming an increasingly common means for classrooms to access information. Unlike earlier classroom technologies like televisions and video recorders, these newer advances are interactive and require the active participation of the learner. No longer is visually presented information viewed

Many museums post items in their collection on the Internet. Teachers can display images in their classroom using a video projector. The Louvre Museum is located at *http://www.louvre.fr/louvrea.htm* and the Metropolitan Museum of Art has a web site at *www.metmuseum.org.*

as a passive experience to be absorbed by the learner. Rather, it is seen as a generative process in which the learner influences and changes the information. Exposure to these information technologies has influenced *how* our students learn as well. Young learners today are far more accustomed to processing multiple visual images in seconds (Jensen, 1998). If you doubt this, compare the editing style of a 1950s-era television show with a recent music video. A comparison of the number of camera and scene changes is likely to be very different, suggesting that today's viewers can process a great deal of information even during very rapid image changes.

Classroom Applications of Technology.   Classroom applications of technologies that are used to construct, share, and interact with information include PowerPoint® presentations like those used by Valerie Hansen in the vocabulary chapter or WebQuests (Dodge, 1995). Ms. Hansen constructed a PowerPoint® presentation to display vocabulary words and their meanings. She also used more advanced aspects of the software to enhance student learning by using the "dissolve" feature to fade out incorrect answers over a period of a minute, thus shaping the responses of those students who were less certain of the correct definition.

WebQuests are another technology tool for gaining attention and supporting long-term learning. A WebQuest is "an inquiry-oriented activity in which most or all of the information used by learners is drawn from the Web" (*http://edweb. sdsu.edu/news/webeye*) and is used to guide students in an investigation of a topic. The teacher plans the WebQuest in advance, and students are typically given a series of questions to guide their search. Specific web sites may be identified and bookmarked by the teacher to provide some frame for the learners to follow, much like lily pads strung across a pond. The good news is that you don't have to create your own WebQuest (although you may choose to do so later). Topics as varied as polar ice caps, eating disorders, and designing paper airplanes are only a click away.

The WebQuest web site has hundreds of lesson plans and can be found at *http://webquest. sdsu.edu.*

Mind Mapping.   A favorite visual display is mind mapping (Buzan, 1979). Mind mapping is described by some as a method of note-taking, however, it is also a technique for learners to develop an organizational structure. Typically, mind mapping relies on the use of color and simple line drawings and graphics to represent the concepts and connections associated with a topic. (A computer application called Inspiration® makes it easy for teachers and students to create mind maps and other webs electronically.) The mind maps are prepared in advance for display on an overhead. As the teacher introduces a new topic, the mind map provides a visual representation of the connections between and among concepts. Like semantic webs, they are typically organized around a word or phrase that represents the central idea. Pictures and words are connected by a series of lines representing linkages. The word "map" is important here, because this visual tool is meant to serve as a guide for students to negotiate their way around the topic.

If you are interested in learning more about mind mapping techniques, take a look at *Mapping Inner Space* by Nancy Margulies (1991).

Thought-Provoking Questions

Like mind mapping and WebQuests, thought-provoking questions are intended to assist students in organizing new information. Like discrepant events, they are meant to appeal to the emotional channels of learning. The use of a provocative question, particularly one that defies a simple answer, has been recognized as a method for promoting interest and sustaining learning by inviting students to formulate an understanding of the material (Brandt, 1992; Muncey, Payne, & White, 1999). These questions may be of a general investigatory nature, as in the K-W-L technique (Ogle, 1986). K-W-L stands for

"What do I **know**? What do I **want** to know? What have I **learned**?" This organizer mirrors the process of scientific inquiry inherent in any investigation. Typically, a teacher will arrange these questions into three columns and then prompt discussion about the new topic of study. Student responses are recorded and then become the guide for subsequent study. This technique has been modified in a number of ways, including K-W-L-Plus (Carr & Ogle, 1987) which adds summarization and K-W-L-H (Wills, 1995) that adds "**How** do I know?" to focus on sources of evidence. The recursive nature of inquiry is emphasized through K-W-L-Q (Schmidt, 1999) when a fourth column for further questions is added at the end of the unit of study.

Later in this chapter we'll examine how K-W-L was utilized in an art class.

Other thought-provoking questions might be more specific to the unit and are likely to encourage an interdisciplinary study. A question like "What is a hero?" is far more interesting than a unit entitled "Heroes of the 20th Century" and is likely to promote greater student interest. Jorgensen (1998) refers to these types of questions as "essential questions" because they are so difficult to answer succinctly. An example of an essential question discussed by Jorgensen is "Can you truly be free if you're not treated equally?"—an invitation to examine the U.S. civil rights movement of the 1950s and 60s. Other essential questions used by educators include:

For more information on interdisciplinary study, see Jacobs, H. H. (1997). *Mapping the big picture: Integrating curriculum and assessment, K-12.* Alexandria, VA: Association for Supervision and Curriculum Development.

- What is the human need to celebrate?
- Is there an art to science? Is there a science to art?
- Mark Twain said, "History is lies agreed upon." Was he right?
- Does an apple a day keep the doctor away?
- Probability and Pop Culture: Are you more likely to hit the lottery or get hit by lightning?

When curriculum units are organized around thought-provoking questions, it provides the teacher with a means for establishing relevance. Learning is enhanced when the relevance of the material is made clear. In fact, information that is not attached to any larger meaning is likely to be quickly forgotten (Jensen, 1998). And remember that relevance is in the mind of the learner, not just the teacher. We know from our own teaching experience that we believe everything we teach is relevant, otherwise we wouldn't bother to talk about it. However, we can also appreciate the importance of relevance from our students' viewpoint. Therefore, it is up to us as instructors to make the relevance explicit. When a curriculum unit is organized around an essential question, and that question is then connected to the assessments and culminating projects of the unit, students can begin to make meaning of the information. After all, when students understand that the information they are reading and writing about will ultimately be utilized to answer the question, they can then appreciate the value of their inquiry.

We've discussed the importance of gaining and sustaining student attention to promote and extend learning. Now let's take a look at how teachers are using anticipatory activities in their content area classrooms.

Strategies at Work

Anticipatory Activities in English

Visual Displays Through Virtual Interviews.   Justin Phillips sometimes teaches by talking to the past. In his ninth-grade English classes he uses creative means to build ideas, information, and historical context that may be absent from his students' frame of reference. Instead of assuming his students have the required background information for a unit of study, he assesses what they know about the main ideas of the unit and fills in the missing links. Making these links interesting, informative and memorable is one of the tools in Phillips' teaching repertoire. He combines a home video camera with simple costumes and props to create a "virtual interview" with historical and contemporary figures, thereby introducing them to his class. This technique serves as an inventive visual display of information to assist his students in fleshing out the details of both historical and fictional characters.

To introduce a group project on biographies, Phillips assumed the identity of Lech Walesa, founder of the Polish Solidarity Movement and 1983 Nobel Peace Prize winner. He scripted a mock interview and then filmed himself in costume. Later, he told his students that they would be seeing Walesa courtesy of a satellite broadcast. Phillips asked "Walesa" a series of questions timed to coordinate with the tape. He later remarked, "I decided that staging a mock interview would surely get their attention, especially if they realized I was the man behind the fake facial hair. It proved to be a success, and I still find myself introducing characters that access students' prior knowledge or build new knowledge on what they already know. I believe I engage students by tweaking the usual. I purposefully complicate what students may expect."

Mr. Phillips has some advice on how to create a successful virtual interview. In addition to the video equipment and costumes, a willingness to engage in a bit of acting is also necessary. The taping, of course, must happen before the class period begins. Prior to the taping, the teacher must select a character and write out a dialogue no longer than a couple of minutes. The conversation should be natural, original and based on texts. Mr. Phillips uses this opportunity to "drill the character" on some difficult questions. He is always sure to include questions students might ask.

The timing and logistics of the interview are important in establishing its believability. When you film the "interviewee," be sure to leave enough time for asking the interviewer questions live. Shake your head in approval of the "question" being asked and send nonverbal signals, including a few "hmms and ums." Don't worry if you veer from the exact words you composed while writing the dialogue. Mr. Phillips has found that the interview is more natural when you get the gist of the response and not focus on the exact words. Remember only the "interviewer" questions are time sensitive, not your taped responses. Once you have signed off, keep the dialogue and practice by reviewing the tape for the in-class performance.

Once you are in class and the students have been prepared, it's show time! Inform the students that the focus character has taken time to join the class live via satellite. Students tend to believe the setup is true, if only for a few seconds, and then go along with you. When this happens, you've got them! Execution is the key. Students will laugh and become excited at their teacher's performance. After the satellite interview and while enthusiasm is still high, be sure to transition to a focus on the text.

Thought-Provoking Questions Through Quick Writes. We refer to brief timed writing activities intended to activate background knowledge and personal experience as *quick writes*. Students seem to like the term because it connotes an event that is limited in duration, and teachers appear to honor the spirit of this anticipatory activity by indeed keeping it brief. We like the key contrasts that Daniels and Bizar (1998) offer between this type of writing event and other process pieces:

- *spontaneous* vs. planned,
- *short* vs. lengthy,

Copy the interview on a DVD to allow students to replay the interview again on the computer.

Quick writes are one of many writing to learn strategies that will be explored in chapter 8.

- *exploratory* vs. authoritative,
- *expressive* vs. transactional,
- *informal* vs. formal,
- *personal* vs. audience-centered,
- *unedited* vs. polished, and
- *ungraded* vs. graded (p. 114).

Quick writes are frequently used in English classrooms at the introduction of a new reading to tap into prior knowledge and reader-related experiences, as well as to initiate a reading/writing connection. The choice of text is crucial, too. Reading multicultural literature can build confidence in fledgling second language readers and writers. When students relate to good literature on a personal level, they discover a purpose for reading and response, and begin to find their writer's voice. Before reading *The Circuit: Stories From the Life of a Migrant Child* by Francisco Jimenez (1997), the students in Rita ElWardi's ESL class participated in a number of anticipatory activities focused on thought-provoking questions related to a quick write designed to accomplish these objectives.

Selected texts should offer quality writing, believable characters, complexity of plot, an engaging storyline, and opportunities for the reader to make unique discoveries.

In order to establish a personal connection with the character and the central conflict in the story, students were asked to write about a moment they remembered well; a moment when they had to say good-bye. Because English language learners need structured support in writing, Ms. ElWardi created a list of guiding questions to help even the most reluctant writers begin to recount such an experience. She reminded her students that these questions are there to provoke thought and should not all be answered. To introduce this activity, she recounted an unforgettable moment when she also had to leave a place and a group of friends. Using the questions as her guide, she modeled how these questions could structure a response. Her questions included:

- Where and when did this take place?
- Who was with you and why?
- Why did you have to leave this place or say good-bye to this person?
- What did you say, and what did the others say to you?
- What did you do during this time?
- What were you thinking before, during and after this moment?
- How did you feel during and after you had to say good-bye?
- How do you feel now that you are looking back at the moment?

While the class began the ten-minute quick write, Ms. ElWardi walked about the room and spoke to students not yet putting pencil to paper. After asking these students a number of questions from the list and making notes, she had gathered enough information to ask them to now write what they had just said to her, and to continue writing down their thoughts, one after another, from that point on. Circling the room again, Ms. ElWardi scanned the responses of students who had stopped writing and asked them a clarifying or detail question that could lead to more writing. Below is an example of one student's response (we've included irregularities in grammar):

On November 15, 1996, it was winter and too cold. At that time I was so sad because I was coming to America. I think I couldn't see anymore my country, my cousins and relatives, my country's church, also my mother. One word was hard to say, for my mother. It was Good-bye. Because I never left my mother for a long time or few days before I came to United States. My feeling was bad like a sad for two weeks before I came to U.S. A. I was counting each day and I thought how do I say good-bye for my mother, cousins, relatives and my country? I was looking all around and I was crying. At last the day, November 15, 1996 came. But at that time I was not sad and I was well. I thought, "Now I can to say good-bye for my mother," and I told to myself. Each minute and hour were decreasing. I was ready and I went to my mother and I hugged. I was looking at the ground and I couldn't say good-bye. Both of us were crying. I remember that time. I never forget I couldn't say good-bye.

With quick writes completed, the class then participated in a collaborative oral language building activity called the Three Step Interview (Kagan, 1992) that encourages students to become active, responsible listeners. In this activity, students are placed in groups of four (Students A, B, C, D), and partner up within their group (A with B, C with D), so that there are two partners in each group. We've included a chart of this activity in Figure 2.1. Using their quick writes as material, each group of four followed these three steps:

Step 1:   Student A recounts her/his "good-bye memory" to student B, while student C recounts the same to student D (2 minutes).

Step 2:   Partners switch roles, and B recounts his/her "good-bye memory" to A, while D does the same with partner C (2 minutes).

Figure 2.1   Three-step Interview Chart

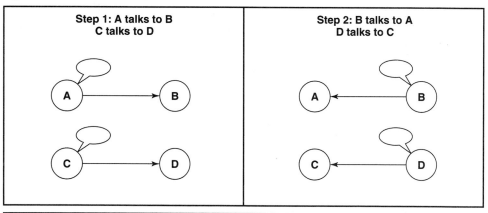

Step 3:   The four members of the group come together in a circle. Now student A must retell his partner's memorable moment to students C & D. Student B then does the same for student A. Then student C retells partner D's memorable moment, and D follows suit (5 to 6 minutes).

The final anticipatory activity to lead into the reading of *The Circuit* came the following day. Ms. ElWardi displayed her own quick write from the previous day on an overhead as a way to demonstrate a writing activity called "Found Poems." Students used words and phrases found in their quick write to compose a poem. She modeled these steps to the class:

Found poems are excerpts of existing texts combined in a poetic form.

Step 1:   Read your quick write aloud from beginning to end.

Step 2:   As you reread the quick write, begin to underline important words and phrases that convey sensory details and express the tone of your writing. (The use of the overhead helps students see exactly what they will be asked to do).

Step 3:   Now read only the words and phrases of your "Found Poem"—a poem you found within your original writing.

Step 4:   Finally, rewrite your poem using an open verse structure.

The students used their own quick writes as the teacher gave individual assistance to a number of students and encouraged others who were attempting to "find their poems." The example below shows the Found Poem that came from the previous student quick write. One can see from the both the writing and the poem that this student has made a personal connection to a conflict central to the story, even before having read it.

Winter
too cold, so sad,
coming to America.
one word was hard to say—
Good-bye.

How do I say it
to my mother,
cousins, relatives,
and my country?

I was counting,
the last day came.
I was counting
each hour, each minute
decreasing.

Looking at the ground,
crying,
I hugged my mother.

I remember that time,
I couldn't say
Good-bye.

Ms. ElWardi strung together several anticipatory activities that had their genesis in one quick write. Her purpose extended beyond activating prior knowledge and personal experience to prepare them for the book they would be reading. She explained that the author was a member of a family of migrant farm workers. She recounted his struggles to learn to read and write, and read aloud the picture book *La Mariposa* (Jimenez, 2000), based on one of the chapters in the book they were about to read. "Francisco Jimenez 'found' his poetry in the words he wrote for *The Circuit*," she told them. "Just as you have found your poetry as well." With that, Ms. El-Wardi's students opened the first page of their book and began to read.

Anticipatory Activities in Social Studies

Demonstration Through Guest Speakers.   Many educators acknowledge the role of experience in learning, especially for adolescents (Dewey, 1938, 1963). The transformative nature of experiences can assist learners in connecting knowledge to its application and variation in the larger world. Experiences can also provoke reflection as students begin to understand that knowledge is not fixed and static, but rather is constantly tested by new experiences (Kolb, 1984). This theory, called experiential learning, has its roots in the work of John Dewey and has been extended by the brain-based research of the past decade. Internships and community service hours are common examples of experiential learning in high school. However, teachers can also bring tenets of experiential learning into the classroom by introducing students to community members who apply the topics of study to their own work. This can be considered a unique form of demonstration through the experiences of others, while serving as an interesting means of introducing a course of study. When the experiences offered through guest speakers are introduced to the classroom, students can clarify their understanding through the eyes of another.

Many nonprofit agencies have speakers bureaus. They offer guest speakers to schools at no cost.

The use of guest speakers in social studies courses is very popular, perhaps because the study of the past and present often converge in the living examples of members of the communities. Historical study of war has been a particularly rich field for guest speakers. A Vietnam war veteran can speak to the experience of being 18 years old and drafted (Poling, 2000). Students can begin to glimpse the meaning of six million dead when they can talk with a Holocaust survivor (Glanz, 1999). Attitudes can change when students meet a citizen of a foreign country (Giannangelo & Bolding, 1998). Guest speakers can also contribute to the understanding of students when they are experts on a topic. Let's look inside a classroom where a guest speaker recently visited.

The three types of vocabulary are general, specialized, and technical. These are discussed in chapter 7.

Mr. Tom Fehrenbacher's world history class had been studying the role of the arts in both reflecting and driving political events. Their inquiry included *Uncle Tom's Cabin* by Harriet Beecher Stowe (1852/1983) and Pablo Picasso's painting "Guernica," an indictment of the 1937 Nazi bombing of a small Spanish town. He wanted to include a study of the "Ring" cycle of operas by Richard Wagner and their influence on Adolph Hitler, but knew that this form of music was unfamiliar to his students. He contacted the local opera society and arranged for a guest speaker to share information on this operatic music form. Mr. Fehrenbacher knew that he would need to prepare his students for their visitor, so he established the purpose and introduced technical vocabulary like *aria, leitmotif,* and *soprano,* and then posted them for easy reference so that these would not be unfamiliar when the guest speaker used them. He also created a form for his students to use during the lecture and charted some of their questions for use during the visit (see Figure 2.2).

Figure 2.2   Student Form for Guest Speakers

Name of Speaker: _____ Date: _____

Purpose of Visit

Unique Experiences

Connections

Questions	**Answers**

When the representative from the opera society arrived, he was delighted to find the students primed for his visit. He gave a brief presentation on the origins of opera in Italy and explained the differences between operas and musicals. He then played excerpts from a selection of operatic works to give the students an idea of the range of the art form, from the light comedies of Mozart to the dramatic works of Bizet. He also included samples of *"Porgy and Bess,"* a twentieth century opera by George Gershwin. Students were able to ask questions and clarify their understanding of the general knowledge of opera. Mr. Fehrenbacher later described the visit as a success and attributed the preparation of the class to the success of the discussion. He also offered advice to ensure a successful visit with a guest speaker:

- *Discuss the purpose and audience in advance.* Furnish specifics in writing about the objectives for the visit—guests welcome this level of detail because it helps them prepare. Make sure that you have discussed any technology needs, including slide projectors, overheads, and CD players. Discuss the number of students involved, and don't surprise the speaker with a few "extras" on the day of the presentation.

- *Prepare the students as well.* A guest speaker who appears unrelated to the current unit of study may be viewed as a "filler" and not central to their understanding of the course materials. Make sure they are familiar with the work of the guest, and have an adequate command of vocabulary and terminology the speaker is likely to use.

- *On the day of the visit, have the room and students organized for the presentation.* Don't waste time with moving furniture and students while the guest stands by.

- *Be an active participant in the presentation.* This is not the time to grade papers—ask questions and make connections for your students. You are modeling the behavior you expect from your students.

- *Have a back-up plan in case the speaker is unable to show.* Emergencies happen and you don't want to be left with lots of down time!

- *Don't forget to write a note of thanks after the visit.* Your mother would be proud. If the speaker is representing their place of work, copy the letter to his or her supervisor.

Thought-Provoking Questions Through Anticipation Guides.   An anticipation guide is a teacher-prepared list of statements that connects to a passage of text. The purpose is to activate prior knowledge, encourage predictions, and stimulate curiosity about a topic (Head & Readence, 1986). These guides are usually constructed for use with texts that are controversial or commonly misunderstood, such as sharks, slavery, or the legal age for drinking alcohol. These guides are useful for promoting class discussion as well, because they can spark debate and foster the inevitable need to consult other sources of information.

Helen Arnold used an anticipation guide in her history class study of the Los Angeles Zoot Suit Riots of 1943. These violent clashes between Mexican-American youths and American servicemen brought in from Southern California military bases are now understood to be racially motivated, but at the time of these events, the Mexican-American community and "zoot suiters" in particular, were blamed for the riots. Ms. Arnold prepared an anticipation guide like the one in Figure 2.3.

Many of the statements do not appear in the text, but rather are inferred from several places in the reading. Some are "think and search" questions that are in-

Figure 2.3   Anticipation Guide

Discuss each statement with your group. Mark your opinion and then read the assigned web site to check your understanding.

True   False

_____ _____   1. When bad times came, Mexicans who had been encouraged to come to LA were now seen as "job stealers."

_____ _____   2. Thousands of Mexicans, some with children born in the US, were sent back to Mexico.

_____ _____   3. Mexicans were the only group to suffer from discrimination and injustice.

_____ _____   4. Headlines in newspapers disapproved of the attacks.

_____ _____   5. The servicemen who took part in the attack were prosecuted.

_____ _____   6. Eleanor Roosevelt blamed discrimination as a root cause of the riots.

_____ _____   7. Today, there is more anti-immigrant sentiment in California.

After reading the assigned text, discuss your answers with your group. You may change any answers you want.

tended to give students experience with putting together answers from more than one sentence (Raphael, 1986). Others require both information from the text as well as their personal experiences—so-called "in the head" questions that often demand more complex answers.

> These and other types of questions are discussed in depth in chapter 4 on questioning.

Perhaps the most challenging part of developing an anticipation guide is identifying a provocative text that will motivate your students to discuss, debate, disagree, and confront their own misconceptions. Once that is done, the steps to creating a guide are fairly simple (Head & Readence, 1986):

Step 1:   *Identify the major concepts in the reading.* What are the main ideas in the passage? Keep it to two or three so the guide won't be too long.

Step 2:   *Consider your students' prior knowledge.* What are they most likely to hold misconceptions about?

Step 3:   *Write five or ten statements pertaining to the reading.* Don't make them all factual—be sure to create open-ended statements as well. Look again to your major concepts to make sure you are creating statements that relate to larger concepts rather than isolated facts.

Introduce the anticipation guide and ask students to complete it before the reading. Encourage small group discussions of the statements, then invite them to read the text passage to confirm or disconfirm their beliefs. Let them know they can change their answers while they read, then follow up the reading with a class discussion of the items and the broader questions generated by the reading. This is an ideal opportunity to connect this activity with a strategy employed by critical readers—the self-assessment of beliefs and assumptions that may be supported or disputed by a reading. After all, it is this cognitive dissonance that challenges all of us to continually refine what we know.

> The anticipation guide provides a visual record of student learning as it scaffolds their growing understanding of the reading.

Anticipatory Activities in Mathematics

Advance Organizers in Algebra.   Secondary students are often required to read extended passages of text containing complex ideas and concepts. A challenge for content area teachers is that the very reading materials essential to learning the content may be too complex for students to process. One method for scaffolding comprehension of text passages is through the use of an advance organizer (Ausubel, 1960). There are two types of advance organizers—expository advance organizers, meant for use with texts containing new material, and comparative organizers, which link new knowledge with previously learned material (Ausubel, 1978). These are not just summaries of the passage—they are meant to contain more complex information than the reading alone offers so that students can gain a sense of how the information is associated with other concepts and ideas. The use of advance organizers with young adults enhances student recall and understanding of the material (Thompson, 1998).

In order to prepare his algebra students for an end-of-course test, Aaron Sage chose a shared reading of poems from *Math Talk* (Pappas, 1991). These unique poems are designed to be read by two voices, or groups of voices. After modeling the performance of one, he assigned a poem to each small group. Their task was to perform the poem for the class and explain the mathematical concepts contained in the poem. The purpose of this lesson was to give students a creative means for reviewing the major mathematical concepts featured on the upcoming test. In addition to the poem, their textbooks, and mathematics notebooks, the groups were given a comparative advance organizer on their assigned poem's topic. For example, one group was given a poem on imaginary numbers. Their advance organizer appears in the box below.

> ### IMAGINARY NUMBERS
>
> This poem discusses imaginary numbers and uses humor to remind us how odd it is to have numbers that "don't exist." Of course, they do exist because they help us to solve equations. An imaginary number is the square root of a negative number. It is called "imaginary" because any number that is squared results in a positive number. It is written as "i" and is defined as $i = \sqrt{-1}$. They are used in physics and engineering.

This advance organizer made connections between the information contained in the poem and knowledge learned from earlier in the year. It is important to note that the advance organizer contained more complex information than the poem itself contained—a hallmark of advance organizers. In this case, the advance organizer was a bridge between the poem, the textbook, and their notes. With advance organizers like these, the teacher can consider both the information contained in the text and the prior knowledge and experiences of the students to create a higher order of associative learning than the text alone can offer.

Anticipatory Activities in Science

Demonstrations in Chemistry.   Perhaps there is no content area more perfectly suited to classroom demonstrations than science. A jaw-dropping demonstration can provoke wonder and inquiry and establish real purpose to subsequent study of a sci-

---

An advance organizer is a much shorter synopsis of the reading that focuses on its major concepts.

See chapter 3 for more details on how Mr. Sage taught this lesson.

The key to scaffolding instruction is accessing students' prior knowledge about the topic.

entific concept. These memorable occasions can also be considered discrepant events because they use the element of surprise to motivate (Wright & Govindarajan, 1995). They may be considered visual displays as well because they activate memory and retention through motion and light. We suspect that inside every good science teacher there is a young child who was mesmerized by a dazzling display of a mysterious scientific concept. In his autobiography *Uncle Tungsten: Memories of a Chemical Boyhood,* Oliver Sacks (2001) recounts life in a household surrounded by parents and siblings deeply involved in the sciences. In a chapter entitled "Stinks and Bangs," he writes of a demonstration he performed as a 10-year-old with his two older brothers:

> Attracted by the sounds and flashes and smells coming from my lab, David and Marcus, now medical students, sometimes joined me in experiments—the nine- and ten-year differences between us hardly mattered at these times. On one occasion, I was experimenting with hydrogen and oxygen, there was a loud explosion, and an almost invisible sheet of flame, which blew off Marcus's eyebrows completely. But Marcus took this in good part, and he and David often suggested other experiments. (p. 77)

Chemistry teacher Robert North uses the "stinks and bangs" of science to motivate and stimulate interest in chemistry. A member of the local American Chemical Society, he recruits 8th graders from middle schools to take an interest in science. He brings a "day of magic" to each feeder middle school and proceeds to dazzle them with a range of demonstrations of chemical wonders, always connecting to the scientific concepts that explain the phenomena.

Many of these same students sign up for chemistry when they reach 11th grade, enticed by the memory of amazing demonstrations and plenty of stinks and bangs. On the first day of the course, he sets a tone for the "Cardinal Chemists," his nickname for those enrolled in his course. While he introduces the rules of the class, he pours a small amount of isopropyl alcohol (2-proponol) into on empty 5-gallon water cooler container. Without explanation, he lights a match at the mouth of the jug and a loud "boom!" results, along with startled gasps and squeals of his new students. He then instructs them to quickly write about what they have just witnessed. After inviting responses from the students, he prompts a discussion on the difference between an explosion and a burn, terminology many of them have just used interchangeably. Mr. North then gives them a few minutes to revise their writing using accurate vocabulary and reviews the rules again, reminding them that they are there for the safety of all. Finally, he moves in for the final point—"Chemistry is a bomb!"

It is important to note that Mr. North's teaching is not all "stinks and bangs." He pairs writing with the demonstrations to give students an opportunity to clarify their understanding and support their inquiry of what is still unknown to them. He is also careful to ground his work in the theoretical underpinnings of each demonstration. Indeed, without this careful attention to the scientific concepts, students are likely to form misconceptions about what they have seen (Roth, McRobbie, & Lucas, 1997). But the powerful responses to anticipatory activities like this one are always part of the instructional repertoire of this teacher. "Science is fun," says Mr. North, "and there's a reason why it should grab their attention."

Freedman (2000) recommends several principles for designing effective science demonstrations:

- *Establish a clear purpose.* The demonstration must be directly related to the scientific concepts being studied.

Neurologist Oliver Sacks has written many biographies of unique individuals who experience the world in nontraditional ways. Many adolescents find these accounts to be particularly interesting.

- *Plan the demonstration carefully.* This is more than just assembling the materials. What other learning experiences will the students have in order to understand the theoretical basis for the demonstration? Plan the related lessons to support student connections to important concepts.

- *Plan for repeatability.* Students may need to see the demonstration again. Be sure to have extra materials on hand for this possibility. Also, be sure that the demonstration you've selected yields reliable and consistent results.

- *Plan for safety.* Although discrepant events like science demonstrations can enhance learning, your students don't need to witness you getting hurt.

- *Consider visibility.* A crowded classroom can make it difficult to see and fully appreciate the demonstration. It can become a safety issue as well for your students if they are jockeying for position. If the sight lines are obstructed in your classroom, consider dividing the class in half and performing the demonstration twice. If the phenomenon you are demonstrating needs to be seen from close range, then perform the demonstration with small groups of students.

- *Don't discount the importance of showmanship.* The literal and figurative "stinks and bangs" of science demonstrations can intrigue your students. Don't be afraid to play it up—your enthusiasm is infectious.

Thought-Provoking Questions in Physics.   Hal Cox, physics teacher, uses thought-provoking questions to follow demonstrations and lab experiments. During a unit on waves, students worked in small groups to complete a lab using slinkies. With slinkies stretched across the floor and a lab sheet to structure their inquiry, they performed a series of experiments to make predictions about wave behavior by manipulating length and tension. During another lab, they used string instruments to study the effect of these variables on sound waves. The following day, they arrived to find a question posted on the overhead—What would happen to the pitch of a string if you changed both the length and the tension on a string?

Students discussed this for a few minutes with their lab groups and then wrote their responses in their science journals. Most of the students were able to connect the concept of wave frequency with the variables. However, he was delighted to see that some of them had also understood that the same pitch could be obtained by manipulating either variable. He then reviewed the lab from the previous day and led a discussion on the successes and challenges the groups had in completing the lab sheet. One of the things we admire about Mr. Cox's approach is the efficiency of this instructional strategy—the entire review process took only ten minutes. By beginning his class with a thought-provoking question, he activated his students' prior knowledge and gave them an opportunity to make connections to newly acquired knowledge.

Providing students with opportunities to discuss content with peers assists them in meeting oral language standards for accountable talk.

Anticipatory Activities in Electives

Thought-Provoking Questions Through K-W-L in Art.   As we had discussed earlier in this chapter, a popular and effective anticipatory activity is K-W-L (Ogle, 1986). Remember that K-W-L (know/want to know/learned) is a method for activating prior knowledge and formulating questions to guide inquiry (see Figure 2.4). Teachers across content area subjects have confirmed the usefulness and flexibility

Figure 2.4   K-W-L Chart

What Do I Know?	What Do I Want to Know?	What Have I Learned?

Figure 2.5   K-W-L Art Inquiry Chart

What Do I Know?	What Do I Want to Know?	What Have I Learned?
He was an artist He was famous He's dead	Why was he famous?	He painted Mona Lisa and The Last Supper
	Does he use the elements of art in his work?	He used line, hatching, shadowing, 3-dimensional shading
	When was he born?	Born 1452
	Where was he born?	Born in Italy
	When did he die?	He died 1519
	What influenced him?	Imagination and creativity
	Was he only an artist?	He was an inventor, scientist, and city planner
	What were the names of his famous works?	Mona Lisa, The Last Supper
	What material did he use for his work?	Red chalk (sanguine) finely sharpened
	What kinds of things did he paint?	In early career, he drew/designed military arms Left-handed

of this technique for introducing a unit of study. Buehl (2001) identifies it as one of the instructional strategies essential in the repertoire of every secondary content area educator.

Jeremy Merrill's Art students are required to conduct in-class research every two weeks on an artist of their choice. Mr. Merrill introduces research methods early in the year and models the first project on a single artist. He shows them a selection of slides featuring the artist's work and invites questions about the paintings. Subsequent research projects are student-directed and encompass every era from medieval to post-modern. K-W-L charts are the initial component of any inquiry, and are expected with every research report. Recently, Hayna researched the life and work of Leonardo da Vinci. (We've included irregularities in grammar). Her K-W-L chart is displayed Figure 2.5.

Teachers and researchers continue to revise and update this time-honored instructional strategy.

Figure 2.6   K-W-L Grading Rubric

K-W-L Research Project Grading Rubric

K=What You Know   **W=What You Want to Know**   **L=What You Learned**

5. Exemplary!
- Completes the K-W-L chart with 7+ entries in each column.
- Demonstrates mastery in his/her writing skills, with little or no grammar and punctuation errors.
- Answers all of the W questions in the L section and includes all of the information in the writing assignment.
- Adds additional information in the writing section that was not part of the W section.

4. Exceeds Standards
- Completes the K-W-L chart with 5–6 entries in each column.
- Demonstrates above average writing skills in grammar and punctuation (errors do not interfere with meaning).
- Answers all of the W questions in the L section and includes all of the information in the written assignment.
- No new information.

3. Meets Standards
- Completes the K-W-L chart with 3–4 entries in each column.
- Demonstrates adequate writing skills in grammar and punctuation (some errors interfere with meaning).
- Answers more than half of the W questions in the L section and includes the information in the writing assignment.

2. Progressing
- Partially completed K-W-L chart.
- Answers less than half the W questions in the L section and includes the information in the writing assignment.

1. No Evidence
- Does not turn in a project for grading.
- Does not make an attempt at the project.

A rubric is an assessment tool that allows teachers to evaluate a student's performance based on established criteria. For sample rubric forms, see *http://www.teachervision.com/lesson-plans/lesson-4522.html.*

Mr. Merrill uses a 5-point rubric to guide the development of the K-W-L. The rubric is intended to guide the entire research process as it is mirrored in the completion of the K-W-L, and includes the written report that is submitted (see Figure 2.6). Formative feedback through peer editing is also featured in the course. Mr. Merrill uses a simple Peer Review Sheet for the peer editor to complete and discuss with the writer (see Figure 2.7).

Mr. Merrill's emphasis on the history of art, as well as its execution, connects past works to the students' original compositions. He has found that using K-W-L charts supports the development of research and inquiry skills among his students while giving him a way to prompt discussion about works of art and their creators.

"It's really the basis for what we do as artists. 'What has been done by others?' 'Where do we want to go with our own art?' 'Now that we've attempted it, what have we learned?' That's the artistic process in a nutshell."

Figure 2.7   Peer Review Sheet

Name: _____

Date: _____

Period: _____

Peer Review Sheet

Number of the paper you graded: _____

Assignment Title: _____

Rubric Score: 1   2   3   4   5

Evidence to support score:

_____

_____

_____

_____

_____

What can the author do to improve the assignment?

_____

_____

_____

_____

_____

Conclusion

Anticipatory activities can enhance the learning and retention of students in content area classrooms. They can also serve to motivate and stimulate curiosity about the topics being studied. Demonstrations, discrepant events, visual displays, and thought-provoking questions are examples of the types of anticipatory activities used by effective teachers.

Demonstrations are typically used to display a theory, concept, or phenomenon. They are a staple of science instruction, but can be utilized in any content area. Demonstrations are particularly useful for English language learners because they foster mental models for concepts. It is important to remember that a demonstration does not replace the need for the theoretical basis for understanding the phenomenon. Discrepant events are useful for gaining attention and creating a lasting impression. These events are characteristically described as surprising or startling. Teachers have found success in using costumes and props to illustrate a character, setting, or era. The growing availability of technology makes it possible to include novel visual displays for illustrating an idea or concept. Web-based programs are a particular area for resources on a variety of phenomenon. Exciting examples of visual displays can be found through the growing number of available WebQuests. Thought-provoking questions are a primary tool for teachers to create anticipatory activities. Examples of thought-provoking questions in this chapter included essential questions, quick writes, found poems, anticipation guides and K-W-L's.

References

Anderson, R. C., & Pearson, P. D. (1984). A schema-theoretic view of basic processes in reading comprehension. In P. D. Pearson, R. Barr, M. L. Kamil, & P. Mosenthal (Eds.), *Handbook of reading research* (pp. 255–292). Mahwah, NJ: Lawrence Erlbaum.

Ausubel, D. P. (1960). The use of advance organizers in the learning and retention of meaningful verbal material. *Journal of Educational Psychology, 51,* 267–272.

Ausubel, D. P. (1978). In defense of advance organizers: A reply to the critics. *Review of Educational Research, 48,* 251–257.

Beasley, W. (1982). Teacher demonstrations: The effect on student task involvement. *Journal of Chemical Education, 59,* 789–790.

Brandt, R. (1992). On Deming and school quality: A conversation with Enid Brown. *Educational Leadership, 50*(3), 28–31.

Brooks, H. B., & Brooks, D., W. (1996). The emerging role of CD-ROMs in teaching chemistry. *Journal of Science Education and Technology, 5,* 203–215.

Bruner, J. S., Goodnow, J. J., & Austin, G. A. (1956). *A study of thinking.* New York: Wiley.

Buehl, D. (2001). *Classroom strategies for interactive learning* (2nd ed.). Newark, DE: International Reading Association.

Buzan, T. (1979). *Using both sides of your brain.* New York: E. P. Dutton.

Carr, E., & Ogle, D. (1987). K-W-L plus: A strategy for comprehension and summarization. *Journal of Reading, 30,* 626–631.

Daniels, H., & Bizar, M. (1998). *Methods that matter: Six structures for best practice classrooms.* York, ME: Stenhouse.

Dewey, J. (1938, 1963). *Experience and education.* New York: Macmillan.

Dodge, B. (1995). *Some thoughts about WebQuests.* Retrieved June 23, 2002 from http://edweb.sdsu.edu/courses/edtec596/about_webquests.html

Eggen, P., & Kauchak, D. (2001). *Educational psychology: Windows on classrooms* (5th ed.). Upper Saddle River, NJ: Merrill/Prentice Hall.

Freedman, M. P. (2000). Using effective demonstrations for motivation. *Science and Children, 38*(1), 52–55.

Giannangelo, D. M., & Bolding, R. A. (1998). Ethnocentrism, geography, and foreign guest speakers: An attempt to change attitudes. *Journal of the Middle States Council for the Social Studies,* 122–126.

Glanz, J. (1999). Ten suggestions for teaching the Holocaust. *History Teacher, 32,* 547–565.

Good, T., & Brophy, J. (2002). *Looking in classrooms* (9th ed.). New York: Harper Collins.

Head, M. H., & Readence, J. E. (1986). Anticipation guides: Meaning through prediction. In E. K. Dishner, T. W. Bean, J. E. Readence, & D. W. Moore (Eds.), *Reading in the content areas* (2nd ed.) (pp. 229–234). Dubuque, IA: Kendall Hunt.

Hurst, B. (2001). ABCs of content area lesson planning: Attention, basics, and comprehension. *Journal of Adolescent & Adult Literacy, 44,* 692–693.

Hyerle, D. (1996). *Visual tools for constructing knowledge.* Alexandria, VA: Association of Supervision and Curriculum Development.

Janney, R., & Snell, M. E. (2000). *Modifying schoolwork: Teachers' guides to inclusive practices.* Baltimore, MD: Paul H. Brookes.

Jensen, E. (1998). *Teaching with the brain in mind.* Alexandria, VA: Association for Supervision and Curriculum Development.

Jimenez, F. (1997). *The circuit: Stories from the life of a migrant child.* Albuquerque, NM: University of New Mexico Press.

Jimenez, F. (2000). *La mariposa.* New York: Houghton Mifflin.

Jorgensen, C. M. (1998). *Restructuring high schools for all students: Taking inclusion to the next level.* Baltimore, MD: Paul H. Brookes.

Kagan, S. (1992) *Cooperative learning.* San Juan Capistrano, CA: Kagan Cooperative Learning.

Kolb, D. (1984). *Experiential learning: Experience as the source of learning and development.* Englewood Cliffs, NJ: Prentice-Hall.

Landauer, T. K. (1975). Memory without organization: Properties of a model with random storage and undirected retrieval. *Cognitive Psychology, 7,* 495–531.

Larsen, J. D. (1991). Pay attention! Demonstrating the role of attention in learning. *Teaching of Psychology,* 18, 238–239.

Lee, C. (2000). Modelling in the mathematics classroom. *Mathematics Teaching, 171,* 28–31.

Margulies, N. (1991). *Mapping inner space: Learning and teaching mind mapping.* Tuscon, AZ: Zephyr.

Muncey, D. E., Payne, J., & White, N. S. (1999). Making curriculum and instructional reform happen: A case study. *Peabody Journal of Education, 74,* 68–110.

Ogle, D. (1986). K-W-L: A teaching model that develops active reading of expository text. *The Reading Teacher, 39,* 564–570.

Pappas, T. (1991). *Math talk: Mathematical ideas in poems for two voices.* San Carlos, CA: Wide World Publishing/ Tetra.

Poling, L. G. (2000). The real world: Community speakers in the classroom. *Social Education, 64*(4), 8–10.

Raphael, T. E. (1986). Teaching question-answer relationships, revisited. *The Reading Teacher, 39,* 516–522.

Roth, W. M., McRobbie, C. J., & Lucas, K. B. (1997). Why may students fail to learn from demonstrations: A social practice perspective on learning in physics. *Journal of Research in Science Teaching, 34,* 509–533.

Sacks, O. (2001). *Uncle Tungsten: Memories of a chemical boyhood.* New York: Alfred A. Knopf.

Schmidt, P. R. (1999). KWLQ: Inquiry and literacy learning in science. *The Reading Teacher, 52,* 789–792.

Smith, F. (1998). *The book of learning and forgetting.* New York: Teachers College Press.

Sprenger, M. (1999). *Learning and memory: The brain in action.* Alexandria, VA: Association for Supervision and Curriculum Development.

Stowe, H. B. (1852/1983). *Uncle Tom's cabin or life among the lowly.* New York: Bantam.

Sylwester, R. (1995). *A celebration of neurons: An educator's guide to the human brain.* Alexandria, VA: Association for Supervision and Curriculum Development.

Thompson, D. N. (1998). Using advance organizers to facilitate reading comprehension among older adults. *Educational Gerontology, 24,* 625–638.

Wills, C. (1995). Voice of inquiry: Possibilities and perspectives. *Childhood Education, 71,* 261–265.

Wright, E. L., & Govindarajan, G. (1995). Discrepant event demonstrations. *Science Teacher, 62*(1), 24–28.

Chapter 3

Read-Alouds and Shared Readings: Not Just for Elementary Anymore

Nancy Frey and Douglas Fisher

The 11th-grade U.S. history classroom is shrouded in darkness, lit only by the soft glow of two colonial-style lanterns. Students have been studying the American Revolution and its effect around the world. They lean in closer as the teacher begins a dramatic reading of *The Midnight Ride of Paul Revere* (Longfellow, 1860/2001). "Listen, my children, and you shall hear. . . " (p. 3). Richly detailed illustrations by Christopher Bing appear on the projector as the reading continues. The two lanterns are lifted high as the poem describes patriot Robert Newman's ascent to the belfry of the Old North Church to signal Paul Revere of the British approach across the Charles River. "For, borne on the night-wind of the Past, through all our history, to the last, in the hour of darkness and peril and need, the people will waken to listen and hear. . . " As the poem concludes, fifteen-year-old Terrell exclaims, "That's the way all poems should be!"

Interest in the practice of read-alouds and shared readings in secondary content area classrooms has increased in the last decade. At one time, public performance of text in high school classrooms was limited to oratory exercises of excerpts from the English canon. It was rare to find narrative or expository text used in content area classrooms, and, in fact, there was some resistance to instruction of any reading strategies in content area classrooms (Price, 1978; Rieck, 1977; Smith & Otto, 1969). However, deeper understandings of the connections between reading and learning have caused content area teachers to reexamine sound literacy practices in their classrooms (McKenna & Robinson, 1990; Ornstein, 1994).

Two literacy practices borrowed from developmental reading theory and customized for secondary classrooms are read-alouds and shared reading. A *read-aloud* is a text or passage selected by the teacher to read publicly to a large or small group of students. A primary purpose for the read-aloud selection is to focus on the content of the text. A *shared reading* is a text or passage that is jointly shared by teacher and student, but is read aloud by the teacher. In shared readings, the students can also

In both read-alouds and shared reading, the reading is done by the teacher, not the students.

see the text, and it is usually chosen both for its content and to draw attention to a particular text feature or comprehension strategy. Let's take a closer look at each of these literacy practices.

Read-Alouds

The practice of reading aloud in public dates to the dawn of written language. Throughout history, town criers shared local news, religious orders proclaimed scriptures, and lectors read classical works and newspapers to Cuban cigar factory workers, paid for by the laborers themselves (Manguel, 1996). Even in widely literate societies, the act of being read to continues to enthrall. Demand for audio books rose 75% between 1995 and 1999, and some estimate that "for every ten print books sold, one audio program is sold" (Block, 1999).

A large body of evidence suggests that being read to by an adult enhances literacy development. For example, young children who are read to are more likely to enter school with higher literacy skills (Anderson, Hiebert, Scott, & Wilkinson, 1985). Likewise, a longitudinal study of students identified as precocious readers (before age 6) revealed that they were more likely to be read to by their parents (Durkin, 1974–1975). Correlational studies demonstrate an association between exposure to read-alouds and positive motivation to read (Greaney & Hegarty, 1987; Morrow & Young, 1997). Conversely, Rosow's (1988) interviews with illiterate adults demonstrated the negative effects when read-alouds are not available. Her data revealed that none of the interviewed adults had any recollection of being read to as a child.

Do you remember being read to as a child? Who read to you?

Effectiveness of Read-Alouds

While read-alouds have been shown to be effective for young children's literacy development, they can also be used to motivate older, reluctant readers (Beckman, 1986; Erickson, 1996). In a study of 1,700 adolescents, Herrold, Stanchfield, and Serabian (1989) found positive changes in attitude toward reading among students who were read to by their teacher on a daily basis. Likewise, a survey of 1,765 adolescents conducted more than a decade later reported that 62% of the participants identified teacher read-alouds as a favorite literacy activity (Ivey & Broaddus, 2001). Students themselves have reported that a preferred instructional practice is having teachers read aloud portions of text to introduce new readings and promote interest (Worthy, 2002). It appears that students appreciate the read-aloud event as an opportunity to share the teacher's enthusiasm and interest in the topic.

Another advantage to the use of read-alouds is the level of text complexity that can be utilized. When text is read aloud by the teacher, students with reading difficulties can access books that might otherwise be too difficult for them to read independently. This is essential in content area classrooms. Text complexity rises rapidly during the secondary school years and students who have reading difficulties often find themselves unable to comprehend the information in content area books. A vicious cycle then begins when these students fail to assimilate the information, further impacting their ability to use it as background information for new content. Thus, the gap continues to widen as students with reading difficulties fall further behind their classmates. It comes as no surprise that student interest and attitudes toward reading also decline precipitously after sixth grade coinciding with the increased reading demand in their content area classes.

While read-alouds alone cannot compensate for these gaps, they can introduce important texts that some students might not otherwise be able to read and comprehend independently. Students without reading difficulties are also likely to benefit. A recent empirical analysis of secondary textbooks revealed that many students were unsure about their comprehension of the readings (Wang, 1996). Read-alouds are a viable strategy for clarifying difficult text.

Teachers should monitor student interest in reading and topics associated with the content. This can be accomplished using an interest survey asking students about their reading preferences.

The Benefits for English Language Learners

English language learners benefit from exposure to read-alouds as well. Adolescents acquiring a new language are subjected to a bewildering array of social, pragmatic, and academic language patterns (Nieto, 1992). Read-alouds create opportunities for the teacher to utilize multiple pathways to promote understanding of the content of the text, including intonation, facial expressions, and gestures (Cummins, 1980).

Read-alouds also support language acquisition for English language learners because it provides fluent language role models (Amer, 1997). The text choice for the read-aloud is also crucial for English language learners. Selection of books that utilize engaging illustrations or photographs adds another dimension to assist students in creating new schema (Early & Tang, 1991).

This also helps students meet and exceed the English language arts standards for listening.

Planning for Read-Alouds in Secondary Classrooms

The successful use of read-alouds in secondary content area classrooms has been well documented. It has been shown to be effective in foreign language instruction (Richardson, 1997–1998), social studies (Irvin, Lunstrum, Lynch-Brown, & Shepard, 1995), and mathematics (Richardson & Gross, 1997). However, text selection can also be daunting for teachers unfamiliar with the range of possibilities associated with their discipline. It is important to note that read-alouds in content area need not be confined to narrative text, or unrelated to the topic of study. In other words, we wouldn't advise the algebra teacher to read from *Canterbury Tales* (Chaucer, 1400/1985)! However, that same algebra teacher might be interested in a read-aloud from *The Number Devil* (Enzensberger, 1998) detailing the intricacies of irrational numbers, referred to by the title character as "unreasonable numbers." Several excellent teacher resources on text selection are available, including *Read All About It!* (Trelease, 1993) and *The Read-Aloud Handbook* (Trelease, 2002). The author of these books has compiled an array of short stories, poems, and newspaper articles suitable for a number of classroom applications. In addition, *Read It Aloud!* (Richardson, 2000) is organized by content areas, including mathematics, geography, music, physical education, and social studies.

Regardless of where you find your readings, make sure it is connected to the content you are teaching.

Each chapter contains examples of readings and recommendations for connecting the texts to the concepts being taught. Figure 3.1 lists picture books that are particularly well-suited for secondary content classrooms.

There are several elements to consider in planning and delivering read-alouds to secondary students. These items also serve as indicators of effective instructional

Figure 3.1   List of Picture Books Across Content Areas

Picture Books for English
Narrative:
Johnson, D. B. (2002). *Henry builds a cabin*. New York: Houghton Mifflin.
Martin, J. (1998). *The rough-face girl*. New York: Putnam & Grosset.
Rohmann, E. (1994). *Time flies*. New York: Scholastic.
Scieszka, J. (1994). *The book that Jack wrote*. New York: Viking.
David, L. (1999). *Beetle boy*. New York: Bt Bound.
Non-narrative:
Aliki. (1999). *William Shakespeare and the Globe*. New York: HarperCollins.
Lincoln, A. (1995). *The Gettysburg address*. Boston: Houghton Mifflin.
Thayer, E. L., & Bing, C. (2000). *Casey at the bat: A ballad of the republic sung in the year 1888*. New York: Handprint
   Books.
Spier, P. (1973). *The Star-Spangled Banner*. New York: Yearling.

Picture Books for Social Studies
Narrative
Cherry, L (1993). *The great kapok tree*. San Diego, CA: Harcourt Brace.
Hesse, K. (Scholastic). *Come on, rain!* New York: Scholastic.
Wiesner, D. (1991). *Tuesday*. New York: Clarion.
Bunting, E. (1989). *Terrible things*. Philadelphia: Jewish Publication Society.
Siebert, D. (1988). *Mojave*. New York: HarperCollins.
Tsuchiya, Y. (1988). *Faithful elephants: A true story of animals, people, and war*. New York: Houghton Mifflin.
Yin. (2001). *Coolies*. New York: Philomel.
Non-narrative
Hart, T. (1994). *Antarctic diary*. New York: Macmillan-McGraw Hill.
Martin, (1998). *Snowflake Bentley*. Boston: Houghton Mifflin.
Sis, P. (1996). *Starry messenger: Galileo Galilei*. New York: Farrar, Straus and Giroux.
Abells, C. B. (1983). *The children we remember*. New York: Greenwillow.
Bridges, R. (1999). *Through my eyes*. New York: Scholastic.
Lincoln, A. (1998). *The Gettysburg address*. New York: Houghton Mifflin.
Smith, D. J. (2002). *If the world were a village: A book about the world's people*. Toronto, Canada: Kids Can Press.

Picture Books for Mathematics
Narrative
Demi. (1997). *One grain of rice*. New York: Scholastic.
Friedman, A. (1994). *The king's commissioners*. New York: Scholastic.
Neuschwander, C. (1999). *Sir Cumference and the dragon of Pi*. New York: Scholastic.
Scieszka, J. (1995). *Math curse*. New York: Viking.
Turner, P. (1999). *Among the odds and the evens*. New York: Farrar Straus and Giroux.
Non-narrative
Pappas, T. (1993). *Fractals, googles, and other mathematical tales*. San Carlos, CA: Wide World Publishing/Tetra.
Parker, S. (1995). *Isaac Newton and gravity*. Broomall, PA: Chelsea House.

Picture Books in Elective Courses
Narrative
Krull, K. (2000). *Wilma unlimited: How Wilma Rudolph became the world's fastest woman*. New York: Voyager.
Laden, N. (1998). *When Pigasso met Mootise*. San Francisco: Chronicle.
Shafer, A. C. (2002). *The fantastic journey of Pieter Bruegel*. New York: Scholastic.
Taylor, C. (1992). *The house that crack built*. San Francisco: Chronicle.
Weatherford, C. B. (2000). *The sound that jazz makes*. New York: Walker.
Non-narrative
Krull, K. (1993). *The lives of the musicians: Good times, bad times (and what the neighbors thought)*. San Diego:
   Harcourt Brace.
Roalf, P. (1992). *Looking at paintings: Dancers*. New York: Hyperion.

Figure 3.2 Read-Aloud Rubric for Self-Assessment

	Successfully implemented	Moderately successful	Just getting started	Not evident
Text chosen appropriate for students' interests and level				
Selection has been previewed and practiced				
Clear purpose established				
Teacher provides a fluent reading model				
Students are engaged in listening				
Teacher stops periodically and questions thoughtfully to enhance focus (literal, interpretive, and evaluative)				
Students engaged in discussion				
Connections to reading and writing				

Comments:

practice for administrative observations. A self-assessment rubric of these same elements appears in Figure 3.2.

1. *Select readings appropriate to content, students' emotional and social development, and interests.* Read-alouds can be especially useful for activating background knowledge and connecting to student experiences.

2. *Practice the selection.* You wouldn't go on stage without rehearsing, would you? Think of the read-aloud as a performance. Rehearsal allows you to make decisions about inflection, rate, and pitch.

3. *Model fluent oral reading.* In addition to exposure to content information, a read-aloud also serves as a place for students to hear fluent oral reading. Reading acquisition for students with reading difficulties, as well as some English language learners, can be inhibited by their own disfluent reading.

4. *Engage students and hook them into listening to the text.* Creating anticipation for the reading, as the teacher did in the *Midnight Ride of Paul Revere* scenario, can activate student interest and increase meaning. When appropriate, pair read-alouds with other supporting materials such as props, diagrams, manipulatives, or illustrations.

5. *Stop periodically to ask questions.* Talk within the text enhances student understanding. Plan questions for critical thinking in advance and write them on a sticky note to remind you. Don't rely only on "constrained questions" (Beck & McKeown, 2001) that can be answered in a few words. For example, "What do you believe was the author's purpose for writing this story?" allows for a more detailed response than "Where did the story take place?" Create inferential questions that invite connections beyond the text as well.

6. *Engage students in book discussions.* This is related to the questioning that is done during the reading. Choose read-alouds that foster further discussion once the reading is complete. Perhaps you may ask students why you chose this particular reading, or how it relates to the current topic of study.

7. *Make explicit connections to students' independent reading and writing.* A read-aloud should relate directly to the content—otherwise, it might have limited applicability in the curriculum. As well, the read-aloud should also connect to other literacy experiences. For instance, the end of a read-aloud event might signal an ideal time to invite students to write a response. Questions raised through the discussion following the reading might also prompt further research and outside reading by students.

Shared Reading

In addition to read-alouds, teachers also extend literacy experiences through shared reading. Shared reading is the practice of reading collaboratively with students. Unlike read-alouds, where only the teacher can see the text, an important feature of a shared reading experience is that students can follow along silently as the teacher reads aloud. Another difference is that in shared reading there is a lesson specifically related to a comprehension strategy, text feature, or reading behavior. As with read-alouds, the practice of shared reading has its roots in emergent literacy practices for young children (Holdaway, 1982).

Shared reading serves as an instructional bridge between the teacher-directed read-aloud and student-directed independent reading. While read-alouds are teacher-controlled and independent reading is student-controlled, these literacy activities provide little opportunity for teacher and students to alternatively take and relinquish the lead. Pearson and Gallagher (1983) proposed a model for comprehension instruction called the gradual release of responsibility. They suggest that using guided practice as a method for instruction allows students to attempt new strategies for eventual use in their own reading. Thus, through instructional practices like shared reading, teachers move from modeling in read-alouds to applying strategies in independent reading.

See chapter 2 for more information on using anticipatory activities.

See chapter 4 for more information on questioning strategies.

See chapter 8 for more ideas on using writing to learn.

The concept behind gradual release of responsibility is that students experience scaffolded instruction that moves them from teacher-modeled activities to student-directed work.

Shared reading is grounded in the sociocultural theory of Vygotsky's zones of proximal development (1978). This allows for scaffolding of information to extend learning through guided instruction. Vygotsky theorized that when students receive support just beyond what they can accomplish independently, they learn new skills and concepts. He defined the zone as

> the distance between the actual developmental level as determined by independent problem solving and the level of potential development as determined through problem solving under adult guidance or in collaboration with peers. (p. 86)

The scaffolded instruction in shared reading extends students' learning. In addition, the learner receives immediate feedback and further prompts to arrive at solutions (Tharp & Gallimore, 1989). While students may not be able to initiate a new strategy alone, they can easily apply one with guidance, further advancing their zone of proximal development.

Thus, shared reading events allow teachers to address comprehension strategies through modeling. For instance, teachers who work with English language learners and students with reading difficulties recognize the power of a daily fluent reading model (Early, 1990). This allows teachers to model prosody (the use of rate, pitch, inflection, and tone) to demonstrate subtle language techniques that influence meaning (Pynte & Prieur, 1996). While read-alouds also present opportunities for modeling prosody, they lack the visual prompts that signal fluent readers. Because students can see the text in shared reading, they can associate the punctuation, layout, spacing, phrase boundaries, and other text cues used by the teacher to make decisions about how the piece should be read and interpreted. Perhaps the most powerful endorsement of this effect comes from students. A survey of 600 adolescents revealed that they attributed their literacy achievement growth to shared reading (Allen, 2001).

Vygotsky, a Russian psychologist, also theorized that humans learn when they transfer information to inner speech.

Implementing Shared Reading

As with all instruction, practical application is as important as the theoretical underpinning. One of the first decisions teachers make in shared reading is how students will interact with the reading. Teachers employ several methods to share the text with students, such as using an overhead projector to display enlarged print on a screen.

This is particularly convenient with use of textbook passages, graphs, or charts. This technique also allows the teacher to highlight words or phrases using overhead markers. At other times, photocopies of a passage can be distributed to each student, with the advantage of encouraging students to become more actively involved with the reading, including making notations directly on the paper. While marking passages in a school textbook is usually discouraged for obvious reasons, this method provides students with guided practice for interacting with text. When teachers construct participatory approaches to text, they assist their students in moving away from ineffective beliefs about reading as a passive experience (Brown, Palinscar, & Armbruster, 1994; Wade & Moje, 2000).

E-books and audio books can be used together to share text with a laptop and data projector while being read by a professional reader.

Selecting Texts for Shared Reading

Text choice is equally important in shared reading, and it differs on several levels from text choice for read-alouds. Recall that a primary purpose for read-alouds is to build background knowledge, often through ancillary text that might otherwise be above the students' independent reading level. In shared reading, teachers focus on a comprehension strategy or a text feature that enables the learner to understand the content of the text. Therefore, the text selected should be at the independent or instructional level of the students. It should also offer the teacher an opportunity to discuss the identified strategy. Examples of comprehension strategies suitable for shared reading instruction include:

- inferencing,
- summarizing,
- self-questioning and self-monitoring,
- text structures (e.g., cause and effect, sequence, problem-solution),
- text features (e.g., headings and subheadings, captions, directions), and
- interpreting visual representations (charts, graphs, diagrams).

Notice that you are using all of these skills as you read this text.

Notice that these comprehension strategies are not the exclusive domain of any one content area; rather, they transcend reading for meaning in any discipline, with any text.

Want to discuss inferencing? Then choose a text that implies attitudes or opinions without stating them outright. Text features and interpretation of visual representations are easily modeled using the course textbook. Self-questioning and self-monitoring (that small insistent voice inside every fluent reader's head that keeps asking, "does this make sense?") can be demonstrated through the teacher's own questions as a reading is shared. If the word "ancillary" in the previous paragraph was a little vague to you (and you noticed) then you are self-monitoring!

As with read-alouds, we find that a self-assessment rubric can be useful for organizing lessons (see Figure 3.3). Some of the elements on this rubric overlap with the features of the read-aloud (for instance, practicing the reading), so we will focus on the unique elements of the shared reading:

1. *Choose text that is appropriate for the purpose.* In the case of shared readings, not only should the text be associated with the content of the class, but it should also provide clear illustrations of the strategy or reading behavior being modeled. For example, a passage about how the biceps muscle of the arm contracts to move a lever (the radius) on a fulcrum (the elbow) is an excellent example of cause-and-effect text, especially if it contains signal words like *accordingly, therefore, as a result,* or *since.*

We've all attended a university class or professional conference where the presenter put a 12-point font overhead on the screen and then said, "I know you can't read this but. . . " Remember how frustrating that was? Don't do this to your students!

2. *Make the purpose of the reading explicit.* If you are modeling a particular strategy, tell your students what it is before you read. Remind them each time you model the strategy.

3. *Decide how the text will be accessible to all students.* If you are projecting the reading on the overhead, make sure the font is large enough for those in the back row to read.

4. *Scaffold, scaffold, scaffold.* This is the foundation of shared reading. Don't assume that they "got it"—teach the strategy or reading behavior explicitly and provide multiple examples. Then have them do it with you during the course of the reading. This leads to the last element of a shared reading. . .

5. *Make sure students are aware of what they are supposed to do with the new knowledge.* A frustration of teachers is that students ask questions like, "Is this going to be on the test?" when the teacher really wanted them to see the usefulness and practicality of what they had been taught. Our experience has been that when students ask questions like this, it is because we have not made it clear what they should

Figure 3.3 Shared Reading Rubric for Self-Assessment

	Successfully implemented	Moderately successful	Just getting started	Not evident
Choice of text is appropriate for purpose				
Selection has been previewed and practiced				
Purpose of reading made explicit and is reflective of student needs				
Text visible to students				
Model provided of fluent reader				
Lesson design reflects scaffolding for student success				
Questions elicit thoughtful response				
Students are aware of what they are expected to do with new knowledge				

Comments:

do with the new information. After you have modeled a strategy, and given them guided practice in using the strategy, you must connect it to their independent reading. When students can apply the strategy independently, the instructional cycle of shared reading is complete.

We've discussed read-alouds and shared reading at length, and have examined both the research and the practical considerations for implementing both in the classroom. Now let's look inside classrooms to see how teachers apply these instructional strategies in the content area.

Strategies at Work

Read-Alouds in English

Read-alouds are a quiet time in the classroom. They can be effectively used throughout the period, whether it be to introduce a new topic at the beginning of class, emphasize a discussion point by returning to quote a text passage, or ending the period with well-crafted prose. Many teachers see this time as an opportunity to hone their students' critical thinking skills. A popular method for creating a focus on critical thinking is the Directed Reading-Thinking Activity (Stauffer & Harrell, 1975). The DR-TA, as it is commonly known, is an instructional technique that invites students to make predictions, then check their predictions during and after the reading. An advantage of the DR-TA is that it assists listeners in clarifying the purpose for the reading. In addition, the DR-TA provides a frame for self-monitoring because the teacher pauses throughout the reading to ask students questions.

Directed Reading-Thinking Activity.   While the steps of a DR-TA may vary slightly in individual practice, the sequence usually consists of the following (Stauffer & Harrell, 1975):

1. *Introduce background knowledge.* Begin the lesson with a discussion of the topic of the reading. Elicit information the students may already know, including personal experiences and prior readings. Discuss the title, cover (if there is one), and any other salient information. Record students' ideas on the board or chart paper.

2. *Make predictions.* Although these predictions can be part of a class discussion, we like to use this as an opportunity to write. Ask questions that invite prediction, such as:

- What do you expect the main idea of this article will be?
- From the title, do you anticipate that the author will be for or against?
- Will this short story have a happy or tragic ending?

After students have written their predictions, extend their writing further by instructing them to explain what evidence they used to arrive at their predictions.

3. *Read a section of text, stopping at predetermined places in the text. Ask students to check and revise their predictions.* This is a crucial step in DR-TA instruction. Identify where the natural stopping points are, then ask students to reread their predictions. Let them know they should change their predictions if necessary and cite new evidence that has influenced their opinions. Repeat this cycle several times through the course of the read-aloud.

4. *After the reading is completed, use student predictions as a discussion tool.* The beauty of a DR-TA may not be apparent until this step. We have all faced the blank stares and shuffled silence of adolescents reluctant to respond to discussion questions. However, when students have written and revised predictions throughout a reading, the tools for discussion lie waiting for them in their own handwriting. "What did you expect to happen before we began the reading?" is easily recalled when the student has a record of his or her thoughts to consult. Another important strategy is embedded in their predictions—it serves as a track record for their thinking processes. The ability to understand one's own thinking—metacognition—is viewed as a key to increased comprehension (Fitzgerald, 1983).

Another version of DR-TA can be found in chapter 4 on questioning.

DR-TA in English.   Lee Mongrue used DR-TA's throughout his extended read-alouds of *Harry Potter and the Sorcerer's Stone* (Rowling, 1997) in his English class. A primary focus of this course is genres (types of literature, such as poetry, folklore and myth, and expository text), and Mr. Mongrue used *Harry Potter* as an entry point into the genre of fantasy. While *Harry Potter* might not be a traditional choice for an English class, he recognized that this semester (the fall of 2001) coincided with the enormous publicity associated with the release of the movie. An experienced teacher, Mr. Mongrue knew the value of student motivation and interest in learning. Therefore, he decided to read excerpts from the book over the course of several weeks. Students read assigned chapters independently in anticipation of the next read-aloud event. He used DR-TA's during some read-alouds to focus their attention on the importance of prediction in reading comprehension (his graphic organizer appears in Figure 3.4). To introduce the book, Mr. Mongrue first led a discussion about the cover art and title. There was much discussion about the word *sorcerer*, which replaced *philosopher* in the title for the American market.

Discussing the cover art engages students and encourages them to make predictions about the text.

They also compared and contrasted the cover art with the photograph of a train featured on a British paperback cover. He then turned to the first chapter, entitled "The Boy Who Lived" and invited students to make predictions about what they might find out in the first few pages. Eric, noting the drawing of a house above the chapter's text, wrote "We'll find out where Harry lives, and maybe where he was born." Mr. Mongrue also added another organizing question—what is normal and abnormal in a magical world?

Mr. Mongrue placed stickies in his copy of the text so that he would know where to stop to invite students to reconsider their original predictions.

Using stickies in books allows teachers to plan questions in advance, as well as ensure a natural stopping point.

After completing the chapter, he led a discussion about the reading. Eric, who had initially predicted that the chapter would be about Harry's living quarters, noted that the author meant the chapter title to serve a second purpose—the reader finds out that Harry was the only survivor of an attack that left his parents dead. In response to Mr. Mongrue's question about normality in a magical world, Anthony remarked, "that's way too normal, when you have to live with people who don't really like you."

It is important to note once again that the class did not complete a DR-TA each time they listened to a read-aloud. By any measure, this would represent overkill, and students would quickly become bored with the activity. At times, he used the read-aloud to introduce an important plot change or event. For instance, Harry's first visit to Diagon Alley in chapter 5 challenged readers with a completely new setting, a number of unfamiliar characters, and detailed information about the workings of a magical society. At other times, he read aloud for the pure pleasure of it. Chapter 14, when a dragon is born in Hagrid's hut, was a particularly enjoyable read-aloud event. (We suspect it was because Mr. Mongrue enjoyed doing the voice of a giant!) This also raises an essential component of a read-aloud event—the teacher's enthusiasm for the text. We witnessed the infectious nature of his joy for the story and how he hooked even the most reluctant students into the book. And lest anyone question whether the book was of a suitable rigor for this class, we should also note that his students averaged a gain in reading levels of 2.1 years in one semester.

Never underestimate the power of a good story, an expressive reader, and a room full of captivated students!

Shared Reading in Mathematics

A critical aspect of reading is *fluency*, the ability to decode and understand words, sentences, and paragraphs in a way that is smooth and accurate. Fluency is closely related to the concept of prosody discussed earlier in this chapter. While the rate of

Figure 3.4 Directed Reading-Thinking Activity

DR-TA for (title) _____

Prediction question(s):

_____

_____

_____

Using the title, your own background knowledge, and any other contextual clues, make your predictions.

Before reading:

During reading:

During reading:

During reading:

After reading:

reading alone is not the only indicator of a good reader, consider the labored reading of a struggling student (Rasinski, 2000). When reading is choppy and disfluent, it becomes difficult to attend to the message behind the words. Meaning for the reader (and listener) is lost in a string of pauses, false starts, and hesitations.

Rereading.   An effective instructional strategy for building fluency is repeated readings (Mastropieri, Leinart, & Scruggs, 1999). Repeated readings are just that—the repeated reading of the same text passage. There is a great deal of evidence to suggest that repeated readings lead to a practice effect. If you are skeptical, try it yourself. Select a passage from this chapter and read it aloud for one minute—be sure to time yourself. When the timer rings, count the number of words you read and record it. Now read the same passage again, beginning at the same starting point, and count the number of words you read during this second one-minute interval. Repeat this cycle one more time and then compare your results. If you are like most readers, you read more words at cycle 3 than you did at cycle 1. Many of you may have read more during each cycle.

If you completed the above exercise, then you have also identified a difficulty with repeated readings. Many students, and especially adolescents, are not terribly motivated to reread. In fact, we often hear them say something like "I read this before! Why do I have to read it again?" And indeed, less able readers often believe that any text only needs to be read once, with no new information to be gained from subsequent readings (Alvermann, 1988). However, fluent adolescent readers recognize that rereading is an important tool for comprehending text, especially dense content area readings (Faust & Glenzer, 2000).

Reader's Theatre.   A popular method for engaging in repeated readings to build fluency and comprehension is Reader's Theatre (Martinez, Roser, & Strecker, 1998-1999). Reader's Theatre is the public performance of a scripted text, but unlike traditional theatre, the lines are not memorized, and props, movement, and other acting devices are not used. Instead, students read the text using prosodic elements while their classmates follow along silently using their own copies.

The success of Reader's Theatre for promoting repeated reading and conversations about meaning seems to be related to the performance itself. Think about what motivates you—if you know that you will be presenting an oral reading for your peers, you are probably going to rehearse, reread, and discuss the methods of performance with your fellow actors. That is precisely what happened in Aaron Sage's 10th-grade algebra class.

Reader's Theatre in Mathematics.   Toward the end of the semester, Mr. Sage needed to prepare students for the end-of-course examination. He used a number of different review techniques, including structured study groups and student presentations.

However, he also recognized that it was important to interject some novelty and inventiveness in the review. During one class period, he used a version of Reader's Theatre (which he entitled "Math Theatre"). Mr. Sage used the book *Math Talk* (Pappas, 1991), an innovative collection of poems of mathematical concepts, written to be read by two voices (or two sets of voices). Mr. Sage began by showing the students a large strip of paper connected to form a continuous band, with a single twist in the loop. With great flourish, he cut the strip down the center, producing not two thinner strips as many had predicted, but rather one larger loop. He then modeled the poem "Mobius Strip" with another teacher and explained the mathematics behind the phenomenon.

Fluency and vocabulary are two of the best predictors of reading comprehension.

Many Reader's Theatre scripts are available at *http://www.aaronshep. com/rt/RTE.html.*

Remember that the emphasis of Reader's Theatre is on oral language development and fluency, not on props, costumes, or dramatic performance.

Next, he divided the class into five groups of students. Each group was assigned a poem to perform. In addition to performing the poem, they were also to explain the mathematical concepts represented by their poem. The poems he chose for this lesson addressed concepts studied during the semester, including square roots, radicals, integers, variables, and imaginary numbers. He included an advance organizer for each group that summarized the main concepts of their assigned poem.

Students rehearsed for 30 minutes or so, and Mr. Sage noted that they repeatedly returned to the text, their notes, the advance organizer, and the algebra textbook in order to support their understanding. After sufficient rehearsal, each group performed their poem, which was displayed on an overhead for all to see. They ended their performance with a review of the selected mathematical concept. Mr. Sage later remarked, "There's no way I would have gotten any of them to read about square roots for half an hour straight, let alone talk about it with their classmates. I think this activity really gave them a different way to find out what they know."

> Refer back to chapter 2 to review Mr. Sage's advance organizer.

Shared Reading in Social Studies

Many teachers use shared readings to demonstrate a *think aloud* technique for explicit modeling (Davey, 1983).

When using a think aloud, the teacher interjects questions and statements as the text is read. For instance, Ms. Richardson, a 12th-grade government teacher, applied this strategy during a shared reading of a newspaper article on a lawsuit that had been recently filed against the school district concerning the use of federal money (Magee, 2002). The class had been studying federal compensatory programs, including Title 1 and the Individuals with Disabilities Education Act, so Ms. Richardson used the article to begin a discussion. She read the sentence "A lawsuit filed in U.S. District Court yesterday includes claims the school district has segregated minority children, deprived them of a decent education and has fostered a hostile and racist environment" (p. B2). She underlined "segregated," "deprived," and "fostered a hostile. . . environment" and then asked herself aloud, "I wonder what are the examples of the charges? And who is filing the suit?" She then went on to explain that a common writing style in newspaper articles is to write the "big ideas" first, then provide supporting details in later paragraphs.

> A think aloud is a metacognitive process that allows students to hear what goes on "inside the head" of a fluent reader.

As she continued to read, she pointed out general statements that connected to the phrases in the opening paragraph. The class quickly noted that the article provided few specific examples, although it did detail the group filing the lawsuit. This led to a spirited discussion about the importance of using several sources of information when learning about current issues. The students all agreed that the newspaper article gave general information about the lawsuit, but not enough to form an opinion one way or the other.

> The journalistic style used in many newspapers is very different from the essays students are accustomed to writing. This can be confusing for students and should be used as a teaching point, along with the content.

Another U.S. history teacher, Helen Arnold, used a newspaper article as a beginning point for a study of the 1942 Zoot Suit Riots in Los Angeles. A community in San Diego county had recently obtained a court injunction aimed at prohibiting 22 alleged gang members from associating with each other. The restriction made it possible for the police to arrest any of the identified people for "flashing gang signs, making loud noises and engaging in other activities in two city neighborhoods" (Ma, 2001, p. A8). Ms. Arnold made an overhead of the newspaper article and distributed copies for the students to make notes on.

> Some shared reading tasks lend themselves to notetaking opportunities for readers, including adding "marginalia"—brief notes in the margins.

The class searched the article for details about the specific activities that might lead to arrest. The found a quote from a police sergeant explaining that they were "activities that may lead to violence" and located a list of prohibited activities in the sidebar. The students were surprised to see that the injunction included wearing clothing associated with the gangs. The article also provided quite a bit of detail on the number and types of crimes associated with the gang members. The class was in wide agreement that the seriousness of the crimes made it necessary to enforce such restrictions.

She then distributed another reading for the class to consider. It was a web site report on the Zoot Suit Riots. The report duplicated a newspaper article from 1942 outlining the "Mexican crime wave" that was occurring in the city. The newspaper called for a crackdown, and reported on grand jury testimony by the head of the sheriff's office investigation that Mexicans had inherited "naturally violent tendencies" from the "bloodthirsty Aztecs of Mexico" (Ayres, 1942/1974). These two shared readings provided Ms. Arnold with a way to discuss point of view when considering texts. She pointed out that when evaluating historical events, it would be unwise to read only one source because the information may or may not be accurate. She believed it vital that her students become adept in seeking multiple perspectives. Tunnell and Ammon (1996) suggest that multiple perspectives are "fundamental to good history teaching" (Robb, 2002, p. 31). Because she wanted them to consider point of view and the author's perspective in reading about the Zoot Suit Riots, she modeled the use of a tool for evaluating information found on the Internet (see Figure 3.5).

> Too often students believe everything they find on the Internet to be of equal value. Critical thinking skills are developed when students learn to evaluate sources of information.

Later in the unit, Ms. Arnold also used a Reader's Theatre play on the riots and an anticipation guide to structure another reading.

Shared Reading in Science

Many content area textbooks contain a great deal of technical information that is presented in tables, photographs, diagrams, and graphs. This is especially true of science textbooks, where students frequently misinterpret complicated diagrams, thus leading them to incorrect conclusions (Wheeler & Hill, 1990). However, because of the complex concepts inherent in science, much of the information needs to be presented in the form of a diagram.

> During standardized tests, students are often required to analyze information presented in diagrams. Using diagrams as shared readings gives students opportunities to practice using this type of information.

Could you imagine learning the elements without a periodic table? Science teachers recognize the role of literacy for science students, especially as it applies to interpreting diagrams and drawings (Bridges, 1986). In many secondary science classrooms, teachers explicitly instruct on graph and diagram interpretation. Antoinette Linton, a 10th-grade biology teacher, also cites testing concerns. "These are just the kinds of things that are on the Golden State Exams (a subject area test for merit scholarships). I've got to make sure they can read and interpret these properly. That's how you think like a researcher."

During a unit on genetics, Ms. Linton reviewed diagrams and tables for displaying scientific information. The students were expected to write a research paper on the ethics of genetic engineering as a final project. Included in the project were the results from a number of labs, including karyotyping, probability, and bird adaptations. Because of the technical nature of these labs, the results needed to be displayed as graphs, diagrams, and tables, with support and explanation in the text. She used a chapter on Mendel's law of heredity from another textbook because the visuals offered good examples for her shared reading lesson. She reminded her students that

Figure 3.5   Web Site Evaluation Tool

URL: _____

1. Title of web site: _____

2. What is the main purpose of the web site? _____
   • Is it selling something?
   • Does it describe a service?
   • Is it an educational site?

3. Who created the web site? _____
   • Is there a contact name?
   • Is it a private company?
   • Is it a school?
   • Is it a government agency?

4. How current is the web site? (When was it last updated?) _____
   • Look at the bottom of the homepage.

5. Are links available to other sites? (Try some of them to make sure they work).

   _____

6. Are there references or citations? _____ If yes, what are they?

   _____

7. What new information did you learn from this web site?

   _____

   _____

8. What information is missing?

   _____

Readability refers to the complexity or difficulty of the text. There are many ways to report readability, including grade level equivalence.

the purpose of displaying data is to compare or to show relationships. She then put a variety of tables from the chapter on the overhead and discussed the characteristics of good visuals, especially the importance of labels and captions. She displayed a series of diagrams from the chapter, including a flow chart illustrating the genetic changes in four generations of beans. With a copy of the diagrams and charts in front of them, they interpreted the displayed data. In cases where the tables or diagrams were ambiguous, they made changes to improve the ease of readability.

Ms. Linton later noted that the shared reading about displaying data was particularly useful in the students' final projects. "After all," she said "what good is knowing all the information if you can't use it?"

Read-Alouds and Shared Reading in Electives

Andy Trakas teaches an elective class titled Tutoring and Mentoring. This class offers a unique opportunity for students to improve their literacy skills by helping others. In addition to supporting their own academic growth, students in the course can also earn internship and community service hours. Mr. Trakas "sells" the course to prospective participants by telling them "you'll learn something about yourself, too." Each morning, his students go to nearby elementary schools to teach younger students.

A Rationale for Cross-age Tutoring.   Cross-age peer tutoring involves an older student, under a teacher's guidance, who helps younger students learn or practice a skill or concept (Cassady, 1998; Giesecke, 1993). Though features vary from program to program, all cross-age tutoring programs provide individualized and personal attention, high levels of interaction, and immediate feedback. The effects of cross-age peer tutoring on the older student are particularly intriguing. A study of 21 adolescents participating in a cross-age peer tutoring program found significant growth in the tutors' reading scores on standardized measures (Jacobson, Thrope, Fisher, Lapp, Frey, & Flood, 2001). According to Gaustad (1993) and Cobb (1998), cross-age tutoring is beneficial because the process allows tutors expanded opportunities to review material, reiterate the purpose of the assignment, and expand their communication skills. A meta-analysis of 65 studies on cross-age tutoring revealed that the practice of students helping one another enhanced classroom instruction and led to higher academic achievement (Cohen, Kulik, & Kulik, 1982). Through purposeful engagement, cross-age tutoring provides the older learners with an authentic reason for practicing in order to improve their reading performance (Haluska & Gillen, 1995; Juel, 1991). Tutoring has been shown to be effective within classrooms as well. Referred to as peer tutoring, classmates are paired to support each other's learning and problem solving. In addition, cross-age or peer tutoring has been found to promote positive reading attitudes and habits (Caserta-Henry, 1996; Newell, 1996). Cohen (1986) suggests that the act of planning instruction for another aids the student in understanding the text.

It is likely that the relatively small difference in ages between tutor and tutee contribute positively to the success of the younger students. Sensitivity and responsiveness to tentative understandings of a concept is seen frequently in cross-age tutoring (Schneider & Barone, 1997). The ability of older students to effectively communicate with younger children may be due to the fact that they are cognitively closer to the tutee, and likely to have experienced similar situations in the recent past (Jenkins, Mayhall, Peschka, & Jenkins, 1974). Feldman and Allen (1979) demonstrated that sixth-graders were more likely to accurately determine understanding through the nonverbal behavior of their third-grade tutees than experienced teachers.

Student-Conducted Read-Alouds and Shared Readings.   An understanding of the reading process is essential in Mr. Trakas' Tutoring and Mentoring class. Students begin the year with study on the characteristics of effective teachers and development of a personal goals statement. They receive instruction on read-alouds and shared reading techniques, principles of reading, and child development. Because they work with emergent and early readers, they pay particular attention to directionality, accessing prior information, rereading for fluency, making predictions, and phonics.

In addition to working with the younger students, Mr. Trakas also emphasizes their own literacy development, particularly through writing. Tutors are expected to maintain reflective journals, develop lessons, and communicate with the elementary teacher. They also propose and write a research paper on a topic related to their experience. Students wrote papers such as, "Reading Strategies at the Elementary Level," "Motivation for Mentoring," and "The Impact of Inspirational and Motivating Teachers."

Possibly the favorite project of the class is the picture book they create for their tutee. The tutors develop a story, edit, illustrate, and publish a picture book that they

Emergent readers benefit from instruction about concepts of print, which includes book handling skills, directionality, and layout of the text.

give to their elementary student to keep. The process of bringing a picture book to publication is an involved one, and students conduct research on what makes a picture book appropriate and effective for read-alouds and shared reading. Their own experiences with interacting with a large volume of picture books over the course of the year also contributes to their understanding of good children's literature. Layout, print size, and complexity of language must all be considered. Illustrations should support and advance the story. And of course, these books are designed with a particular student in mind. Background knowledge and interests play an important role in shaping the text. Picture books produced have included stories on friendship, Pokemon, and skateboarding. An especially creative young man known widely for his interest in graffiti crafted a story about a boy who learned to write through tagging! (Don't worry—the book's message also emphasized the importance of tagging only where it is invited.)

As we said earlier, tutors benefit as well. In the three years that Tutoring and Mentoring has been offered, counselors and other teachers have come to expect that students will make gains in reading. Students in Mr. Trakas' course average a 1.5 year gain in reading scores, as measured by the Gates-MacGinitie Reading Test (MacGinitie, MacGinitie, Maria, & Dreyer, 2000). Individuals have been known to make more than two years' progress in reading during this course. None of these results should be surprising, notes Mr. Trakas. "They're immersed in literacy. They talk about it, read about it, and write about it. There's a 'trampoline effect.'" Perhaps the best indicator of all is the number of students who have re-enrolled in the class—30%. Several students have joined the Future Educators Club, and several are now studying at local universities with the intent of entering the teaching profession. As Mr. Trakas promises them all on the first day—"you'll learn something about yourself."

Conclusion

The decision to use a read-aloud or shared reading is based on the purpose and the text selected. Teachers do both, but usually on different days.

Read-alouds and shared reading are two instructional practices borrowed from elementary reading practice and customized for secondary content area use. A *read-aloud* is a text or passage selected by the teacher to read publicly to a small or large group of students. A primary purpose for the read-aloud selection is to focus on the content of the text. A *shared reading* is a text or passage that is jointly shared by teacher and student. In shared readings, the students can also see the text, and it is usually chosen both for its content and as a way to draw attention to a particular text feature or comprehension strategy.

A summary of tips for using read-alouds and shared readings in the classroom appears in Figure 3.6.

Read-alouds and shared readings increase content knowledge.

When considering read-alouds and shared readings for your own practice, always keep in mind the focus of your course. While we believe strongly that students should see their teachers regularly engaged in the act of reading for pleasure, we do not suggest that large portions of instructional time should be spent on using readings that are unrelated to your instructional purposes.

The teachers in this chapter made a strong case for their purposes in selecting a particular piece, and clearly saw these experiences as an important way to advance student learning. Having said that, do not underestimate the influence of a teacher who shares a newspaper story that concerned them, an email that made them laugh, or a cartoon that made them think. When students see their teachers reading a variety of genres, they begin to see possibilities in their own literate lives.

Figure 3.6 Summary of Effective Strategies for Using Read-Alouds and Shared Readings

- Read-alouds and shared reading events do not need to be long to be effective. A short, powerful passage has far more impact than a long, dull reading. Plan on about five minutes a day, and increase gradually as your students' stamina for listening improves.
- Rehearse in advance. Remember that one goal is to provide a fluent language model. That requires a bit of rehearsal so that you can bring the proper expression and inflection to the text.
- Choose readings that are meaningful to you and are connected with the course content. Comprehension increases when connections are made, so don't assume that your students understood the relevance of your selection. Be explicit that the information from the selected reading fits into your course of study.
- Determine in advance where you're going to stop. Look for the natural breaks in a piece. Selected passages can either be read in a single reading, or extended over a few class periods. If the reading will continue on another day, stop at a point where you can elicit predictions about what is yet to come.

References

Allen, J. (2001). *Yellow brick roads: Shared and guided paths to independent reading 4–12.* Portland, ME: Stenhouse.

Alvermann, D. E. (1988). Effects of spontaneous and induced lookbacks on self-perceived high- and low-ability comprehenders. *Journal of Educational Research, 81,* 325–331.

Amer, A. A. (1997). The effect of the teacher's reading aloud on the reading comprehension of ESL students. *ELT Journal 1997, 51*(1), 43–47.

Anderson, R. C., Hiebert, E., Scott, J., & Wilkinson, I. (1985). *Becoming a nation of readers: The report of the Commission on Reading.* Washington, DC: National Institute of Education.

Ayres, E. D. (1942/1974). Edward Duran Ayres report. In M. S. Meier & F. Rivera (Eds.) *Readings on La Raza: The twentieth century* (pp. 127–133). New York: Hill and Wang.

Beck, I. L., & McKeown, M. G. (2001). Text talk: Capturing the benefits of read-aloud experiences for young children. *The Reading Teacher, 55,* 10–35.

Beckman, J. (1986). Turning reluctant readers into lifetime readers. *English Journal, 73,* 84–86.

Block, D. G. (1999, November 11). Spoken word still a stronghold. *TapeDisc Business: The International Business Magazine for Media Manufacturers.* Retrieved April 13, 2002, from http://www.tapediscbusiness.com/tdb_nov99/11spoken.htm

Bridges, B. (1986). Science and reading: A winning combination. *Clearing House, 60*(2), 56–58.

Brown, A. L., Palinscar, A. S., & Armbruster, B. B. (1994). Instructing comprehension-fostering activities in interactive learning situations. In R. B. Ruddell, M. R. Ruddell, & H. Singer (Eds.), *Theoretical models and processes of reading* (4th ed., pp. 757–787). Newark, DE: International Reading Association.

Caserta-Henry, C. (1996). Reading buddies: A first-grade intervention program. *The Reading Teacher, 49,* 500–503.

Cassady, J. K. (1998). Wordless books: No-risk tools for inclusive middle-grade classrooms. *Journal of Adolescent & Adult Literacy, 41,* 428–433.

Chaucer, G. (1400/1985). *The Canterbury tales.* (D. Clark, Trans.). Oxford: Oxford University Press.

Cobb, J. B. (1998). The social contexts of tutoring: Mentoring the older at-risk student. *Reading Horizons, 39,* 50–75.

Cohen, J. (1986). Theoretical considerations of peer tutoring. *Psychology on the Schools, 23,* 175–186.

Cohen, P. A., Kulik, J. A., & Kulik, C. C. (1982). Educational outcomes of tutoring: A meta-analysis of findings. *American Educational Research Journal, 19,* 237–248.

Cummins, J. (1980). The cross-lingual dimensions of language proficiency: Implications for bilingual education and the optimal age issue. *TESOL Quarterly, 14,* 175–187.

Davey, B. (1983). Think aloud: Modeling the cognitive processes for reading comprehension. *Journal of Reading, 27*(1), 44–47.

Durkin, D. (1974–1975). A six year study of children who learned to read in school at the age of four. *Reading Research Quarterly, 10,* 9–61.

Early, M. (1990). Enabling first and second language learners in the classroom. *Language Arts, 67,* 567–575.

Early, M., & Tang, G. M. (1991). Helping ESL students cope with content-based texts. *TESL Canada Journal, 8*(2), 34–44.

Enzensberger, H. M. (1998). *The number devil: A mathematical adventure.* New York: Metropolitan.

Erickson, B. (1996). Read-alouds reluctant readers relish. *Journal of Adolescent & Adult Literacy, 40*, 212–214.

Faust, M. A., & Glenzer, N. (2000). "I could read those parts over and over." Eighth graders rereading to enhance enjoyment and learning with literature. *Journal of Adolescent & Adult Literacy, 44*, 234–239.

Feldman, R. S., & Allen, V. L. (1979). Student success and tutor verbal and nonverbal behavior. *Journal of Educational Research, 72*, 142–149.

Fitzgerald, J. (1983). Helping readers gain self-control over reading comprehension. *The Reading Teacher, 37*, 249–253.

Gaustad, J. (1993). Peers and tutoring. *ERIC Digest, 79*. Office of Educational Research and Improvement. [ERIC Document Reproduction Service No. ED 354 608].

Giesecke, D. (1993). Low-achieving students as successful tutors. *Preventing School Failure, 37*, 34–43.

Greaney, V., & Hegarty, M. (1987). Correlates of leisure-time reading. *Journal of Research in Reading, 10*(1), 3–20.

Haluska, R., & Gillen, D. (1995). Kids teaching kids: Pairing up with cross-grades pals. *Learning, 24*(3), 54–56.

Herrold, W. G., Jr., Stanchfield, J., & Serabian, A. J. (1989). Comparison of the effect of a middle school, literature-based listening program on male and female attitudes toward reading. *Educational Research Quarterly, 13*(4), 43–46.

Holdaway, D. (1982). Shared book experience: Teaching reading using favorite books. *Theory into Practice, 21*, 293–300.

Irvin, J. L., Lunstrum, J. P., Lynch-Brown, C., & Shepard, M. F. (1995). Enhancing social studies through literacy strategies. *Bulletin 91*. National Council for the Social Studies, Washington, DC.

Ivey, G., & Broaddus, K. (2001). "Just plain reading:" A survey of what makes students want to read in middle school classrooms. *Reading Research Quarterly, 36*, 350–377.

Jacobson, J., Thrope, L., Fisher, D., Lapp, D., Frey, N., & Flood, J. (2001). Cross-age tutoring: A literacy improvement approach for struggling adolescent readers. *Journal of Adolescent & Adult Literacy, 44*, 528–536.

Jenkins, J. R., Mayhall, W. F., Peschka, C. M., & Jenkins, L. M. (1974). Comparing small group instruction and tutorial instruction in resource rooms. *Exceptional Children, 40*, 245–250.

Juel, C. (1991). Tutoring between student athletes and at-risk children. *The Reading Teacher, 45*, 178–186.

Longfellow, H. W., & Bing, C. (1860/2001). *The midnight ride of Paul Revere*. New York: Handprint.

Ma, K. (2001, August 12). Gang unit out in force. *North County Times*, pp. A1, A8.

Manguel, A. (1996). *A history of reading*. New York: Penguin.

Magee, M. (2002, June 1). Parents file federal suit against S.D. schools. *The San Diego Union Tribune*, B2.

MacGinitie, W. H., MacGinitie, R. K., Maria, K., & Dreyer, L. G. (2000). *Gates-MacGinitie Reading Test, 4th Edition, Forms S and T*. Itasca, IL: Riverside.

Martinez, M., Roser, N. L., & Strecker, S. (1998–1999). "I never thought I could be a star:" A reader's theatre ticket to fluency. *The Reading Teacher, 52*, 326–334.

Mastropieri, M. A., Leinart, A., & Scruggs, T. E. (1999). Strategies to increase reading fluency. *Intervention in School and Clinic, 34*, 278–283, 292.

McKenna, M. C., & Robinson, R. D. (1990). Content literacy: A definition and implications. *Journal of Reading, 34*, 184–186.

Morrow, L. M., & Young, J. (1997). A collaborative family literacy program: The effects on children's motivation and literacy achievement. *Early Child Development and Care, 127–128*, 13–25.

Newell, F. M. (1996). Effects of a cross-age tutoring program on computer literacy learning of second-grade students. *Journal of Research on Computing in Education, 28*. 346–358.

Nieto, S. (1992). *Affirming diversity: The sociopolitical context of multicultural education*. White Plains, NY: Longman.

Ornstein, A. C. (1994). Curriculum trends revisited. *Peabody Journal of Education, 69*(4), 4–20.

Pappas, T. (1991). *Math talk: Mathematical ideas in poems for two voices*. San Carlos, CA: Wide World Publishing/ Tetra.

Pearson, P. D., & Gallagher, M. C. (1983). The instruction of reading comprehension. *Contemporary Educational Psychology, 8*, 317–344.

Price, R. D. (1978). Teaching reading is not the responsibility of the social studies teacher. *Social Education 42*, 312, 314–315.

Pynte, J., & Prieur, B. (1996). Prosodic breaks and attachment decisions in sentence parsing. *Language and Cognitive Processes, 11*, 165–191.

Rasinski, T. V. (2000). Speed does matter in reading. *The Reading Teacher, 54*, 146–151.

Richardson, J. S. (1997–1998). A read-aloud for foreign languages: Becoming a language master. *Journal of Adolescent & Adult Literacy, 41*, 312–314.

Richardson, J. S. (2000). *Read it aloud! Using literature in the secondary content classroom*. Newark, DE: International Reading Association.

Richardson, J. S., & Gross, E. (1997). A read-aloud for mathematics. *Journal of Adolescent & Adult Literacy, 40*, 492–494.

Rieck, B. J. (1977). How content teachers telegraph messages against reading. *Journal of Reading, 20*, 646–648.

Robb, L. (2002). Multiple texts: Multiple opportunities for teaching and learning. *Voices from the Middle, 9*(4), 28–32.

Rosow, L. V. (1988). Adult illiterates offer unexpected cues into the reading process. *Journal of Reading, 32*, 120–124.

Rowling, J. K. (1997). *Harry Potter and the sorcerer's stone*. New York: Scholastic.

Schneider, R. B., & Barone, D. (1997). Cross-age tutoring. *Childhood Education 1997, 73,* 136–143.

Smith, R. J., & Otto, W. (1969). Changing teacher attitudes toward teaching reading in the content areas. *Journal of Reading, 12,* 299–304.

Stauffer, R. G., & Harrell, M. M. (1975). Individualized reading-thinking activities. *The Reading Teacher, 28,* 765–769.

Tharp, R. G., & Gallimore, R. (1989). *Rousing minds to life: Teaching, learning, and schooling in social context.* New York: Cambridge University Press.

Trelease, J. (1993). *Read all about it! Great read-aloud stories, poems, and newspaper pieces for preteens and teens.* New York: Penguin.

Trelease, J. (2002). *The read-aloud handbook* (5th ed.). New York: Penguin.

Tunnell, A. M., & Ammon, R. (1996). The story of ourselves: Fostering multiple perspectives. *Social Education, 60,* 212–215.

Vygotsky, L. S. (1978). Mental development of children and the process of learning. In M. Cole, V. John-Steiner, S. Scribner, and E. Souberman (Eds. and Trans.), *Mind in Society: The development of higher psychological processes.* Cambridge: MA: Harvard University Press.

Wade, S. E., & Moje, E. B. (2000). The role of the text in classroom learning. In M. L. Kamil, P. B. Mosenthal, P. D. Pearson, & R. Barr (Eds.), *Handbook of reading research* (Vol. III, pp. 609–628). Mahwah, NJ: Lawrence Erlbaum.

Wang, J. (1996). An empirical assessment of textbook readability in secondary education. *Reading Improvement, 33,* 11–15.

Wheeler, A. E., & Hill, D. (1990). Diagram-ease. Why students misinterpret diagrams. *Science Teacher, 57,* 58–63.

Worthy, J. (2002). What makes intermediate-grade students want to read? *The Reading Teacher, 55,* 568–569.

Chapter 4

Questions, Questions Everywhere

DOUGLAS FISHER, NANCY FREY, AND CHRISTINE JOHNSON

The strains of a familiar tune fill the air in room 408. The music fades, anticipation grows, but Alex Trebek does not appear. In his place, however, by popular demand of the ninth graders, is Mr. Troop, their English teacher. Poised at the lectern, he faces the wipe board that is covered with twenty-five color-coded cards, numerically indexed and arranged in five neat rows. Today's quiz game is titled "Maya Angelou." Each row is labeled with today's topics: Personal Life, Short Stories, Poetry, Writer's Craft, and Achievements. The class has completed the study of her life and works, and they are ready for showtime—another episode of Poetry Jeopardy.

With pleasurable expectation, the six teams of students squirm in their seats. Mr. Troop draws from the selected category box and announces, "Achievements!" Bells ring out and Team A wins the call. Hugo, the spokesperson, selects a blue card for ten points. With a commanding voice Mr. Troop reads, "President Clinton's inaugural poem." His team encourages Hugo and, taking a deep breath, he replies, "Angelou wins the Grammy Award." Mr. Troop, shaking his head, responds, "Incorrect."

Team C captures the opportunity to ring their bell and to gain recognition from Mr. Troop. He asks, "What is your answer Team C?" Murmuring excitedly, the team points to Diana, who clears her throat and asks, "For what did Maya Angelou win the Grammy Award?"

Mr. Troop smiles and exclaims, "Correct! You answered in the form of a question." With that reply, Team C earns the ten points that are celebrated with cheers from the teammates.

Why is Mr. Troop teaching this way? What theory or research supports his instruction? How does this activity contribute to his students' literacy? How does he know whether his students are learning? The answer lies in the queries themselves: Mr. Troop is using questioning as a means for instruction. If questions are not asked, then expected application to meaningful context will be limited (Routman, 2000).

Traditionally, teachers use questioning more than any other method for developing comprehension. Questions help the teacher assess whether students understand the text (Durkin, 1978-1979). However, in organizing daily lessons, teachers are inclined to plan thinking activities where the learners' potential to question the text is diminished because the teacher dominates the questioning (Busching & Slesinger 1995). Conversely, less time is dedicated to student questioning. In addition, questioning loses its effectiveness when teachers require students to swallow and regurgitate facts before they have had an opportunity to chew and digest information. Another drawback of teachers' routine questioning habits is that their questions too often focus on literal comprehension rather than critical thinking, even in content areas like mathematics (Wimer, Ridenour, & Thomas, 2001), and especially when working with students perceived as struggling readers (Allington, 1983; Durkin, 1978-1979; Gambrell, 1983).

Reading researchers report from their classroom observations at the elementary level that the majority of questions are teacher-generated, explicit and require only one correct answer (Armbruster et al., 1991; Block, 2001). An important series of studies on the questioning habits of teachers was conducted by Cazden (1986, 1988). Like others before her, she found that classroom instruction is dominated by a particular cycle of questioning known as IRE: Initiate, Respond, and Evaluate (Mehan, 1979; Dillon, 1988). The IRE pattern of questioning is familiar to all—the teacher initiates a question, students respond, and then the teacher evaluates the quality and accuracy of the responses. Here's an example of IRE:

Teacher: Why was the battle of Gettysburg important? (Initiate)

Student: The Union army defeated the Confederate army. (Respond)

Teacher: Good. (Evaluate) Why else was it important? (Initiate)

Here's the difficulty with that question—the student could have also answered that it was the northernmost battle of the Civil War, or that 54,000 people died, or that Abraham Lincoln delivered a famous speech at a memorial service on the site. Instead, the question is low-level and consists of a teacher-directed query that excludes any discussion or debate among students. A classroom where IRE is the dominant form of discourse quickly becomes a passive learning environment dependent on the teacher for any kind of discussion. The danger, of course, in the overuse of an IRE pattern of questioning is that the teacher alone becomes the mediator of who will speak and who will not (Mehan, 1979). The students learn that the only questions worth considering are those formulated by the teacher. Ironically, the teachers in Cazden's study (1988) reported that they wanted a student-centered, constructivist classroom, yet clung to IRE as their dominant instructional method for inquiry. If you doubt the pervasiveness of this questioning pattern, then eavesdrop on kindergartners "playing school." Invariably, the five-year-old "teacher" will engage in this questioning pattern with his or her "students." If only all teaching behaviors were this easy to teach!

Creating Quality Questions

From these studies it is evident that many students have little practice in answering implicit questions in elementary school and may be ill-equipped to formulate and respond to questions requiring critical thinking at the secondary level. In secondary schools it is imperative to create a classroom culture of inquiry. However, these same adolescents are likely to require teacher modeling to engage in inquiry. One way teachers can accomplish this is through effective questioning strategies. The

Literal comprehension refers to information related to discrete facts like names and dates, rather than information that requires the student to draw inferences.

If you want to gain insight into how your students perceive you as a teacher, invite them to teach for a day!

goal of these restructured questions should be to monitor and guide the ways that students construct and examine meaning in reading, writing, talking, listening, and reflecting.

The self-monitoring of understanding that comes from self-questioning is underutilized by poor readers. In turn, these struggling readers learn to dislike reading because it is unsatisfying and the concepts of textbook language are unfamiliar. Their comprehension skills then fail to advance because they do not read, reinforcing a cycle of failure (Stanovich, 1986). However, a basic expectation of content area learning is that students learn a variety of strategies and engage in a variety of activities in order to convert new information into learned information. We know that in content area learning, the students develop meaningful understanding gradually, and not in a single brief and isolated experience (Lapp, Flood, & Farnan, 1996). Therefore, instruction must routinely incorporate questioning techniques that encourage active participation and high response opportunities for students. Questioning is central to the two tools in every teacher's arsenal—scaffolding and coaching (Roehler & Duffy, 1991).

Scaffolding is an instructional approach that begins with what the student knows, then extends their understanding through supported learning experiences. Scaffolding is especially useful when teaching English language learners and struggling readers.

When teachers use these strategies to ask probing questions, students grow in their thinking processes. At the same time, teachers should share with their students the reasons for their questions. Additional research suggests that instructional questioning strategies that focus on inferences and main ideas equip the students to respond with improved recall and understanding (Raphael, 1984). This is achieved through higher-order questioning.

What Are "Higher-Order" Questions?

If you have read the previous pages, you have probably inferred that some questions are better than others. You have seen phrases like "low-level" and "higher-order" questions. But what distinguishes types of questions? How do you determine what sorts of questions are appropriate? A review of the work of Benjamin Bloom is helpful to understand questioning.

In 1956, Benjamin Bloom, an educational psychologist at the University of Chicago, published a series of handbooks on the domains of learning—psychomotor, affective, and cognitive. The handbook devoted to the cognitive domain outlined a classification system that described six levels of competence. This classification system, referred to commonly as Bloom's taxonomy, has become a cornerstone in the description of questions used in the classroom and on tests (Bloom, 1956). Bloom described these competencies; we've included a sample question to illustrate each one:

Level 1—Knowledge: States facts, terms, and definitions.

    Sample question: What is the capital of California?

Level 2—Comprehension: Change the information to compare to another form.

    Sample question: Explain why Sacramento was selected as the state capital.

Level 3—Application: Solve a new problem using information.

    Sample question: What city in California would you choose as the state capital today?

Level 4—Analysis: Identifies components and infers causes or motives.

    Sample question: Why do you believe that the legislature chose to move the state capital from San Jose to Sacramento?

Level 5—Synthesis: Create a new product using information in a novel way.

Sample question: Design a state capital for California that will be useful throughout the 21st century.

Level 6—Evaluation: Make judgements and defend opinions.

Sample question: Assess the suitability of the present state capital and make recommendations for future development.

The questions got more difficult, didn't they? This is where the terminology of higher- and lower-order questions comes from.

Knowledge and comprehension questions are sometimes referred to as literal questions because they require the student to draw upon memorization or location of facts. In other words, the answers to these types of questions are usually located verbatim in a text. They are also the easiest questions to compose and test. Guszak (1967) estimated that 70% of the questions asked in a typical classroom are knowledge or comprehension questions. That means that only 30% of the queries required students to apply knowledge in unique ways, or to construct understanding by assembling disparate information. It is the imbalance between literal and non-literal questions that is problematic, not the questions themselves. Brophy and Good (1986) noted that students who have experience with lower-order questions do well on tests of basic skills because these tests mirror this type of question.

Tests do not consist only of basic skills; they also demand that students can draw inferences, justify answers, and defend opinions. These same higher-order skills are also widely recognized as critical for adult success (Pithers & Soden, 2000). Therefore, classrooms should include ample experiences in responding to questions that require students to analyze information, identify problems, develop original solutions, and formulate opinions. These are also the more difficult questions for teachers to develop. Let's take a look at a variety of questioning techniques that are utilized across content areas.

Strategies at Work

Questioning the Author (QtA)

Questioning the Author (QtA) is a text-based strategy that invites the reader to interact with the information and build meaning from the content by analyzing the author's purpose (Beck, McKeown, Hamilton, & Kucan, 1997). These questions, referred to as queries by Beck et al., are meant to serve as discussion prompts that invite students to develop ideas rather than restate information directly from the text. Queries require the students to take responsibility for thinking and for constructing understanding. As students wrestle with ideas and concepts while reading, their inquiry moves into deeper levels of meaning in narrative and expository texts by moving beyond the stated facts and becoming involved with issues. The students realize that the author is challenging them to build their ideas and concepts. As a result, collaborative discussion follows the open-ended and author-oriented queries. Table 4.1 contains a table of QtA queries designed by these researchers.

The goals of QtA are always the same: to construct meaning of text, to help the student go beyond the words on the page, and to relate outside experiences from other texts. The way to achieve these goals is discussion enriched by the student's world and their own personal histories. QtA involves the teacher as well as the whole

Today's standardized tests not only assess basic skills, they increasingly demand test takers utilize more sophisticated strategies like prediction, inferring, and synthesizing information.

Table 4.1   **Questioning the Author Prompts**

Goal	Query
Initiate discussion	What is the author trying to say? What is the author's message? What is the author talking about?
Focus on author's message Linking information	That's what the author says, but what does it mean? How does that connect with what the author already told us? What information has the author added here that connects or fits in with _____?

Identify difficulties with the way the author has
    presented information or ideas
	Does that make sense?
	Is that said in a clear way?
	Did the author explain that clearly? Why or why not? What
	    do we need to figure out or find out?

Encourage students to refer to the text because
    they have misinterpreted, or to help them
    recognize that they have made an inference
	Did the author tell us that?
	Did the author give us the answer to that?

Beck, I. L., McKeown, M. G., Sandora, C., Kucan, L., & Worthy, J. (1996). Questioning the author: A yearlong classroom implementation to engage students with text. *Elementary School Journal, 96,* 385–414. Used with permission of the University of Chicago Press.

class as they collaboratively build understanding during the reading. During this process the teacher participates in the discussion as a facilitator, guide, initiator, and responder. The role of the teacher is not to dominate the conversation, but to lead the students into dialogue with open-ended questions. The teacher strives to elicit the readers' thinking while keeping them focused in their discussion (McKeown & Beck, 1999). The students' answers are not evaluated in this procedure because QtA is designed to engage the readers with the text, not to rate the accuracy of their responses. We recently saw Mrs. Melanie Scott use QtA queries in her English class as she introduced the poem "Annabel Lee" by Edgar Allen Poe (1849/1966). Let's take a peek.

Some teachers record the questions developed during QtA for later use.

Questioning the Author in English

Poe is a new author for the students, who do not yet have the background knowledge of his life or works. The students will work with ideas they have generated during this shared reading to gain meaning of his poetic narration. After reading aloud the first stanza, Mrs. Scott draws their attention to Poe's message and listens to their responses.

"What is Poe talking about in this poem? Is he the speaker in "Annabel Lee?" Let's look for clues in this poem about this. What is Poe's message?"

Voices echo, "Death. Love. Sorrow. Marriage."

With a smile and a nod, Mrs. Scott alerts the class to listen to the rhyme, rhythm, and sounds of the words as she continues to read aloud. During her reading, Mrs. Scott pauses and asks, "Do you feel that Poe really loves Annabel Lee?"

The class shouts, "Yes!" One student confirms, "Of course he does."

Mrs. Scott keeps probing. "How do you know that he loves her?"

Eric immediately replies, "Because he talks about angels in heaven were jealous of Poe's and Annabel's love. But, I don't get it when he talks about him being a child, and her, a child."

Josh adds, "Yeah, on Valentine's Day, I see little angels with hearts, bows and arrows on cards. Are Poe and Annabel Lee sweethearts? Are they grown-ups or are they kids?" Carolina calls out, "I think that maybe they were teenage lovers and the angels are symbols of their love."

As the students generate thoughts and questions, Mrs. Scott is doing less and the students are doing more. She guides them through the next stanza, then stops and asks, "Have you ever loved someone? Think about how you felt at that time. How did you feel when that person left?" The class remains silent. Waiting, she encourages the students to think about Eric's and Carolina's ideas. "What is the 'reason' that Poe refers to in the following lines? What is Poe really saying when we read,

> And this was the reason that, long ago,
> In this kingdom by the sea,
> A wind blew out of a cloud, chilling
> My beautiful Annabel Lee . . ."

When students generate questions, the instruction shifts from a teacher-centered approach to a student-centered one.

"He blames the angels for Annabel Lee's death because maybe, she got very sick and died. Poe can't really explain how she got sick, so he tells us the wind came from the angels, and it made her sick," offers Tanisha.

Shaking his head, Thomas interjects, "How can the wind come from the angels and how can the wind make Annabel Lee sick?"

Instead of answering Thomas, Mrs. Scott responds with a question to dig deeper. Mrs. Scott inquires, "Is the information about Annabel Lee's death as important as the previous information about their love?"

Murmurs fill the room and some student voices are heard above the rest.

"Maybe it isn't important for us to know how she died, because Poe would have told us," says Roberto.

"Or he really didn't know," Joelle interjects.

"I think it's important that Poe and Annabel Lee loved each other and when she died, he still thought that they were married," offers Ting.

Engaging the students in the final segment of text, Mrs. Scott reads aloud the last stanza. She then asks, "If you could, would you bring Annabel Lee back to Poe? Why do you think this way?"

Tanisha replies, "Definitely, I would bring her back to life, because Poe's in a lot of pain. He's sleeping by her side in the tomb!"

Eric retorts, "I wouldn't. Once you die, it's never the same when you come back. People change all the time."

This is an example of a Writing to Learn activity, discussed in more detail in chapter 8.

To prevent this comment from leading the students onto another tangent, Mrs. Scott reveals an important fact from Poe's life that they had not known. "Mr. Poe died two days after he wrote this poem. If you could speak to Mr. Poe right now, what would you say to him? Take ten minutes to write your response and then you'll share them with the class."

With the stated prompt, Mrs. Scott sparks the students' thinking about Poe as both author and speaker and provides an opportunity for the students to write their thoughts. Using their written responses, the students then interact with each other and Mrs. Scott using class discussion practices including *marking, turning back, revoicing,* and *recapping.* Marking is repeating students' comments in a manner that draws attention to certain ideas. Turning back occurs when the teacher turns the responsibility of the conversation back to the students. Revoicing involves restating student words to add clarity; it is the "in other words" approach. Recapping the discussion reviews key points and provides closure.

These discussion techniques are taught at the beginning of the year. At this point in the course, students are able to use these skills during class discussions.

Concentrating on the quality and depth of meaning that students are constructing during the reading and discussion of "Annabel Lee," Mrs. Scott keeps the focus on the topic while guiding the discussion and helping to clarify confusion. Her in-depth questioning allows the students to transform the author's ideas into their ideas and to challenge the author's words in order to make connections to the text based on their constructive thinking and curiosity.

ReQuest

ReQuest (Manzo, 1969) is another useful questioning technique designed to assist students in formulating questions and answers based on a text passage. This procedure also builds background knowledge and vocabulary through discussions, and helps readers develop predictions about the reading. Through modeling and feedback, students are provided an example, then have an opportunity to apply the strategy.

Designed first for one-to-one instruction, ReQuest has been used as a group activity as well.

The ReQuest process is a simple one to implement in the secondary classroom. The teacher chooses a passage of text, then designates short segments within the passage. When ReQuest is introduced, it is advisable to conduct the first round so that the teacher is the one to answer questions generated by the students. The teacher/respondent keeps the book closed during the questioning, and students may be requested to rephrase questions if necessary. Manzo cautions that the teacher must answer to the best of his or her ability. The student/questioners have their books open and check the teacher's answers against the text. Once this phase is complete, the roles are reversed. After reading the next segment of text, the teacher, with book open, becomes the questioner, while the students answer. As before, those who are answering the questions can ask to have the question restated or clarified. This cycle is repeated two or three times until students have the background knowledge and vocabulary to make predictions about the remainder of the reading. Once students are familiar with ReQuest, the sequence can be utilized in small groups to support their understanding of the text. ReQuest can be also be tailored to suit the specific needs of students. For instance, questions can include those related to specific vocabulary featured in the reading. Respondents can also be asked to validate their answers with evidence from the text. Task cards for a student-led small group ReQuest procedure appear in Figure 4.1. Let's watch Mrs. Rita Peña's class of English language learners use ReQuest.

A text segment can range from one sentence to an entire paragraph, based on the needs of the students.

ReQuest in Social Studies

Today the students are engaged in learning how to compose questions and apply questioning strategies that help in comprehending a passage from their textbook entitled, "The Rise of Chinese Civilization." They have had previous experience with ReQuest and the emphasis of this lesson is on using multiple sources for locating information to answer questions. Because her students are English language learners, she is always interested in refining their oral language skills. Mrs. Peña reminds the class of the words used in formulating questions, especially *who, what, when, where, why,* and *how.* "I'm going to show you how I make questions that I ask the author, my peers, the teacher and myself, " she says as she draws a circle on the board and divides it into quarters with the respective labels: author, peers, teacher, self. The teacher then explains that she will use headings and captions in the text to formulate her questions.

Remember that English language learners need multiple opportunities to practice their speaking and listening skills–the basis of writing and reading.

Rather than reading silently, Mrs. Peña invites her students to participate in a shared reading, "China—The Land and the People." After reading three sentences,

Figure 4.1   ReQuest Task Cards

Questioner Task Card

1. Read the first passage silently. Pay attention to the information it contains.

2. Think of questions to ask. Try to use your own words, not exact phrases from the passage.

3. Keep your book open while you ask your question. Listen to the answer, then check to see if it is accurate. If it is not, ask another question to help the person arrive at the correct answer.

4. When finished, change roles. Repeat 2–3 times.

Respondent Task Card

1. Read the first passage silently. Pay attention to the information it contains.

2. Think of questions you might be asked. Check the passage you just read for possible answers.

3. Close your book and answer each question you are asked. You can ask the questioner to rephrase or clarify a question you do not understand.

4. When finished, change roles. Repeat 2–3 times.

Mrs. Peña pauses and invites a student to ask a question of the class. Henok asks the class, "Why is it that the Chinese are calling themselves the 'Central Country'?"

Margarita replies, "Because it is the cultural center of the world."

Mrs. Peña reads the second paragraph and invites another student to pose a question. Flordia says, "Why would China want to change its name to the People's Republic of China?"

When no one has an answer, Mrs. Peña points to the quarter-circle marked "questions for the teacher."

Students then ask her about the history of the name change and the reasons. After explaining the political changes that swept China over the last century, they return to the text.

In paragraph three, the students are introduced to countries bordering China. Tran asks, "How did China get along with its neighbors who were hunters and herders?"

Anna responds, "I don't understand the question."

Mrs. Peña asks Anna, "What do you need to do to understand the question? Would you like for me to write it on the board so you can see it?" When Anna responds affirmatively, the teacher posts the question on the board and clarifies the *who, what,* and *how* information. Her explanation focuses on vocabulary and context clues found within the text. Confidently Gabriela answers, "They shared things like food, ideas, talk and money."

Mrs. Peña repeats, "What did you need to do to understand the question?"

Gabriela replies, "Reread the text for who, what, and how."

Mrs. Peña instructs the class to read the next paragraph silently and write questions for their peers on index cards. They read about the Hwang Ho River and its flood plains and record questions on their index cards. When they finish reading, Mrs. Peña returns to the question circle on the board and directs the students to the quarter that reads "questions for peers." She then says, "Reread your questions and ask the person sitting next to you some of them."

A buzz immediately begins. One student is overheard saying, "I found out the Hwang Ho River is also called the Yellow River. It has two names." Other pairs compare information, clarify understanding, and even return to the text.

In this classroom, ReQuest has become a valuable means for English language learners to formulate questions and locate accurate answers. Perhaps more importantly, these students benefit from opportunities to use language in a precise fashion. These questioning events allow them to refine and restate their questions so that they will yield the information they are seeking, which supports the development of their metacognitive strategies (Ciardiello, 1998).

> Remember that metacognition is the ability to think about one's thinking.

Directed Reading–Thinking Activity (DR-TA)

The complex processes of reading require strategies to be practiced before, during, and after reading. The awareness of the necessity of these strategies and the ability to conscientiously activate them is referred to as *metacognition*. The Directed Reading-Thinking Activity (DR-TA) is an excellent instructional tool for modeling these reading processes using either expository or narrative text. DR-TA allows the readers to increase their metacognitive skills so that they become aware of their own thinking processes and develop the ability to regulate, evaluate, and monitor them. Struggling readers seldom make effective use of metacognitive strategies (Haller, Child, & Walberg, 1988). Even among more fluent readers, metacognitive knowledge in expository reading often lags behind. A study of middle school students without reading difficulties found that their metacognition in content reading mimicked the levels seen in elementary students reading narrative text (Craig & Yore, 1995). On the other hand, these strategies can be learned if they are explicitly explained, modeled, and regularly included in literacy instruction (Helfeldt & Henk, 1990).

Stauffer (1969) describes DR-TA in three basic steps: predicting, reading, and proving. Students are instructed to continually ask themselves three questions:

- What do I think about this?
- Why do I think so?
- How I can prove it?

At each segment of the text, the readers predict aloud, read to confirm, stop, and engage in the self-questioning. The DR-TA assists students in recognizing that the text is split into sections that build upon each other (Richardson & Morgan, 1994). Because the text is divided into smaller portions, students can focus on the process of responding to higher-order questions. Students make predictions about specific sections of the text and then read the next segment to confirm or alter their predictions.

> It is important that students make and revise their predictions as they read.

The segmentation of the text is a critical part of teacher preparation for a DR-TA. This chunking of text information is a distinctive element of critical thinking instruction because it allows the reader to concentrate on both larger concepts and smaller supporting details. To prepare a content area reading for your students, read the text closely to determine where the natural stopping points are located. These may occur at the end of a paragraph, or before a major heading. We've included a teacher preparation checklist to assist you in preparing a DR-TA lesson (Figure 4.2).

A typical sequence of instruction for a DR-TA looks like this:

1. *Activate background knowledge.* The teacher elicits purposeful predictions to explore the students' prior knowledge relative to the reading assignment by asking

Figure 4.2   Teacher Checklist for Planning a Directed Reading-Thinking Activity

☐ **Select a focus text** _____

☐ **Activate Background Knowledge**
Prediction questions related to title, headings

_____

_____

Questions related to student experience

_____

_____

☐ **Develop Vocabulary**
Target vocabulary

_____   _____

_____   _____

_____   _____

How will students learn target vocabulary? (concept maps, vocab cards, etc).

_____

☐ **Text Organization**
☐ Cause and effect   ☐ Description   ☐ Problem/solution
☐ Temporal sequence   ☐ Compare/contrast   ☐ Other _____

☐ **Springboard Questions**

_____

_____

_____

☐ **Independent Reading**
Students who will need extra support

_____   _____

_____   _____

☐ **Review, Reinforce, and Evaluate**

Small group discussion focus _____

Large group discussion focus _____

questions about the title, headings, and any charts or pictures featured in the reading. Prediction or speculation aids students in setting a purpose for reading and increases their attention to text objectives and their motivation to read (Nichols, 1983).
These prereading questions also serve to activate and build background knowledge
(Nessel, 1988). The new text is discussed with regard to the previous assignments so
that the students can make relevant connections. Students may be invited to write
their predictions, which are reviewed and shared after the reading (Lapp, Flood &
Farnan, 1996).

2. *Develop vocabulary.* It is essential that vocabulary is introduced prior to reading. Students need multiple opportunities to read and use new words so that they can learn how they relate conceptually to one another. By introducing vocabulary at the beginning of a DR-TA, you are signaling readers to their importance to the piece of text being examined (see chapter 7 for more information on vocabulary).

3. *Identify significant patterns of text organization.* Some patterns are cause and effect, description, problem/solution, temporal sequence, and compare/contrast. Students can scan text quickly to determine what general text structures they should anticipate.

For information on text structures, see chapter 1.

4. *Ask springboard questions.* Ask questions that align with the purpose for reading and focus the students' thinking before reading (Lapp, Flood, & Farnan, 1996). Prepare questions that target some of the main ideas of the reading, and utilize their predictive questions as well. Craft questions that are not readily answered in a few words, but rather are higher-level in nature. Students will revisit these questions as they read, supporting their search for possible answers. We have found it helpful to post these springboard questions on the board so that students can refer to them during the reading.

5. *Read the selection.* Identify the stopping points in the passage for students to use during the DR-TA. Remind them that they will read the text and monitor their own comprehension using the three central DR-TA questions: *What do I think about this? Why do I think so? How I can prove it?* These questions scaffold students' self-regulation of metacognitive strategies while reading. While the students are reading, circulate and assist students in making notes that answer these questions.

6. *Review, reinforce, and evaluate.* After the reading is completed, have students move into small discussion groups and share their predictions. In particular, they should focus on the revisions they made to their predictions, and what parts of the reading led them to those revisions. Lead the whole class in a discussion of the springboard questions and ask students to support their responses using the text. Additional questions are likely to evolve, and should be connected to further reading or projects related to the content.

The practice of the DR-TA is demonstrated in Mrs. Christine Johnson's social studies class. We're just in time to view a video. Let's take a seat.

DR-TA in Social Studies

The students in this 11th grade social studies class are studying the rise of industrialization and immigration at the turn of the 20th century. These dual trends intersected tragically in the sinking of R.M.S. Titanic on Sunday, April 14, 1912. Mrs. Johnson is using documentary film clips as well as key scenes from the popular movie "Titanic" (Landau & Cameron, 1997) to help students understand the event. She uses reproductions of newspaper accounts from the era, including the *St. Louis Dispatch* and the *New York Tribune*. Students will also read modern accounts of the event and an article on the recovery effort.

Using popular culture items such as movies engages students and allows them to see connections between what they're learning in school and their activities outside of school.

Mrs. Johnson asks the class, "After seeing the video presentation of the Titanic accident, what are your thoughts and feelings about this tragedy? Write all you know. You have five minutes." Time is called and the students share their thoughts and feelings. They begin to brainstorm prior knowledge using the KWL strategy to focus on the assigned text. Mrs. Johnson follows with the question, "What would you like to

For information on KWL and other iterations of KWL, see chapter 2.

know about the Titanic?" The students write their questions and hold them aside for later inquiry after reading the newspapers. She asks for the students to share their questions as she writes some of them on the board. The students seem anxious to respond as well as to question.

Anna reads, "Why didn't they listen to the warnings? Why didn't they look hard enough for an iceberg?"

Isaac asks, "What did they do to the ship that made them think that it was unsinkable? How long does it take an iceberg to disappear?"

"I want to know why didn't they have enough life boats for everyone?" asks Cesar.

Marco adds, "Who were some of the people in first class? I would like to know about them in more detail."

Latasha wonders, "Who were the survivors and are they still alive? Are they scared to go on trips in a boat?"

"Whose fault was it?" asks Josie.

Mrs. Johnson identifies each question as either literal or interpretive level. She challenges the students to extend their thinking as strategic readers and to answer their own questions in the final step of the KWL strategy.

Next, Mrs. Johnson introduces relevant vocabulary, including *steerage, disaster, panic, transmit, SOS,* and *dispatch*, all of which appear in the news articles. She constructs a concept map to visually represent both the definitions and relationships among the target words. She also reviews the organization of the texts they are about to read. "We will read and question the text, so that we can build an understanding of the human experience in this tragic event." She adds, "Newspaper text is often organized in a temporal sequence that tells a chronological description of events. We will pay close attention to see how this structure is used in our articles." Two other articles analyze the event from the research conducted on the wreck site. She explains that these texts are organized for cause and effect. To help students differentiate cause from effect, Mrs. Johnson points out that a cause may have one or more effects and an effect may have one or more causes. She emphasizes, "The cause must always precede the effect. The following signal words will help you identify the cause and effect pattern: reasons why, if . . . then, as a result, therefore, because." She writes the signal words on the board.

For more information on vocabulary instruction, see chapter 7. In addition, chapter 6 has examples of graphic organizers.

Then she posts springboard questions taken from student KWL charts to stimulate predicting, searching, and verifying information:

- Why didn't Captain Smith want the crew to announce that the ship was sinking?
- Why did Jack Phillips, the radio operator, think the disaster was his fault?
- What does SOS signify? What signal did it replace? Explain.
- Why did it take so many years for anyone to reach the wreck of the Titanic?
- What have you learned about this disaster?

Mrs. Johnson reads aloud the first news report, titled, " 'Save Our Souls' was Titanic's Last Appeal." She encourages her students to follow the way she constructs meaning using the three central DR-TA questions: *What do I think about this? Why do I think so? How I can prove it?* She guides the students with her questions and think aloud responses through the reading process. Systematic questioning helps to structure thinking in a manageable order so parts of the new text fit together with their prior knowledge. Using a step-by-step questioning procedure, she helps the students to understand the organization of the text. "What are the 5Ws (Who? What? Where? When? Why?) and How? These are questions we ask ourselves to find the information. Let's also think about what happened first, second, third?" "What is the result of these events?" This directed questioning guides the students for their independent reading and leads them toward higher-level thinking (Ryder, 1991).

After her guided preparation, the students participate in a pair/share reading of their assigned news articles. Chunks of text on the same topic will be interpreted using the DR-TA and springboard questions. Mrs. Johnson monitors the students as they read to achieve individual levels of understanding.

Shifting Responsibility From Teacher to Students. Over time, her teaching role will shift from generating questions to coaching students to generate and respond to their own questions. She advises them to use a timeline or graphic organizer to show the sequence of details and again directs the students to the posted springboard questions. The students are alerted to read between the lines because the answers are not explicitly stated. She informs the students that some of these questions require thinking and searching because the text information is implicit. She reminds them, "Implicit means you have to link main ideas with support/specific details to arrive at an answer. When you connect ideas with details to find the answer, you become a critical thinker."

After reading, the students review their answers to verify their understanding and accuracy. Their responses are shared in a whole-class discussion. Mrs. Johnson reviews the learning processes they used, including mapping, questioning, reading, and writing; then summarizes the events of the tragic voyage of the Titanic. The students are asked to reread, this time skimming and scanning, in order to write more extensive responses to the springboard questions. The readers revisit their selections to link information acquired from their video observations, questions/answers and discussions.

The guided discussion focuses on the participants' roles. Mrs. Johnson points out that the common link human behavior connects the series of events that led to the sinking of the Titanic and its aftermath. Students support their statements with evidence from the texts, and their written responses serve as talking points for their conversations.

The final stage of the DR-TA is the post-reading and Mrs. Johnson requires the students to apply what they know. She assigns them the role of newswriters. As reporters, the students are to write a news article on the effects of the Titanic's sinking on the world today. In applying what they learned to a new situation, the students develop an extended perspective of their knowledge.

Question-Answer Relationship (QAR)

The question-answer relationship (QAR) strategy describes four types of questions: *Right There, Think and Search, Author and You,* and *On Your Own* (Raphael, 1982, 1984, 1986). It is based on the three categories of question classification described by Pearson and Johnson (1978): *text explicit* (the answer is directly quoted in the text); *text implicit* (the answer must be implied from several passages in the book); and *script implicit* (requires both the text and prior knowledge and experiences). A classroom poster on Question-Answer Relationships appears in Figure 4.3.

Posting comprehension tools like QAR in the classroom assists students in applying the strategy after the initial instruction has been completed.

QAR requires teachers to model the different levels of questions that are associated with a text. QAR should not be confused with Bloom's taxonomy of questions (Bloom, 1956) because QAR "does not classify questions in isolation but rather by considering the reader's background knowledge and the text" (McIntosh & Draper, 1996, p. 154). In addition to serving as a tool for teachers to develop questions, it is

Figure 4.3   Question-Answer Relationship Chart

In the text. . .	In the text. . .
RIGHT THERE	THINK AND SEARCH
When was the Declaration signed?	*What are some of Thomas Jefferson's notable accomplishments?*
The Declaration of Independence was adopted on <u>July 4, 1776</u>.	<u>The Declaration of Independence</u> was adopted on July 4, 1776. John Hancock signed first, and <u>Thomas Jefferson, the author</u>, signed as a delegate of Virginia. He later became <u>the third president of</u> the United States.
Answers to Right There questions are in the text. The words in the question usually through match a sentence in the text.	Answers to Think and Search questions are in the text. The answer is compiled segments of several sentences.
In your head. . .	In your head. . .
AUTHOR AND YOU	ON YOUR OWN
What influence did participation in the development of the Declaration have on the signers?	*If you were a delegate of the Second Continental Congress, would you sign?*
Answers to Author and You questions are not in the text. You need to consider both what the author has told you and what you already know about the topic.	Answers to On Your Own questions are not in the text. You need to consider your personal experiences to answer.

also a framework for students to apply in answering questions. QAR is a student-centered approach to questioning because it "clarifies how students can approach the task of reading texts and answering questions" (Raphael, 1986, p. 517). A comparison chart illustrating the relationship between these concepts of text questioning can be found in Figure 4.4.

It is advisable to pair both "right there" and "think and search" questions to encourage the learner to self-assess for uncertainties. This inquiry interaction promotes more personal involvement than using questions with separate phrases of isolated facts (Busching, 1995). In contrast, "author and you" and "on your own" questions invite the reader to integrate personal experiences and prior knowledge into their responses. These inferential and evaluative questions require the reader to make connections between text, self, and world (Keene & Zimmerman, 1997). During this time, the reader must deduce, infer, connect, and evaluate (Leu & Kinzer, 1995; Raphael, 1982, 1986).

The instructional power of QAR lies in the explicit instruction of identifying what type of question is being asked, and therefore what resources are required to answer the question. Raphael (1984) notes that less effective readers are often puzzled by where to locate answers to questions based on a reading. Some students rely only on the text, sometimes fruitlessly searching for an answer that is just not there. Con-

> When students can connect text with their own experiences or other texts, they are able to understand and remember information efficiently.

Figure 4.4 Question-Answer Relationship Comparison Chart

QAR Strategy	Category	Description
Right There	Text explicit	The question is asked using words from the text and the answer is directly stated in the reading.
Think and Search	Text implicit	The questions are derived from the text and require the reader to look for the answer in several places and to combine the information.
Author and You	Script- and text implicit	The question has the language of the text but in order to answer it, the reader must use what he/she understands about the topic. The answer cannot be found directly in the text, but the text can provide some information for formulating an answer. The information is implied and the reader infers what the author meant by examining clues in the text.
On Your Own	Script implicit	The question elicits an answer that comes from the reader's own prior knowledge and experiences. The text may or may not be needed to answer the question.

versely, other students rarely return to the text for any answers, believing that they can only depend on information they can recall from memory. By teaching the relationship between questions and answers, students can apply the framework to answer more efficiently and accurately.

The QAR framework can typically be taught in one lesson. We advise the teacher to read aloud a small segment of text and ask a question about what was read. The teacher reflects aloud on the selection and answers the question. What is critical is to identify the level of the question and the source of the answer. When students learn to classify questions and locate answers, they learn to recognize that the reading process is influenced by both the reader and the text. Eventually, students are ready to formulate original questions in response to text. To see students in action, let's visit Mr. Robert North's science class.

QAR in Science

The chemistry students follow Mr. North's voice and pointer as it moves from line to line of the text displayed on an overhead projector. He is engaging his students in a shared reading that describes and explains the nature of solvents, solutes, and solutions. Directing his attention to the students, he informs them that in order to learn the information, they will use the QAR strategy. Mr. North has modeled QAR and taught it to his students, and frequently supports his novice chemists in shared and independent readings. Today, the students are using QAR in a whole class activity. They will be answering questions and generating new questions for their classmates to answer.

Mr. North reads aloud, "It is important to realize that agitation affects the rate in which a solute dissolves." He stops and asks, "What affects the rate that a solvent dissolves?"

The class unanimously answers, "Agitation."

Making the type of question explicit shifts responsibility to students.

As noted in chapter 7, when students know Latin and Greek affixes and roots, they are able to apply them to new vocabulary.

He quizzes, "What kind of question did I ask?"

Together they respond, "Right there."

Mr. North continues reading aloud. "Agitation cannot influence the amount of the solute to be dissolved in a solution. In the solution, the dissolving medium is the solvent." He deliberately repeats the last statement and students raise their hands as if on cue.

Serina is acknowledged and she asks, "What is the solvent?"

Mr. North nods and checks the class, "Are you ready? What kind of question is Serina asking?"

Without hesitation, they shout, "Right there!" And they add, "The dissolving medium is the solvent."

Before he reads the remaining text, Mr. North skims the second paragraph. He notes the term *thermodynamics*. "Someone make my day and tell me what that word means. We've met the word before."

When no one responds he continues, "Let's divide the word into two. *Thermo* means what? *Dynamics* means what?"

Rosario replies, "Thermo means temperature."

April adds, "I think dynamics means change." As the students answer, Mr. North writes their definitions on the transparency.

By clarifying vocabulary without using a dictionary, Mr. North taps into his students' prior knowledge and reminds them how to discover meaning by looking for context clues. "That's an On Your Own question, folks."

Mr. North returns to the passage of the text that explains the nature of a saturated solution. He poses the question, "What is sodium chloride?"

Phan calls out, "Salt."

Mr. North asks with a knock on the desk, "What kind of salt?"

Brian adds, "Table salt."

Mr. North then queries, "If I dissolved a box of salt in a beaker of water, can I dissolve two more boxes in the same beaker? Any educated guesses?"

Serina quizzically states, "How big is the box and how big is the beaker?"

Jorge chimes in, "Serina's right, Mr. North, because the answer to your question depends on the amount of solute and solvent. We need to know more information. It's an Author and You question." At this point, the students must rely on their own understanding about solutions, as well as inferential information in the text.

Mr. North encourages the students' responses with a compliment and another probing question. "What if we agitated the solution, would that influence the amount of salt that goes into the solution?" This is a Think and Search question because the answer can be constructed by linking information from several parts of the text.

Phan, jumping out of his seat, replies, "No. The agitation would increase the rate at which it dissolves, but not the amount that dissolves."

"Mr. Phan Nguyen, you made my day!"

Ahmed asks, "Mr. North, you were talking about thermodynamics. So what's the temperature of the solution going to be?"

"Very good question, Ahmed. How would the temperature influence your answer to my question? That's an On Your Own question, and a great segue." Mr. North continues, "Today you covered all the points of our shared reading. Different variables like temperature, volume of solution, and quantity of solutes are crucial in answering our scientific questions. Tomorrow during lab, we will do experiments that change the respective variables. And we'll answer Mr. Ahmed's question at that time."

Mr. North's chemistry class knows that QAR is a useful strategy for locating answers and his budding chemists recognize that question-answer relationships involve explicit and implicit text language. Mr. North's learners also realize that their experiences and knowledge contribute to their questions and answers. As a result of these teaching and learning practices, Mr. North is strategically developing and improving these students' literacy abilities in order to enhance their understanding of the content.

Using Questioning for Study (SQ3R, SQ4R, and SQRQCQ)

Effective questioning is essential for reading and class discussion. The ultimate purpose of teacher questioning is to teach students to formulate their own questions as they read, for this is a tool that will support their comprehension of text. It is also at the heart of three popular study strategies, SQ3R (*survey, question, read, recite, review*), SQ4R (*survey, question, read, reflect, recite, review*), and a customized framework for mathematics called SQRQCQ (*survey, question, read, question, compute, question*).

SQ3R is a systematic way of studying text to support the student's reading by previewing, skimming, and setting purpose questions before actual reading. This study system, originated by Robinson (1946), includes a series of steps that are offshoots of teacher modeled reading lessons, including DR-TA. While students read to learn, they utilize the following steps of SQ3R:

S	Survey	Skim text for headings and charts
Q	Question	Turn headings into questions
R	Read	Read to answer questions
R	Recite	Answer questions and make notes
R	Review	Reread for details and unanswered questions

- *Survey* the text to acquire its essence from headings, charts, bold print terms.
- *Question* the material. Turn each section heading into a question or set of questions.
- *Read* with the purpose of answering the questions.
- *Recite* the answers to the questions after reading and without looking back in the text, then making notes on learned concepts.
- *Review* what has been read and try to answer from the text all the self-questions to evaluate responses and summarize important information.

The sequence utilized in SQ3R is intended to echo the behavior of effective readers. As students *survey* the material before reading, they predict what the material will be about, what prior knowledge will be relevant, and which strategies will be useful in approaching the new text. They formulate *questions* in anticipation of the content they are about to encounter. The students' prior knowledge and use of *reading* strategies assist them in constructing meaning of the content area text. However, their comprehension does not necessarily lead to learning that is meaningful and useful. Learning takes place when the new information becomes an interactive part of existing knowledge. Therefore, they *recite* answers to their own questions and make notes for later use. They then *review* the text, rereading for details and to clarify questions that remain unanswered (Armbruster et al., 1991).

The metacognitive sequence utilized by SQ3R is a clear model of the reading behaviors of effective readers, yet it seems to be underutilized in many secondary classrooms. Vacca and Vacca (1999) suggest that this may be due to the way SQ3R is

By understanding what effective readers do, we can teach more uncertain readers some of the skills needed to improve comprehension.

taught. Because there is a prescribed set of steps to be followed, there is a temptation to teach the strategy through rote memorization only, with little time spent on the purpose for each step. When students perceive strategies like these to be an instructional exercise with no real purpose beyond the lesson, they are unlikely to generalize them to other settings. Even more importantly, they will not adopt the approach into their metacognitive repertoire, thus defeating the purpose of teaching the strategy in the first place. Although it will take longer, we strongly urge teachers to invite students to discover *why* the steps are useful.

SQ3R has inspired several adaptations for guiding students to study and learn from text. These include SQ4R (*survey, question, read, reflect, recite, review*), and like its predecessor it is implemented across the content areas. SQ4R (Thomas & Robinson, 1972) adds a reflective step after the initial reading to make connections to what is already known. In addition to these learning strategies, there is the SQRQCQ (*survey, question, read, question, compute, question*), which assists mathematics learners to interpret and use the needed textual information in solving word problems (Fay, 1965).

SQRQCQ is an effective framework for solving mathematical word problems because its steps form a systematic approach to determining the information provided in the question, and the mathematical operations necessary to arrive at the correct answer. Like SQ3R, it has a series of steps to be followed:

S	Survey	Skim to get the main idea of the problem
Q	Question	Ask the question that is stated in the problem
R	Reread	Identify the information and details provided
Q	Question	Ask what operation needs to be performed
C	Compute	Solve the problem
Q	Question	Does the answer make sense?

- *Survey* the question to get the essence of the problem. This first reading is for general understanding.
- *Question* what the problem is asking. Restate the question using your own words, being careful not to lose the technical terminology in the problem.
- *Reread* the problem to locate details and eliminate unnecessary information, if applicable.
- *Question* the problem again. What operations are necessary to solve the problem?
- *Compute* the answer.
- *Question* again. Does the answer make sense? Does it answer the question posed in the problem?

It is not uncommon for students to be intimidated by word problems. Frameworks like SQRQCQ can increase student confidence because they learn a systematic approach to solving problems. It also encourages elimination of extraneous information meant to distract the student.

Mr. David Skillman implements skillful questioning techniques like SQRQCQ to meet the diverse levels of the English language learners in his geometry class. He adapts questions that require knowledge of facts and mathematical processes before introducing higher-level questions related to concepts and principles. His students use the series of questions to reach a correct answer. Let's join him and his class as they tackle a geometry word problem.

Like many instructional approaches, these strategies change depending on the needs of students and the text. What they all have in common is attention to questioning as a means for learning.

Mathematics teachers recognize the importance of teaching flexible problem solving approaches, not just memorization of algorithms.

SQRQCQ in Mathematics

The 11th-graders in Mr. Skillman's class successfully met yesterday's challenge of cutting and assembling a geometric puzzle to visually prove the Pythagorean Theorem, but struggled with applying the principle in word problems. The class agreed that the fifth problem on their assignment was particularly vexing. Mr. Skillman first engaged in reflective questioning on his own:

- Are the students unable to work with the given information (vocabulary)?

- Are the students unable to apply the Pythagorean Theorem?

Based on the feedback from the students, he decides that there is reason to believe that both vocabulary and application may lie at the heart of the problem, so he leads them through an SQRQCQ sequence. He reminds them of this familiar strategy for solving word problems and provides guided instruction to find the solution to this one—determining the hypotenuse formed by a fallen tree.

Mr. Skillman quickly reads aloud the problem to get the general idea and he instructs his English language learners to survey the illustration of the fallen tree and its metric measurements. He asks, "What is the problem?"

Survey

Alberto responds, "We don't know how many meters of tree are left."

Looking for details and being sure not to mention too much detail, Mr. Skillman scans the problem. He says as he draws a vertical line on the board, "There's a great big tree. How tall is the tree?"

The class replies, "36 meters."

"How many feet roughly is a 36 meter tree? Does anybody know? How many feet are approximately in one meter?"

Jessica answers, "About three."

Mr. Skillman picks up a yardstick and shows its length to support the visual relationship between meters and feet. "What is three times thirty-six?" Mr. Skillman is asking these questions to involve the students in examining and applying visual information to mathematical concepts. Students are busy calculating and they arrive at an answer of 108 feet. Now they have a visual understanding of the tree's height.

Mr. Skillman has them restate the question posed by the problem and invites them to write it down. "What happened to this poor tree?" he says, then answers himself, "It broke off, crack, bang!" He then rereads the problem to identify further details. He adds the new details to his drawing of the fallen tree. While he labels the given measurements, he asks, "Is 24 meters part of the tree?"

Question

Reread

Maria shakes her head, "No. It's part of the ground."

Mr. Skillman expands Maria's answer. "It's the distance from the tree trunk to the top of the tree, as it lies on the ground." Pointing to the board drawing, Mr. Skillman questions again, "How long is this line? I can only use x for its length." He writes $36-x$ over the fallen section of the tree. He repeats, "The original height of the tree is 36 meters, but the tree broke above the ground at the height of x, so my fallen part is $36-x$."

Question

He asks, "What process for solving this problem should we use? Do I have enough information to do the Pythagorean Theorem?"

The class enthusiastically shouts out, "Yes!"

Mr. Skillman confirms with a smile, "Yes, I sure do." He writes on the board:

$$a = x, b = 24, c = 36-x.$$

Compute

"Using the Theorem $a^2 + b^2 = c^2$, I can substitute for all of these values and I need to solve for x." He cautions the class about computing the problem. "There could be a little trouble in solving this one. When using Pythagorean, what will you have to do with $36 - x$?"

Alfredo answers, "You have to square it."

Mr. Skillman writes the equation on the board and encourages, "It looks to me that you're ready to solve the problem. Aren't you glad that you have calculators?" The students proceed to solve the algorithm.

While the students enter the information into their calculators, Mr. Skillman interacts one-on-one with the students to see if they are grasping the computing process. When they've finished Mr. Skillman asks, "Does your answer make sense? Check it against the facts in the problem and substitute your answers in the problem."

It is worthwhile to note Mr. Skillman's method for reading word problems from the students' perspective. He read quickly with the students, however in their initial reading, students read at a moderate pace (slower for English language learners) so they could get the general ideas of the word problem for later discussion and application. Drawing the figure with its numerical relationships was also helpful for supporting their understanding. Mr. Skillman's methods are typical of the critical thinking skills required for mathematical application.

The students then read to look for details and interrelationships. They again self-questioned by asking, "How do I solve it?" The students continued by asking, "What does x equal and how is the other information shown? What do I know and what don't I know?" They set up their equation by translating the words of the problem into an equation. Only then were they ready to compute the answer. Finally, the students questioned whether their answers made sense and tested their answers through substitution in the equation.

When the teacher repeatedly models a strategy like SQRQCQ to solve a problem students have struggled with, there is an increased likelihood that they will later use it independently. Furthermore, students make connections across content areas when literacy strategies are available to construct meaning from a text.

Student-Generated Questioning in Electives

Perhaps the ultimate sign that questioning strategies have been integrated into student learning can be seen in Ms. Dinah Nesbit's Child Development Careers class. This course is an elective in the Regional Occupational Program (ROP). Students enrolled in the class are pursuing a certificate in early childhood education for an eventual career in licensed day care and preschool programs. Course work includes planning and delivering instruction that is consistent with principles of child development. Ms. Nesbit's students are preparing to read aloud stories and question their listeners, all kindergartners at a local elementary school.

The ROP classroom is abuzz with activity. Ms. Nesbit has just announced to her class that they will read to their kindergarten charges tomorrow. The students are excited and anxious about their teaching visit. Sensing her students' motivation, Ms. Nesbit uses this opportunity to review questioning strategies that will help their "little buddies" understand the story, *The Quest for One Big Thing* (Fancher, 1998). She stresses that asking questions is not the goal; understanding and learning from hearing the story is the goal. Ms. Nesbit advises, "Sometimes it's helpful to have the children repeat a question before they attempt to answer it." She continues, "And if the child answers your questions, what follow-up questions will encourage him to think more deeply?"

Question

Teachers can also use follow-up questions to balance their questioning to include literal and evaluative queries.

Enrique responds, "I would ask, what makes you say that?"

Andre chimes in, "I'd say, how do you know that?"

Ms. Nesbit takes the lead and asks, "What do you do if the children ask you a question? How could their questions help you as the teacher of the story?"

"From their questions we can see if the kids understand the story or if they are mixed up," offers Lila.

"What do you think about posing 'what if' questions?' asks Ms. Nesbit.

Carlos joins the discussion. "The kids like when I ask 'what if' questions because they can use their imagination and answer the way they like to."

"They think 'what if' questions are fun," Louisa agrees. "I've seen them asking each other that kind of question when they're playing."

"Can anyone give an example of a 'what if' question you could use with this story," asks Ms. Nesbit.

Angel volunteers, "What if you were a circus bug that was helping with the harvest in the story? What would you do?"

"You did that so well, Angel. Let's try posing an open-ended question to solve the harvest problem," challenges Ms. Nesbit.

Angel hesitates and Leslie jumps in and questions, "How would you get the One Big Thing back to the bug colony?"

Ms. Nesbit smiles with satisfaction as she records their questions on the board. She writes a list of the questions the students have identified during the review of QtA and QAR. Then Ms. Nesbit directs the students to write specific questions about the characters, setting, events, and message of the story.

These are common elements of fiction and are found in nearly every narrative story.

After preparing their questions, the students share their inquiry choices and write them on small sticky notes to serve as reminders when they read the story aloud. Ms. Nesbit points out the importance of questioning as a teaching strategy as well as a strategic approach to learning. "When we elicit ideas through questions as teachers and learners, we gain information and valuable insight into our own thinking processes. When we demonstrate strategic ways of reading, we stimulate thinking for our peers and other learners, namely the kindergartners."

We couldn't help but notice that Ms. Nesbit's focus on questioning strategies has benefited her own students as well. Their awareness and practice of questioning strategies guides their own comprehension. As a result, the process of applying strategies to content area study becomes internalized as students use questioning techniques in the context of a group activity or independent reading.

Conclusion

The range of questioning strategies discussed in this chapter provides teachers and learners with ways to monitor and guide their construction and examination of meaning in reading, writing, talking, listening, and reflecting. These strategies serve as methods for modeling guiding questions, clarifying questions, expanding questions, and revising questions. By maintaining a balance between asking and answering questions, the teacher returns responsibility for critical thinking to the students. The use of effective questioning also directs and focuses students' reading, thereby energizing the reading by inviting students to make connections to both personal experience and prior knowledge.

We'll return to questioning again in chapter 9 when we examine reciprocal teaching.

References

Allington, R. L. (1983). The reading instruction provided readers of differing abilities. *The Elementary School Journal, 83,* 548–559.

Armbruster, B., Anderson, T., Armstrong, J., Wise, M., Janisch, C., & Meyer, L. (1991). Reading and questioning in content areas. *Journal of Reading Behavior, 23,* 35–59.

Beck, I. L., McKeown, M. G., Hamilton, R. L., & Kucan, L. (1997). *Questioning the author: An approach for enhancing student engagement with text.* Newark, DE: International Reading Association.

Beck, I. L., McKeown, M. G., Sandora, C., Kucan, L., & Worthy, J. (1996). Questioning the author: A yearlong classroom implementation to engage students with text. *Elementary School Journal, 96,* 385–414.

Block, S. (2001). Ask me a question: How teachers use inquiry in a classroom. *American School Board Journal, 188*(5), 43–45.

Bloom, B. S. (1956) *Taxonomy of educational objectives: The classification of educational goals: Handbook I, cognitive domain.* New York: Longmans.

Brophy, J., & Good, T. (1986). Teacher behavior and student achievement. In M. Wittrock (Ed.), *The handbook of research on teaching* (3rd ed.) (pp. 328–375). New York: Macmillan.

Busching, B. A., & Slesinger, B. A. (1995). Authentic questions: What do they look like? Where do they lead? *Language Arts, 72,* 341–351.

Cazden, C. B. (1986). Classroom discourse. In M. Wittrock (Ed.), *Handbook of research on teaching* (3rd ed.) (pp. 432–462). New York: Macmillan.

Cazden, C. B. (1988). *Classroom discourse: The language of teaching and learning.* Portsmouth, NH: Heinemann.

Ciardiello, A. V. (1998). You ask a good question today? Alternative cognitive and metacognitive strategies. *Journal of Adolescent & Adult Literacy, 42,* 210–219.

Craig, M. T., & Yore, L. D. (1995). Middle school students' metacognitive knowledge about science reading and science text: An interview study. *Reading Psychology, 16,* 169–213.

Dillon, J. T. (1988). *Questioning and teaching: A manual of practice.* New York: Teachers College Press.

Durkin, D. (1978-1979). What classroom observations reveal about reading comprehension. *Reading Research Quarterly, 14,* 481–533.

Fancher, L. (1998). *The quest for one big thing.* New York: Hyperion.

Fay, L. (1965). Reading study skills: Math and science. In J. A. Figurel (Ed.), *Reading and inquiry* (pp. 92-94). Newark, DE: International Reading Association.

Gambrell, L. (1983). The occurrence of think-time during reading comprehension instruction. *Journal of Educational Research, 77*(2), 77–80.

Guszak, F. J. (1967). Teacher questioning and reading. *The Reading Teacher, 21,* 227–234.

Haller, E. P., Child, D. A., & Walberg, H. J. (1988). Can comprehension be taught? A quantitative synthesis of "metacognitive" studies. *Educational Researcher, 17*(9), 5–8.

Helfeldt, J. P., & Henk, W. A. (1990). Reciprocal question-answer relationships: An instructional technique for at-risk readers. *Journal of Reading, 33,* 509–514.

Keene, E. O., & Zimmermann, S. (1997). *Mosaic of thought: Teaching comprehension in a reader's workshop.* Portsmouth, NH: Heinemann.

Landau, J. (Producer), & Cameron, J. (Writer/Director) (1997). *Titanic* [Motion picture]. United States: Paramount Pictures.

Lapp, D., Flood, J., & Farnan, N. (Eds.) (1996). *Content area reading and learning: Instructional strategies* (2nd ed.). Boston: Allyn & Bacon.

Leu, D. J., & Kinzer, C. K. (1995). *Effective reading instruction K–8* (3rd ed.). Upper Saddle River, NJ: Merrill/Prentice Hall.

Manzo, A. V. (1969). ReQuest procedure. *Journal of Reading, 13,* 123–126.

McIntosh, M. E., & Draper, R. J. (1996). Using the question-answer relationship strategy to improve students' reading of mathematics texts. *Clearing House, 69,* 154–162.

McKeown, M. G., & Beck I. L. (1999). Getting the discussion started. *Educational Leadership, 57*(3), 25–28.

Mehan, H. (1979). *Learning lessons.* Cambridge, MA: Harvard University Press.

Nessel, D. (1988). Channeling knowledge for reading expository text. *Journal of Reading, 32,* 225–228.

Nichols, J. N. (1983). Using prediction to increase content area interest and understanding. *Journal of Reading, 27,* 225–228.

Pearson, P. D., & Johnson, D. D. (1978). *Teaching reading comprehension.* New York: Holt, Rinehart, and Winston.

Pithers, R. T., & Soden, R. (2000). Critical thinking in education: A review. *Educational Research, 42,* 237–250.

Poe, E. A. (1849/1966). *Complete stories and poems.* Garden City, NY: Doubleday.

Raphael, T. E. (1982). Teaching children question-answering strategies. *The Reading Teacher, 36,* 186–191.

Raphael, T. E. (1984). Teaching learners about sources of information for answering questions. *Journal of Reading, 27,* 303–311.

Raphael, T. E. (1986). Teaching children question-answering relationships, revisited. *The Reading Teacher, 39,* 516–522.

Richardson, J. S., & Morgan, R. F. (1994). *Reading to learn in the content areas.* Belmont, WA: Wadsworth.

Roehler, L. R., & Duffy, G. G. (1991). Teachers' instructional actions. In R. Barr, M. L. Kamil, P. Mosenthal, & P. D. Pearson (Eds.), *Handbook of reading research* (Vol. II). (pp. 861–883). Mahwah, NJ: Lawrence Erlbaum.

Routman, R. (2000). Teacher talk. *Education Leadership, 59*(6), 32-35.

Ryder, R. J. (1991). The directed questioning activity for subject matter text. *Journal of Reading, 34,* 606–612.

Stanovich, K. E. (1986). Matthew effects in reading: Some consequences of individual differences in the acquisition of literacy. *Reading Research Quarterly, 21,* 360–407.

Stauffer, R. G. (1969). *Teaching reading as a thinking process.* New York: HarperCollins.

Thomas, E., & Robinson, H. (1972). *Improving reading in every class: A sourcebook for teachers.* Boston: Allyn & Bacon.

Vacca, R. T., & Vacca, J. L. (1999). *Content area reading: Literacy and learning across the curriculum* (6th ed.). New York: Longman.

Wimer, J. W., Ridenour, C. S., & Thomas, K. (2001). Higher order teacher questioning of boys and girls in elementary mathematics classrooms. *The Journal of Educational Research, 95*(2), 84–92.

Chapter 5

Getting It Down: Teaching Students to Take and Make Notes

DOUGLAS FISHER, NANCY FREY, AND LEE MONGRUE

"Students, I am going to make you STARS. Just you wait!" They hear these words at the start of every school year, and, by the end of each year, Advancement Via Individual Determination (AVID) students (Swanson, Marcus, & Elliott, 2000) have taken a real "shine" to Cornell notetaking (e.g., Pauk, 2000). This is so powerful that alumni who come back to tutor current AVID students fondly recall the first time they learned Cornell notetaking from Ms. Penczar, their AVID teacher.

Today, however, her students roll their eyes upward and give each other that "Yeah, right" look when she announces that notetaking is an AVID expectation. Classroom drama escalates as students learn that their weekly notebook grade depends on their notetaking in every academic class. Some students have second thoughts about AVID, but there isn't time to complain. Placing a transparency on the overhead projector (Figure 5.1), Ms. Penczar begins giving step-by-step directions on Cornell notetaking.

She begins by drawing a vertical line down a piece of paper, about a third of the way across the paper. Without a pause, Ms. Penczar begins her lecture, expecting notes to be taken. "She's serious!" they realize, and quickly follow suit, listening and

 Figure 5.1   AVID Notetaking Format

BE A STAR

The Cornell Notetaking Strategy

S = Set up the format.

T = Take text or lecture notes.

A = After class, revise your notes.

R = Review and study your notes.

Figure 5.2   Ms. Penczar's Skeleton Outline

S =

     a.

     b.

     c.

T =

     a.

     b.

     c.

     d.

     e.

A =

     a.

     b.

     c.

     d.

     e.

R =

     a.

     b.

     c.

     d.

writing as Ms. Penczar comments, "Left of the vertical line is for questions about the notes you have written on the right." The students see how easy it is to organize notes as they participate in a lecture titled "How to Be a STAR." Ms. Penczar's transparency, bit by bit, takes the form of a skeleton outline (Figure 5.2), but the students quickly fill a page with both the guidelines and structure of Cornell notetaking (Figure 5.3).

Figure 5.3   A Sample Student Page of Notes Based on the Outline

S = Set up the format.

   a. Put name, class, date in upper right hand corner.
   b. All notes need a title.
   c. Draw a line down the length of the paper about one third of the way in (about three inches).

T = Take text or lecture notes.

   a. Paraphrase the text or lecture in the right-hand column.
   b. Decide important information.
   c. Use whatever it takes to cue your memory system. You may, for example, use capital printing, underlining, arrows, or even pictures.
   d. Don't worry about spelling. If you know what you meant, that is what counts. Later, you can check a reference for proper spelling.
   e. Use abbreviations that work for you. Develop your own shorthand.

A = After class, revise your notes.

   a. As soon as possible, edit your notes. Reread and look for places to make additions, deletions, or clarifications.
   b. Work with a partner whenever possible.
   c. Use a highlighter or underlining to emphasize important points.
   d. Note any points that need to be clarified in class.
   e. Now fill in the left hand column with questions, symbols and pictures, and memory keys.

R = Review and study your notes.

   a. Review notes regularly—after class, at least weekly, and before a test.
   b. Cover the right column with blank paper. Either rewrite the right column or review aloud.
   c. Paraphrase answers.
   d. Reflect. Summarize the notes. Relate the subject to yourself and your personal experience.

When her lecture is complete, Ms. Penczar asks, "Well, what do you think I want you to do now?" It takes them just a moment to realize that their notes have relevance to what they now must do with them. The next ten minutes are devoted to revising and editing notes. They begin working in pairs, rereading their notes to find places to make additions, deletions, or clarifications. Highlighters start to brighten a line of notes here and there, and important phrases are underlined. As a class, they see how easy it is to complete the left-hand column with questions, symbols or pictures, and memory keys. When she asks them how they would study for a test on this information, they fold over the right side of their paper and answer the questions they have written. Ms. Penczar then says, "Well, you've just passed your first quiz in AVID; now don't tell me you can't do this in other classes." And now that they have had a bit of success, any second thoughts about AVID are dispelled, replaced with confident thoughts about success in high school and college. Though none in her class quite realize it yet, this first notetaking experience is a valuable one. It has set an example that hundreds of students have followed throughout both their high school and college years.

Why Teach Students How to Take Notes?

During a recent conversation with a group of teachers, we asked them about the strategies they use to teach students to store and retrieve information from class lectures and textbooks. Interestingly, notetaking was a given, something that all students should do. As one of the teachers said, "we all know how to take notes, and we all have our own ways of doing so. We don't need to teach students to take notes; they come to us knowing this already." Another teacher countered with, "while people may have different ways of taking notes, I do believe that it's a skill that can be taught. I also believe that students need to be shown how to take notes–good notes–that they can use later." We concur with the second teacher and hope that secondary school teachers focus instruction on this area. We believe that this difference in opinion is based on the omnipresence of notetaking in secondary and postsecondary schools. We also believe that all students can learn to take effective notes; the key is to identify for students why their notes can be useful to them later. As Jim Burke (2002) noted:

> Taking notes is an essential skill, one that has many other subskills embedded within it. Taking good notes trains students not only to pay attention but what to pay attention to. It teaches them to evaluate the importance of information and the relationship between different pieces of information as they read textbooks and articles. It also teaches them to organize that information into some format that serves their purposes. After all, we take different notes if we will use them to write a research paper. (p. 21)

How did you learn how to take notes? How do you use your notes to learn and remember?

Setting Students Up for Successful Notetaking

While it is important to teach students how to take and use notes effectively, educators also have a responsibility to organize their lectures in ways that make it possible to create notes. It is instructionally sound to introduce the sequence of topics and concepts for the day's class because it prepares students for learning. This simple preview also gives students a way to organize their notes. Once previewed, students should expect that the sequence will not be drastically altered and that the teacher will present concepts in an organized fashion. Detailed information, including technical vocabulary, names, dates, and formulas, should be presented visually as well as verbally, and well-timed pauses should be used to give students time to record this information. Signal words and phrases like "this is important" or even "be sure to write this down" will alert students to include items in their notes. Ending the class with a review enhances memory and retention and allows students to make corrections to their day's notes.

Lecture is one way to share information with students. However, they should be brief and focused, with opportunities for learners to apply the information through student-directed learning activities.

See chapter 10 for further discussion on signal words.

Distinguishing Notetaking From Note Making.   Before we venture any further, a definition or two is in order. We use the term *notetaking* to refer to students' written notes from a lecture or class discussion. We use the term *note making* to refer to the slightly different phenomenon of recording notes from printed materials. While many of the instructional strategies are the same, we have to remember that students cannot go back again for more information in notetaking (e.g., the lecture is over) while they can in note making (by rereading the text).

In terms of research on notetaking and note making, the evidence is fairly conclusive. Better notetakers generally do better in school and specific types of notetaking produce better results (e.g., Faber, Morris, & Lieberman, 2000; Kiewra, Benton, Kim, Risch, & Christensen, 1995). The reasons for this are interesting. Dating back to the seminal work of DiVesta and Gray (1972), the evidence suggests that notetaking requires both a process and a product function. It seems that both of these are important to produce results—improved comprehension and retention of material.

Process and Product Functions.   The process function—recording the notes—and the product function—reviewing notes later—are both required to create valuable notes (e.g., Henk & Stahl, 1985; Katayama & Crooks, 2001). Stahl, King, and Henk (1991) refer to this as the "encoding and external storage functions" (p. 614). The encoding function requires students to pay attention to the lecture while they write. This, in turn, allows students to transform information and deepens their understanding. The external storage function allows students an opportunity to review their notes, and thus the main ideas presented, before using the information on a test, essay, or lab.

Students sometimes view notetaking as a process function only—to scribe. When notes are used in subsequent learning activities, students see the value in quality notes.

In addition to the use of graphic organizers used in notetaking, a number of common formats have been suggested. Figure 5.4 contains "12 time-honored criteria for successful notetaking" (Stahl, King, & Henk, 1991, p. 615). They have also developed an assessment and evaluation system for teaching students about notetaking called NOTES (Notetaking Observation, Training, and Evaluation Scales).

Figure 5.4   General Notetaking Procedures

Date and label notes at the top of the page.

Draw a margin and keep all running lecture notes to one side.

Use other side for organization, summarizing, and labeling.

Indent to show importance of ideas.

Skip lines to indicate change of ideas.

Leave space for elaboration and clarification.

Use numbers, letters, and marks to indicate details.

Be selective.

Abbreviate when possible.

Paraphrase.

Use underlining, circling, and different colors of ink to show importance.

Cover one side of notes to study.

From: Stahl, Norman A., King, James R., & Henk, William A. (p. 615). (1991, May). Enhancing students' notetaking through training and evaluation. *Journal of Reading, 34* (8), 614–622. Reprinted with permission of Norman A. Stahl and the International Reading Association. All rights reserved.

See chapter 6 for information on graphic organizers.

NOTES (found in Figure 5.5) provides teachers with a specific way of giving students feedback on their current performance in notetaking. The assessment page focuses on current habits of notetaking while the evaluation criteria provides a rubric for teachers to use when reviewing a page of notes with a student (see Figure 5.6). Each of these tools is useful for teachers who wish to give their students an important study skill. Beyond this, there are specific approaches to notetaking and note making that will be explored by the teachers highlighted in this chapter.

Strategies at Work

Notetaking in English

Herrell (2000) identifies dictoglos as one of 50 effective instructional strategies for teaching English language learners.

Students walk into Mr. Herrera's classroom and are welcomed with a wide, ear-to-ear grin. Within this comfortable atmosphere, his ninth-grade students are taught responsible listening and notetaking practices using a strategy called *dictoglos* (Wajnryb, 1990). The purpose of this strategy is to give students experience hearing and recording English spoken fluently.

Teaching Students to Listen.   To begin the dictoglos activity, Mr. Herrera asks his students to listen to a read-aloud. As noted in the chapter on read-alouds, he is careful to choose a passage that will immediately engage his students and relate to a unit of study. Finding his "actor within," students sit in silence, their eyes intent with anticipation, focused on their teacher-storyteller as he roams the room reading. Today Mr. Hererra has selected the writing of Tupac Shakur (1999) to introduce his poetry unit. Once his students are hooked, Mr. Herrera asks them to listen to the same text, read two more times aloud. During these next two read-alouds, they must try to take notes on what they hear so that they can recreate the text as accurately as possible. Consistent with the dictoglos strategy, he provides his students with a few minutes to write what they remember after each read-aloud.

The use of texts reflecting popular culture can serve as an effective means of teaching the universality of themes across time and societies.

After two attempts at writing exactly what they heard, students pair up and share what they have written and attempt to add more to their notes. Two pairs then join and the four students collaborate to recreate the text verbatim. By this time, students have reviewed their notes, and listened to and read others' notes, as they add and revise their own.

Mr. Herrera finds that by giving his students practice in dictoglos they will become better notetakers and skilled listeners. He notes several benefits to teaching notetaking in this way. First, when the students initially hear the text, and even during the second and third reading of the passage, they must listen carefully and maintain an intense focus for the entire reading. This practice teaches students to block out other distractions, a necessary skill for taking notes during a lecture. Most lectures are not repeated and students must record information during their one-time opportunity. Second, students must learn to focus on the most important phrases during their first writing attempt, selecting only the key words that carry the meaning, even if some of the details are not yet scripted. This practice is also essential to good notetaking because one cannot write everything one hears. As students learn how to listen for key phrases, their notes become more valuable to them as study aids. Thus, with periodic practice of dictoglos, ninth-grade English students practice elements of good notetaking—selective listening and scripting of key phrases. They gain skills necessary for success in other content area classrooms by this non-threatening, engaging, collaborative activity.

Figure 5.5 Assessment for NOTES

	Never	Sometimes	Always
Prelecture			
1. I read assignments and review notes before my classes.			
2. I come to class with the necessary tools for taking notes (pen and ruled paper).			
3. I sit near the front of the class.			
4. My notes are organized by subjects in a looseleaf notebook.			
5. I have a definite notetaking strategy.			
6. I adapt my notetaking for different classes.			
Lecture			
1. I use my pen in notetaking.			
2. I use only one side of the page in taking notes.			
3. I date each day's notes.			
4. I use my own words in writing notes.			
5. I use abbreviations whenever possible.			
6. My handwriting is legible for study at a later date.			
7. I can identify the main ideas in a lecture.			
8. I can identify details and examples for main ideas.			
9. I indent examples and details under main ideas to show their relationship.			
10. I leave enough space to resolve confusing ideas in the lecture.			
11. I ask questions to clarify confusing points in the lecture.			
12. I record the questions my classmates ask the lecturer.			
13. I am aware of instructor signals for important information.			
14. I can tell the difference between lecture and nonrelated anecdote.			
15. I take notes until my instructor dismisses class.			

Figure 5.5   Continued

	Never	Sometimes	Always
Postlecture			
1. My notes represent the entire lecture.			
2. I review my notes immediately after class to make sure that they contain all the important points of the lecture and are legible.			
3. I underline important words and phrases in my notes.			
4. I reduce my notes to jottings and cues for studying at a later date.			
5. I summarize the concepts and principles from each lecture in a paragraph.			
6. I recite from the jottings and cues in the recall column on a weekly basis.			
7. I use my notes to draw up practice questions in preparation for examinations.			
8. I ask classmates for help in understanding confusing points in the lecture.			
9. I use my notes to find ideas that need further explanation.			
10. I am completely satisfied with my notetaking in my courses.			
11. I can understand my notes when I study them later.			
12. I use the reading assignment to clarify ideas from the lecture.			

From: Stahl, Norman A., King, James R., & Henk, William A. (p. 617). (1991, May). Enhancing students' notetaking through training and evaluation. *Journal of Reading, 34* (8), 614–622. Reprinted with permission of Norman A. Stahl and the International Reading Association. All rights reserved.

Notetaking in Mathematics

During a summer school mathematics class, Doug Williams steps into an Algebra II classroom and all eyes do a second take. The familiar smile of the school principal is easily recognizable, but the suit and tie have been replaced with a shirt that speaks volumes about what is in store for them. The front reads, "Each One, Teach One!" The back reads, "My lethal weapon is my mind." As this week unfolds, students teach each other and discover the power of their minds as they learn and use the language of mathematics.

Teaching Students to Use an Outline Framework.   Mr. Williams begins his lesson by focusing students on the structured notetaking that they will refer to regularly as they proceed through each lesson. Kiewra, Benton, Kim, Risch, and Christensen (1995) refer to this style of notetaking as an *outline* framework. Essentially, Mr. Williams will provide students an outline or format that they can use to take notes.

Figure 5.6   Notes Evaluation Criteria

Value Points and Descriptors of Notetaking Habits

Format	4	3	2	1	0
Use of ink	I use pen consistently.		I use pen and pencil.	I use pencil.	
Handwriting	Others can read my notes.		Only I can read my notes.	I can't read my notes.	
Notebook	I use a looseleaf binder.		I use a spiral notebook.	I don't use a notebook.	
Use of page	I leave enough space for editing.		I leave some space for editing.	My notes cover the page.	

Organization	4	3	2	1	0
Headings	I use new headings for each main idea.		I use headings inconsistently.	I don't use headings for changes in main ideas.	
Subtopics	I group suptopics under headings.		I don't indent subtopics under headings.	My subtopics are not grouped.	
Recall column	I use cue words and symbols to make practice questions.		I use cue words in a recall column.	I don't use a recall column.	
Abbreviation	I abbreviate whenever possible.		I use some abbreviations.	I don't abbreviate.	
Summaries	I summarize lectures in writing.		I write a list of summary lecture topics.	I don't summarize.	

Meaning	4	3	2	1	0
Main points	I identify main points with symbols and underlining.		I list main points.	I don't list main points.	
Supporting details	I show the relationships between main ideas and details.		My notes list details.	I don't list details.	
Examples	I list examples under main points.		I list some examples.	I don't record examples.	
Restatement	I use my own words.		I use some of my own words.	I use none of my own words.	

From: Stahl, Norman A., King, James R., & Henk, William A. (p. 618). (1991, May). Enhancing students' notetaking through training and evaluation. *Journal of Reading, 34* (8), 614–622. Reprinted with permission of Norman A. Stahl and the International Reading Association. All rights reserved.

While outline formats differ, Kiewra et al. (1995) suggests that the outline framework helps students understand the internal connections within the content.

Mr. Williams knows that mathematics is a language in and of itself and that the correct use of terms is vital for comprehension. In order to establish a target vocabulary, Mr. Williams tells the class, "Please take out three sheets of paper. Everyone will take notes." This is clearly an expectation for all, but any anxiety is quickly allayed with the following statement, "I'll tell you what to write." The gentle directiveness in his style encourages students to negotiate with each other and take risks in this learning community.

Random notetaking, when students haphazardly record anything they think is relevant, is less effective for supporting recall of information.

Students follow his direction and fold each sheet of paper into quadrants (4 boxes) and draw vertical and horizontal lines to separate the four areas. He poses the question, "While you are doing that. . . why is it important to take notes in class?"

Anthony responds, "So that you can remember."

"Remember what? And when?" Mr. Williams probes a bit further.

Gabriela offers, "At home, when you are doing homework, you can look at your notes to remind you how to do the problem, and what it looks like."

"You've got it. These notes will guide your work with me, with your partners, and on your own. Now, write this down." He then introduces, term by term, all of the words necessary for the day's lesson on the addition and subtraction of polynomials. He asks students to write one term per quadrant in the top left corner of the box until they run out of words. The list of terms for the day looks like this:

polynomial	equation	like terms
monomial	binomial	trinomial
degree	standard form	coefficient
leading coefficient		

Under each term, Mr. Williams asks students to identify the prefixes and roots in each of the words and to note other words that contain the prefix or root. Once they understand the component parts, he asks them to define the term. Mr. Williams, engaging his students in vocabulary development practice and notetaking, begins with the first word and asks, "What do you know about the prefix, 'poly?' What other words do you know that start this way?" As they determine the meaning of each term, he returns to the list on the board and writes the definition that both he and the class have agreed upon. He then says, "Now write this." Slowly, the class is building a word wall, and when this notetaking practice is complete, every student in class will have his or her own glossary of mathematical terms. From that point on, students refer to their notes as Mr. Williams uses the terms. An example of one of the quadrants of the outlined framework can be found in Figure 5.7.

Mr. Williams understands his new class well as he changes pace from structured notetaking to creating equations - out of the bananas, grapes, and plums he has distributed to each table. (Yes, you are correct in assuming that the students are really eating this up!) Students learn the concept of a "term" in mathematics by using the pieces of fruit as manipulatives.

He first creates his own equation by placing four bananas, six grapes, and two plums on the front table and asks the students to write an equation based on the fruit information. As students respond, he urges them to use their notes. "I'm looking for the vocabulary from our list that fits." He sees them glancing from him to their notes, as they negotiate with their table partners an explanation to his question. He has given each group a piece of cardboard with "WORKING" written on one side and "READY" written on the other. He reminds them to use the table signs, turning them to "WORKING" or "READY" as appropriate. This lets him know how much time students need to complete the task. He then guides them to writing the following equation:

$$4B + 6G + 2P =$$

Next, the students are required to create their own equations, and to explain them, using the target vocabulary at their side. One group of students immediately turned their sign to WORKING and created two bunches: seven plums and six grapes. After a brief discussion, they turned their sign to READY, and Mr. Williams

Student understanding of prefixes and roots supports transportable vocabulary across content areas.

Figure 5.7   Sample Mathematics Notes

Polynomial	Equation
* "poly-" means many * Other words–polyester, polygraph, poly-phonic, polyunsaturated * "-nomial" means terms * Other words–binomial * A polynomial has many terms and has a constant multiplied by one or more variables raised to a nonnegative integral power	
Like Terms	**Monomial**

joined their table with his question, "What have you created? Remember, use the notes you have on vocabulary terms."

They glance again at their notes as Ashley begins, "We've created a polynomial that is specifically a binomial. With an equal sign it becomes an equation." They then write the equation on their paper:

$$7P + 6G =$$

Mr. Williams asks, "Why can't you go to **13 PG**?"

Eric responds, "You can't because they're not like terms."

This brief moment provided Mr. Williams with a valid assessment of the information he had just introduced and gave students an authentic opportunity to use the target vocabulary from their working notes.

Note Making in Social Studies

"What questions might we ask about the Cold War, just by looking at this page of text?" Ms. Tsai queries her U.S. History class as they participate in a pre-reading activity to prepare for the next chapter in their text. She knows that creating a skeletal note structure of the text is a powerful pre-reading skill her students must acquire in order to become effective notetakers and note makers.

The table signs like WORKING and READY help teachers gauge time needed for the task and create a sense of friendly competition and collaboration.

While the instructional strategies are similar, remember that note making typically focuses on gaining information from texts while notetaking focuses on lectures and class discussions.

Using Technology and Notetaking. Ms. Tsai uses a combination of Directed Notetaking Activity [DNA] (Spires & Stone, 1989) and computer-assisted outlining (Anderson-Inman, 1996) as she engages her students in history lessons. DNA is a process approach to notetaking that includes three instructional principles:

1. a structured format for taking notes commonly referred to as the split page method;

2. a self-questioning strategy for monitoring levels of involvement before, during, and after notetaking; and

3. direct, explicit teaching of the notetaking process adapted for notetaking instruction from Pearson's model (1985) for teaching reading comprehension. (Spires & Stone, 1989, p. 37)

Consistent with the DNA process approach, Ms. Tsai wants her students to become familiar with the structure of the text, preview the targeted vocabulary, form questions, question themselves and others, and gain background knowledge from all of the charts, maps, illustrations, photographs and captions.

Stepping into the classroom, one can see how Ms. Tsai incorporates this note making activity with the use of a PowerPoint® presentation, a series of maps pertinent to the geographical areas and time period, and chart paper to list student-generated questions. She orchestrates a class discussion that requires the students to refer to their own notes, follow a multimedia display of text and maps on two separate screens, and contribute to the new set of notes that she transcribes into a PowerPoint® display. The expanding PowerPoint® presentation Ms. Tsai creates with her students' guidance becomes another structure for them to incorporate into their note making as they read the text. As Anderson-Inman (1996) notes, computer-assisted outlining does not confine students to pre-determined amounts of space in which to take notes. Further, computer-assisted outlining allows for multiple additions, modifications, and deletions.

> This teacher uses PowerPoint® because of its linear format. Another effective software program for teaching notetaking is Inspiration® which is discussed in chapter 6 on graphic organizers.

With books open, Ms. Tsai and her students skim the chapter, page by page, as they contribute ideas to the class notes displayed on one of two screens set up at opposite ends of the room. An outline of the chapter takes shape as the class decides on bullets for main ideas, from the headings and subheadings of each textbook page and their discussion notes. Ms. Tsai then leaves empty bullets under each main idea, areas requiring support information, to be completed later as students read each section of the chapter.

Engaging Students at Multiple Levels. Students are required to preview any visual aids on each text page, such as graphs, charts, pictures, diagrams and maps, and add pertinent bulleted information to their skeleton outline. They also list all of the italicized and boldface terms in the vocabulary section of their notebooks. These terms become the target vocabulary, to be incorporated into their notes, with definitions added. As part of her DNA instruction, Ms. Tsai periodically asks students to consider their level of participation in the notetaking activity. She may ask students to think about their level of motivation, their purpose for listening and participating, or if they are separating main ideas from details.

> Students need to know how to think about these visual and graphic representations of information, as well as how to synthesize details across them.

Using Notes in Class. When the skeleton outline is complete, Ms. Tsai uses it in a PowerPoint® presentation as she gives the students an overview of the chapter. On subsequent days, she will use the maps on the walls as contextual aids and she will have students begin posing questions based on the main ideas of the bulleted outline.

The series of student-generated questions are added to a growing list of questions on a chart in the front of the room.

As her students review their notes regarding the Allies' plan for the postwar world Tsai repeats the question, "What questions might we ask about the rationale of the Truman Doctrine?" She asks them to consider how geography and politics impacted the Truman Doctrine. She hopes for a deeper level of thinking than that required when students simply memorize facts.

"Do you think Truman's economic aid contributed to the containment of communism in Europe after the war? Why?" She smiles as she surveys the scene of students flipping through notes taken over the past week of lecture, class discussions and textbook facts. A student scribe writes these questions on the large sheet of chart paper attached to the wall. Now the students have access to the map on the overhead projector displayed on the front screen as well as the notes they have constructed from the textbook. Tsai guides their thinking by the questions being written on the chart paper hanging next to the data projector screen. This screen now displays the main idea of this discussion: **The Truman Doctrine.**

Tsai hits the return button on her podium and a subtopic bullet appears while the cursor blinks expectantly.

"OK? What do you think? Look over your notes, look at the map, and consider the world of the late 1940s. Europe is crippled; America has emerged from the war as a world leader. What do you suppose were some of President Truman's reasons for asking the U.S. Congress to give economic aid to Turkey and Greece?"

Brian hesitates at first, then with confidence reads from his notes, "Truman believed that the U.S. should support those countries that were fighting communism. And since Turkey and Greece were weak after the war, they were ripe for a takeover."

"Hmm, good point," says Tsai as she types into her power point template. The vacant bullet is now filled with a summary of Brian's idea: **Stop the spread of communism.** Her students know she means business when the new notes incorporate Brian's ideas and they copy this point into their notes. A few others begin to search their notes and textbooks for information to share. Tsai recognizes the familiar reaction of students who know that their ideas are validated. She deliberately uses her students' questions and ideas—either on the chart paper or the PowerPoint® template—to validate their thinking. She believes that the synthesis of students' questions and concerns with historical data is evidence that they are making meaning.

"Yeah, but some Americans believe that we were just messing in other countries' business." Jose interrupts Brian.

"Yeah, like I heard that is what is going on in the Middle East now." Miriam interjects.

Tsai pauses, she does not type that idea into the note making frame visible on the screen. Instead she asks the class if that is a question to include in the growing list of ideas to consider in the future. Most students agree that it should be part of future class discussions. The class scribe adds *9/11* to the chart paper.

Miriam waves her hand and Tsai nods in her direction and asks, "Did you find other information in your notes to add to the Truman Doctrine?"

Miriam reads from her class notes. "Because America was the only nation with money to help we had to do something to stop the possibility of more war." Tsai smiles and types the next bullet: **$400 million in economic and military aid.**

"Ok. Do you think this idea was only a generous act or could there be other reasons for the Doctrine?" Tsai flips on the overhead projector that lights up the room

By returning to their notes during later lessons, students begin to appreciate the value of their notes.

with a map of Europe with the Mediterranean Sea, the Black Sea and surrounding countries and begins the conversation.

Structured Outline Support Before, During and After Activities.   This repeated practice and use of note making demonstrates to students the ease and efficacy of structuring notes before reading, during independent reading of the text, and in class discussions. Students also learn to monitor their involvement and comprehension so that they can change behaviors if they are not learning. The combination of the Directed Notetaking Activity (DNA) and computer-assisted outlining ensures that students move gradually toward independent skills in note making.

Notetaking in Science

When Ms. Hoenstein teaches life skills (known to many adolescents as sex ed), she never has a problem with getting attention. On the contrary, the students are very interested in the topics for discussion; the air is charged with anticipation, anxiety and nervous giggles. Since many adolescents have not yet developed mature responses to this topic, Ms. Hoenstein uses notetaking to facilitate safe and mature discussions. Throughout the year she travels from room to room and building to building teaching 78 separate classes that encompass over 1,200 students.

> Because students can refer back to notes, they are able to affirm information.

Ms. Hoenstein uses a split page method or Cornell notetaking method (e.g., Pauk, 2000). Students are taught to draw a vertical line down the page with about 1/3 of the paper to the left of the line and 2/3s of the paper on the right. In addition, they leave room at the bottom (about 2 inches) to summarize their notes. A sample page is found in Figure 5.8. Ms. Hoenstein asks students to write their notes on the right side of the paper, their reactions and questions on the left side of the paper, and their summary of the information on the bottom of the page.

"Please, write this down, S-T-D, one letter below each other," says Hoenstein. "As we discuss the topic of sexually transmitted diseases, I will often use these three letters instead of the words they represent." Ms. Hoenstein scans the room and takes in about thirty adolescent and curious faces. A few wide eyes and muffled giggles tell her about the tenor of the class. "Now, write your own definition for each of the words–sexually transmitted disease." Based on her classroom experiences and knowledge of effective teaching practices, she gently guides her students into areas of sexuality that require a learning atmosphere that is safe and open.

> To ensure that students are engaged with the delicate topics, teachers can ask students to take notes during lectures and class discussion.

Following their individual work at creating a definition for STDs, Ms. Hoenstein invites students to share with the class. Jessica tries the first word and says, "sex, you know, sex." LaDonna adds to that, "it means doing it, but you can get a disease by just touching other people." As the conversation continues, the students create a working definition of STD and have a great deal of information in their notes. Next, Ms. Hoenstein turns to the class and says, "Some STDs can be deadly. If or when you become sexually active, you must become aware of how to avoid infection as well as how to seek treatment in case you are infected. You may recall some of the ideas you learned in eighth grade, or from your parents, or even information you picked up from friends. While I write on the board the scientific words that name some of the STDs, you write the names that you know in your notes and we'll compare. Please write these on the left side of a new page of notes and skip about five lines between each one. As we learn the definitions of these diseases and the causes, as well as the treatments, write that information on the right side of your page of notes. You

 *Figure 5.8* Sample Split Page Note Format

Name: _____ Date: _____ Class: _____ Page: _____

may ask me questions for clarification or write your questions and reactions on the left side, just below the names of the disease we are discussing."

Notetaking That Encourages Personal Response and Dialogue. Hoenstein believes that structured notetaking not only gives students a chance to categorize important information, but also provides them with options to deal with awkward and embarrassing feelings. "It opens avenues for students to react to controversial material privately," suggests Hoenstein. "As we work on these controversial and critical issues, students may have feelings and emotions that are triggered. Writing these notes often opens doors that allow them a non-threatening tool for deeper personal learning." She also believes that notetaking allows students to react privately to sensitive material before they pose a question or enter into a class discussion.

"It has been my experience that structured notetaking facilitates dialogue which is needed as we learn about human sexual behavior. Since human behavior is affected as much by feelings as by knowledge, this notetaking strategy promotes dialogue which will inevitably include sensitive issues that may provoke intimate feelings."

Notetaking in Electives

When English language learners are introduced to their first research paper, the question, "How do I do research?" is as important as the question, "What do I research?" In Marie Butler's Culture Studies class, no "How" question is left unanswered. In fact, her students master each research skill, step by step, in a scaffolded process that fosters confidence and success for developing writer/researchers.

Notetaking and the Research Process.   Ms. Butler begins the process by explaining what research is. The terms *research, sources of information, bibliography, research questions, research grid*, and *paraphrase* are all introduced as key steps in this process. Her students begin to understand that writing a research report will guide them to learn more about something they are interested in. Ms. Butler gives students the chance to choose what they want to investigate about their subject. She explains the process in the following way:

> The purpose of a **research report** is to collect and present information about your topic in order to share what you have learned. It is an opportunity to explore different **sources of information**: newspapers, magazines, books, encyclopedias, and the Internet.
>
> Research takes time, because you must find the information, then read it and take notes. It is important to keep a record of the sources you plan to use in your report. The final section of the report will be a **bibliography**, which lists in a particular format each source you used, which we will practice and learn.
>
> As you locate and search through resources about your topic, you must select only a few (five or six) major ideas to write about. These ideas will become your list of **research questions**. You will collect information to answer each of these questions by using a **research grid** for notetaking.

The first step in the research process is identifying possible research questions. To get students underway, they are required to produce a minimum of five research questions. The following are examples of the "think and search" research questions that her students wrote:

As stated in chapter 7, when students are able to preview vocabulary before discussion and readings, their understanding of the material is increased.

See chapter 4 for more discussion of think and search questions.

1. Research topic: Tenochtitlan
   - Why and where was the location of Tenochtitlan chosen?
   - What was the structure of the city?
   - How was life in Tenochtitlan?
   - What important events took place in Tenochtitlan?
   - Why and when did the city fall?

2. Research topic: Gandhi

- What was Gandhi's childhood like?
- Why was the spinning wheel important to Gandhi?
- What was Gandhi's position or job?
- How many times was Gandhi arrested?
- What did Gandhi do for his people?
- When was Gandhi assassinated and why?
- Why is Gandhi important?

Learning How to Document Information Sources. Students practice the important skill of documenting information in bibliographies before going to the library. First, Ms. Butler and her students identify the various sources available, then she shows them how each type of resource is documented in a bibliography of a research paper. Teachers know that practicing what has just been explained is the key to understanding, and in Ms. Butler's class this next step makes all the difference. Ms. Butler arranges her class in stations, each station having multiple examples of one particular resource. Groups of students take turns at each station as they practice recording each resource in the correct fashion, following written instructions and a sample page of a bibliography. When students have completed all of the stations, they have experienced how to document a variety of sources including newspapers, magazines, books, encyclopedias, and Internet information. In this staged classroom activity, students apply newly learned notetaking skills that will help them document their own resources correctly and effectively as they do authentic research.

Using a Matrix Format for Notetaking. Now that students are ready to begin their research, Ms. Butler introduces a *matrix* format for notetaking that will facilitate this process. According to Kiewra, Benton, Kim, Risch, and Christensen (1995), a matrix format builds on the outline format. While both provide students with specific information about internal connections, the matrix format emphasizes the relationships that exist across topics. As they note, "information across topics can be drawn more easily and quickly from a matrix than a linear representation" (p. 174). While not all content lends itself to the matrix format, the task Ms. Butler had in mind was perfect for this style of notetaking.

Ms. Butler introduces the "research grid" (see Figure 5.9) and students write their five or six "think and search" research questions in the boxes across the top of the grid. They enter the sources they found in the left-hand column of the grid so that they will be able to remember where the information came from when they cite it. This is also helpful when they must return to a specific source for additional information.

Students then look through each source and find all of the information they can about each of their questions. They write chunks of information, not complete sentences, in each notetaking box. Students examine each source and find information that answers their question. They continue this form of notetaking until each column is completed with information from all of the sources. Students now have a framework for their research paper.

Next, they must write an introductory paragraph and one or two paragraphs for each of the columns. These paragraphs answer their "think and search" questions. Students know they can structure their written response by turning each question into a topic sentence for each informational paragraph.

This practice reduces the possibility of plagiarism while building the skills of strategic readers and writers of informational text.

Figure 5.9   Research Grid

	Question/Topic			
	Write question/ topic 1 here	Write question/ topic 2 here	Question/topic 3	Question/topic 4
List source 1 from your bibliography here	Write notes about question/topic 1 from source 1 here	Write notes about question/topic 2 from source 1 here		
List source 2 here	Write notes about question/topic 1 from source 2 here	Repeat the process in all the spaces ➔ ↓		
List source 3 here				
List source 4 here				
List source 5 here				

Source/Reference (list sideways on grid)

Conclusion

In nearly every high school or college classroom students will be required to take notes from lectures and books. The reasons for this are sound–students who understand notetaking and note making do better on tests and essays. These students also learn more of the content. However, most students do not have sophisticated notetaking strategies. Instead, they rely on haphazard collections of facts and details that are not systematic. This process problem is compounded as many of these same students do not organize and review their notes later. Thus, teachers in secondary schools should provide students with systematic instruction in notetaking and note making. In addition to this type of instruction, we believe that teachers should provide students with feedback on their notes. Specific feedback on notetaking skills, through a process such as NOTES (Stahl, King, & Henk, 1991), will guide students to independence in this most important study skill.

Remember that a goal of notetaking instruction is to teach the usefulness of both the process and the product.

References

Anderson-Inman, L. (1996). Computer-assisted outlining: Information organization made easy. *Journal of Adolescent & Adult Literacy, 39*, 316–320.

Burke, J. (2002). Making notes, making meaning. *Voices from the Middle, 9*(4), 15–21.

Divesta, F. J., & Gray, S. G. (1972). Listening and note taking. *Journal of Educational Psychology, 63*, 8–14.

Faber, J. E., Morris, J. D., & Lieberman, M. G. (2000). The effect of note taking on ninth grade students' comprehension. *Reading Psychology, 21*, 257–270.

Henk, W. A., & Stahl, N. A. (1985). *A meta-analysis of the effect of notetaking on learning from lecture.* Paper presented at the 34th meeting of the National Reading Conference, St. Petersburg, FL. [ED258533].

Herrell, A. L. (2000). *Fifty strategies for teaching English language learners.* Upper Saddle River, NJ: Merrill/Prentice Hall.

Katayama, A. D., & Crooks, S. M. (2001). Examining the effects of notetaking format on achievement when students construct and study computerized notes. *Learning Assistance Review, 6*(1), 5–23.

Kiewra, K. A., Benton, S. L., Kim, S., Risch, N., & Christensen, M. (1995). Effects of note-taking format and study technique on recall and relational performance. *Contemporary Educational Psychology, 20,* 172–187.

Pauk, W. (2000). *How to study in college* (7th ed.). Boston: Houghton Mifflin College.

Pearson, P. D. (1985). Changing the face of reading comprehension instruction. *The Reading Teacher, 38,* 724–738.

Shakur, T. (1999). *The rose that grew from concrete.* New York: Simon & Schuster.

Spires, H. A., & Stone, P. D. (1989). The directed notetaking activity: A self-questioning approach. *Journal of Reading, 33,* 36–39.

Stahl, N. A., King, J. R., & Henk, W. A. (1991). Enhancing students' notetaking through training and evaluation. *Journal of Reading, 34,* 614–622.

Swanson, M. C., Marcus, M., & Elliott, J. (2000). Rigor with support: Lessons from AVID. *Educational Leadership, 30*(2), 26–27, 37–38.

Wajnryb, R. (1990). *Grammar dictation.* Oxford, England: Oxford University.

Chapter 6

Picture This: Graphic Organizers in the Classroom

Nancy Frey, Douglas Fisher, and Rita ElWardi

With notes in hand or markers in their grip, groups of students gather at tables to design poster-size graphic organizers in the shape of a mountain on large sheets of white butcher paper (see Figure 6.1 for a generic version of the story grammar chart). At one table, five students take on different tasks to complete the activity on time. At the foot of their story mountain, one group member, Chuong, has drawn a rectangle labeled "Setting" to hold bulleted phrases indicating the place and time of the story, *The Circuit: Stories From the Life of a Migrant Child* (Jimenez, 1997). Above "Setting" float cloud-like clusters of information labeled "Title & Author" and "Characters: Protagonist & Antagonist."

Two other members of the group, Lupe and Thao, work as partners. They check notes and confer together as they combine ideas and compose summary sentences that lead up to the summit of the mountain. An empty rectangle labeled "Climax" perches on the mountain peak. The two girls first write a sentence in pencil and ask Chuong to check the structure and spelling before they add it to the sequence of events strips that slowly climb the mountain. "Chuong, how is this?" Lupe asks as she reads aloud. "The family packed their belongings in cardboard boxes, loaded Carcanchita and drove to Fresno to look for work."

Chuong checks the structure and spelling of their sentence, gives them an "O.K." and continues sketching the rest of the story mountain components. He slides an arrow down the other side of the story mountain, pointing to another empty rectangle, and writes the word "Resolution" inside.

Two others in the group, Naima and Abdurashid, don't agree on the content of the box labeled "Conflict," so they decide to add a second box with the subtitles "man vs. society" in one, and "man vs. self" in another. "Maybe there are two conflicts in this story," Naima suggests. "One is that the migrant family has to struggle to survive against poverty and always find work from place to place."

Abdurashid adds, "But the other is that Francisco has to find the courage in himself to go to school and get help so that he can learn to read. Remember when we did the response journal about why he was crying when they had to

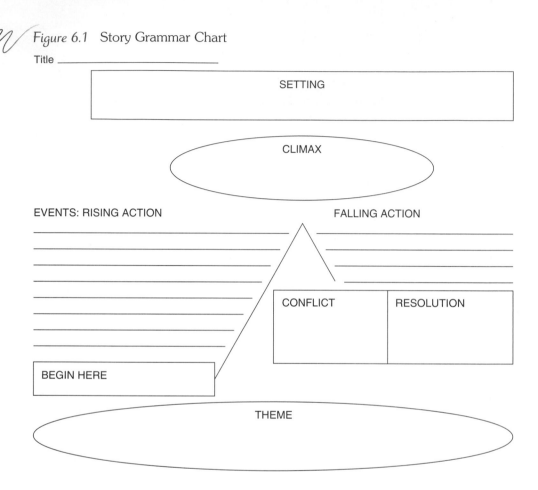

Figure 6.1 Story Grammar Chart

Title _____

SETTING

CLIMAX

EVENTS: RISING ACTION   FALLING ACTION

CONFLICT   RESOLUTION

BEGIN HERE

THEME

leave one place? I wrote that it was because he hated to start going to a new school again."

Chuong joins the discussion, wondering aloud if "man vs. nature" is also a conflict since the migrant workers had to work in the hot sun. "From dawn to dusk," he reads from his notes. They give him a look, nod, and add a third "Conflict" box, then move on to consider the empty box labeled "Theme" centered at the base of the mountain.

Abdurashid reminds everyone, "We didn't talk about the theme in class. This time, we're supposed to decide for ourselves."

"So, what do you think it is?" asks Chuong. They all glance over at the bulletin board filled with information about each literary term.

Abdurashid reads the definition, "The theme is the message, buried under the story. We must dig deep to find its meaning." He then asks his group, "So, what did we learn, what message do we get?"

"That family had to stick together to survive. Is that a message about family values?" Naima wonders.

Just then their teacher, Ms. ElWardi, walks by and listens in, so they wait for her response. She nods her head, but then looks puzzled and asks, "Hmm, and the title, *The Circuit,* does that have anything to do with a message?"

They know that is all the information they are going to get from her, so Chuong goes back to his work on "Resolution," Naima writes a statement about family support under "Theme," and Abdurashid checks his notes on the significance of the title, as the teacher sounds the ten-minute warning.

Graphic organizers are a popular tool for promoting and extending student understanding of concepts and the relationship between them. These visual displays of information, often arranged in bubbles or squares with connecting lines between them to portray conceptual relationships, are commonly found in many secondary classrooms. Howe, Grierson, and Richmond (1997) surveyed teachers to find out what content area reading strategies they perceived as being most useful. While 82% recommended that graphic organizers like concept maps should be used frequently, only 59% admitted that they used it often. This disparity may be due to the perceived difficulty of preparing them in advance.

    In the scenario above, the students used a graphic organizer to engage in several complex learning processes. The small group creating the story mountain graphic organizer used oral language, reading, and writing to arrive at an understanding of the structure of the story they had just read. Graphic organizers have been shown to be a valuable tool for allowing students to make nonlinear visual representations of the concepts being studied in their content area classes. While using teacher-created graphic organizers is beneficial for ordering information and making connections, the goal is always to move students to the development of their own graphic organizers.

Books like Wood, K. D., Lapp, D., & Flood, J. (1992). *Guiding readers through text: A review of study guides.* Newark, DE: International Reading Association have a variety of graphic organizers for teacher use.

Teaching and Learning With Graphic Organizers

Why Use Graphic Organizers?

Robinson (1998) traces the origins of graphic organizers to the advance organizer work of Ausubel (1960). As you may recall from our discussion in chapter 3, advance organizers are brief textual statements that summarize the main points of the upcoming reading, as well as offer explicit connections to larger concepts that may or may not be discussed in the text. They are used as a prereading strategy to assist students in organizing the information through schema building. Advance organizers were immediately a popular instructional strategy, and interest soon turned to finding novel ways to use them. Barron (1969) used advance organizers arranged in a nontraditional manner to display vocabulary in ways that represented connections between words, arguably one of the first graphic organizers. While advance organizers are always used as a prereading strategy, subsequent studies demonstrated that graphic organizers were more effective during and after the reading (Shanahan, 1982).

Graphic Organizers Facilitate Comprehension.   Comprehension is the ability to derive meaning from text and requires students to mobilize strategies when they do not understand. However, it is more than just understanding—it is being consciously aware of what needs to be done in order to support one's own learning, planning and executing the strategies, then reflecting on the their effectiveness. The opportunities presented through graphic organizers activate these comprehension strategies and metacognitive skills. Alvermann and Van Arnam (1984) found that graphic organizers prompted students to reread text passages in order to clarify understanding. Another study found that students became more active readers when they had a graphic organizer to aid them (Alvermann & Boothby, 1982).

Metacognition is the ability to think about one's thinking.

Graphic Organizers Support Students Who Struggle With Literacy.   Graphic organizers have been shown to be of great assistance to students with learning disabilities. These tools can scaffold information to assist students in constructing written products (James, Abbott, & Greenwood, 2001). They are also effective in promoting recall of information (Dye, 2000). The efficacy of graphic organizers appears to extend to students with learning difficulties as well. For example, Lovitt and Horton (1994) studied instructional practices to support students with learning disabilities in general education classrooms, and recommended graphic organizers as an effective means for modifying difficult science textbooks. Their usefulness in the science classroom extends beyond the book—they are also effective for portraying complex science models to students with disabilities (Woodward, 1994).

When Can I Use a Graphic Organizer?

The strength of any instructional strategy is not only in its use, but in its timing. The science of teaching may be in knowing what to do; the art of teaching lies in knowing when to do it. The same is true for graphic organizers. These visual displays provide students with an opportunity to construct their understanding of a subject in ways that are less linear and therefore better suited for representing complex relationships. Depending on when they are used, they can activate prior knowledge, encourage brainstorming, record events in detail, or serve as a review of the topic. In all cases, they are a means of building comprehension.

Instruction in text comprehension is often spoken of in three categories: before, during, and after reading. Likewise, graphic organizers can support comprehension instruction at each of these key junctures. Take prereading strategies, for instance. Graphic organizers can alert students to important ideas they will encounter during an upcoming reading. Wood, Lapp, and Flood (1992) suggest using a Pattern Guide (Herber, 1970) as an anticipatory activity for informational text passages. Key concepts are selected in advance and written on note cards. The edges of these cards may be cut to resemble a puzzle piece, and the page number where the information appears is logged on the back. Students then reassemble the statements and record them in their notes. In this way, students utilize prior knowledge, as well as their understanding of how information is organized, to predict what they will soon read in their textbook. An example of a pattern guide on cell division appears in Figure 6.2. The goal of this activity is not to predict the correct jigsaw—after all, an elementary student could accurately assemble the cards using the shapes or the page numbers written on the back. The purpose of a Pattern Guide is to "help them develop a cluster of knowledge" (Wood, Lapp, & Flood, p. 49) before reading the technical information in the text.

Graphic organizers are not confined to prereading experiences. They can also be utilized during reading. When used in this manner, the graphic organizer resembles a note making tool. The teacher may partially construct a graphic organizer based on previously taught information. However, blanks are strategically used to represent the likely location of a key piece of new vocabulary or concepts. An example of this type of graphic organizer can be viewed in Figure 6.3. As students read and encounter new information, they add them to the graphic organizer. The advantage of this method over traditional note making lies in the portion of the graphic organizer created by the teacher, for it continually draws the student's eye back to material learned prior to the reading. In this way the graphic organizer serves as a kind of structured note making system for the student.

Modifications should be based on the student's Individualized Education Plan IEP).

See chapter 2 for more ideas about anticipatory activities.

See chapter 5 for a discussion of note making.

Mitosis in Cell Division

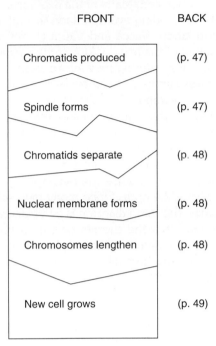

	FRONT	BACK
	Chromatids produced	(p. 47)
	Spindle forms	(p. 47)
	Chromatids separate	(p. 48)
	Nuclear membrane forms	(p. 48)
	Chromosomes lengthen	(p. 48)
	New cell grows	(p. 49)

𝒲 Figure 6.3   Graphic Organizer for Use During a Reading

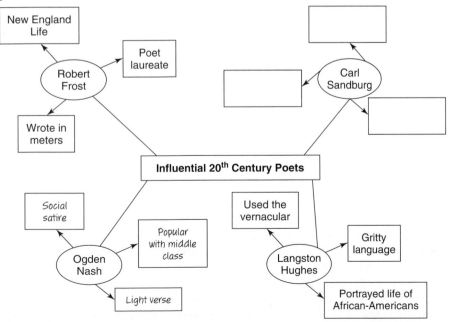

The most popular use for graphic organizers is as a post-reading instructional activity. Like those used before and during readings, charts used after a reading are intended to increase comprehension. Many of the examples shown later in the chapter were conceived as a post-reading event; indeed several are used as test reviews of previously taught information. Vacca and Vacca (1998) point out that strategic readers seek out the structure of the text, looking for the organizational patterns that will give them a framework for ordering new information. When matched carefully with text, graphic organizers can help students clarify the connections and relationships they are finding in the reading. Venn diagrams are an excellent example of a graphic organizer traditionally used after a reading. (We say "traditionally" here, but you will see an art teacher use the same graphic organizer as a prereading tool later in the chapter.) This ubiquitous chart features two overlapping, though not congruent, circles. The portions of the circle that do not overlap are used for contrasting two ideas, phenomenon, or events, while the overlapping portion in the center is reserved for similarities shared by both. Since many high school textbooks contain compare/contrast passages, the Venn diagram is an ideal graphic representation of such readings. Keep in mind that the success of a particular graphic organizer in boosting comprehension lies in matching it carefully with the text. It may be this difficulty that prevents so many teachers, like those in the study by Howe, Grierson, and Richmond (1997), from using graphic organizers more frequently.

You've probably determined the structure of this text—opening vignette, research base, and strategies at work–and could create a graphic organizer for each chapter.

What Are the Types of Graphic Organizers?

Graphic organizers are a component of a larger category of instructional aids called adjunct displays (Robinson, 1998). Advance organizers and outlines are two other forms of adjunct displays, because they serve as complementary devices for representing the information contained in a text. Hyerle (1996) reminds us that these devices are important because they allow us to "stor[e] information outside the body. . . [because] human beings are the only form of life that can store, organize, and retrieve data in locations other than our bodies" (p. x). However, graphic organizers have been shown to be more effective for this function than outlines (Kiewra, Kauffman, Robinson, DuBois, & Staley, 1999), perhaps because they allow for nonlinear representations of relationships across concepts.

So let's define a graphic organizer. They come in a variety of forms and go by a number of names, including semantic webs, concept maps, flowcharts, and diagrams. While there are a myriad of versions, they all have a few things in common. Each of them portrays a process or structure in a way that relies on relative position and juxtaposition of words or phrases that are bound by a shape or line. Frequently, they also feature lines to depict associations between and among ideas. Robinson (1998) categorizes graphic organizers into four groups: *concept maps, flow diagrams, tree diagrams,* and *matrices.*

Concept Maps.   Concept maps are what most people first visualize when they think about graphic organizers. They are shape-bound words or phrases radiating from a central figure that represents the main idea or concept. Lines connect the shapes and may contain words to further explain the relationship. A concept map on the relationship between the reader and the text might look like that in Figure 6.4.

Concept maps are favored by many educators because they lend themselves to quick and efficient illustrations of complicated ideas. Hyerle (1996) reminds us that concept maps should not be used as fill-in-the-blank worksheets to copy a diagram

Figure 6.4 Concept Map

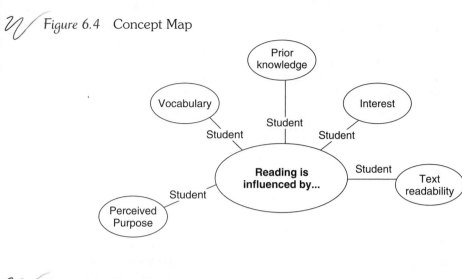

Figure 6.5 Flow Diagram

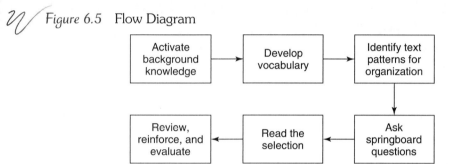

that has already been created by the teacher, because the power of the concept map lies in the learner's opportunity to "negotiate meaning" (p. 32). Instead, he advises that students be allowed the freedom to construct their own concept maps, even though they may vary from the teacher's schema.

Flow Diagrams. A second type of graphic organizer is the flow diagram. These visual displays are ideal for processes, event sequences, and timelines. Flow diagrams are derived from flowcharts, but they differ in the ways they are constructed. Flowcharts utilize a standardized vocabulary of shapes to describe an operation or procedure. For instance, oval shapes signal the beginning and ending of the procedure while a diamond shape contains questions. Flow diagrams do not adhere to these rules, although they do contain shape-bound text. Arrows show the direction or sequence of the topic illustrated. A flow diagram of a Directed Reading-Thinking Activity (Stauffer, 1969) could look like the one in Figure 6.5. A DR-TA is a format for making and confirming or disconfirming predictions to gain detailed information from a text passage. Again, as with concept maps, students should be encouraged to create their own flow diagrams, rather than fill in a predetermined number of boxes.

DR-TAs are discussed in chapter 5.

Tree Diagrams. Tree diagrams are another type of graphic organizer. Like the others, they are suitable for specific purposes. Tree diagrams are most frequently used to categorize and classify information. They are commonly used in mathematics,

Figure 6.6   Tree Diagram

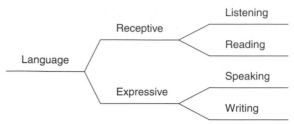

particularly to represent probability, such as in repeated tosses of a coin. A tree diagram of the elements of language is found in Figure 6.6.

Tree diagrams can be constructed on the horizontal, as displayed above, or on the vertical. They typically radiate from a general concept ("language") to a primary level of classification ("receptive" and "expressive"). Supporting categories branch off the primary level of information ("listening," etc.). With each additional level, a greater degree of detail is introduced.

Matrices.   A final commonly used adjunct display is the matrix. A matrix is an arrangement of words or phrases in a table format to be read both horizontally and vertically. Like many graphic organizers, matrix designs show relationships, either by comparing and contrasting concepts, or by classifying attributes. Another type of matrix display is a synectic chart (Gordon, 1961). This organizer is meant to foster creative thinking by requiring the learner to link disparate ideas. This type of creative thinking exercise demands that students look for analogies to explain relationships. It begins with a term to be defined and discussed. Students may look up the definition and record it. Then they brainstorm a list of related words that:

- are *similar* to the focus word;
- describe what the word *feels like* (a stretch for many students);
- are *opposite* of the focus word;
- are *similar* to the focus word, but not the same as those listed before; and
- *redefine* the focus word.

This exercise is best done in small groups, where students can discuss each attribute to construct the matrix. Dictionaries and a good thesaurus are helpful tools in completing this type of graphic organizer. If generating words and phrases is too difficult, the teacher can supply a list of words that have been cut apart into small slips of paper to create a word sort. A synectic matrix on language might look like the one found in Figure 6.7, with a blank for your use in Figure 6.8.

Figure 6.7   Synectics Matrix

Similar	Feels Like	Opposite	Similar	Redefine
Talking	recognition	silent	tongue	It separates and unites
communicate	My identity	quiet	Poetry	It is art
speech	intelligence	still	prose	Makes me human

Figure 6.8   Synectics Matrix

Directions: This is a brainstorming activity designed to activate your creative thinking. Think about the word or topic below and allow your imagination to flow. Work with your group to complete as many of the cells in the matrix as you can. Remember, in brainstorming no answer is wrong; editing can take place later.

Word or Topic: _____

Similar	Feels Like	Opposite	Similar	Redefine

After constructing the matrix, students can then use their brainstormed ideas to formulate an inquiry. For instance, the students who made the matrix in Figure 6.7 might investigate the similarities and differences between prose and poetry, the association of language and intelligence, or the use of language in animals and humans.

How Can I Teach the Use of Graphic Organizers?

Like all good teaching strategies, graphic organizers must be introduced carefully to students. On the surface, they are such a simple tool that there is a temptation to merely distribute them out and ask students to fill them in. Unfortunately, without proper scaffolding, graphic organizers can be reduced to the level of a fancy worksheet, completed only to satisfy the teacher. Organizers are visual illustrations; a tool to help students understand, summarize and synthesize the information from texts or other sources. As students create graphic representations, they manipulate and construct organizational patterns for the informational or narrative text. The students become actively involved in concrete processing of abstract ideas in print form. Here are some considerations to move from teacher-centered to learner-centered instruction for creating and interpreting graphic organizers:

- Introduce a specific type of graphic organizer by showing how it represents the structure of a text or concept.
- Model how to use the graphic organizer with a familiar text that the students have read. Emphasize that there is no one "right way" to use a graphic organizer, although there are wise practices (legibility, striking a balance between too little and too much information) that make them more helpful over time.
- Show the class examples of graphic organizers you have created for yourself so that they can see the usefulness of the tool.
- Give students questions to guide them to the important information they should seek in the text.

- When students become more practiced, choose a new text, or new information, and have them apply the same graphic organizer. Create guiding questions with the students then pair them to complete the process.
- Give students many opportunities to practice using the graphic organizer in pairs, moving toward independent use.
- As students add to their repertoire of graphic organizers, be sure to provide lots of blank copies that are readily accessible. Many teachers keep an open file in the room containing labeled folders of graphic organizers.

With practice and reflection on the process and its benefits, students may begin to alter or design their own graphic organizers. When this happens, celebrate! It's a sign you've done a great job in teaching an important tool for learning.

How Can Graphic Organizers Be Used for Assessment?

Formative assessment is used throughout the unit to inform instruction. Summative assessments are administered at the end of the unit to measure cumulative student learning.

Although we have emphasized the practicality of graphic organizers to represent learning as it is being constructed, we don't want to overlook their usefulness as an assessment tool. The goal of assessment, after all, is to provide students with an opportunity to demonstrate what they know. While this is traditionally done with tests that limit students to selecting a correct answer (multiple choice, true/false, and matching tasks), the true measure of understanding is the ability of the learner to construct an answer (Why do you think essay tests are so hard?). Extended essays can be time-consuming to grade, particularly if it is a formative (mid-unit) assessment.

Graphic organizers offer an opportunity for students to construct an answer while allowing the teacher to quickly assess their understanding (Lewin & Shoemaker, 1998). We witnessed this in a physics classroom when the teacher assigned students to work in small groups to create a concept map representing the states of matter. Several groups created a map that looked like the one in Figure 6.9. While all of these manifestations had been discussed during previous classes and dutifully recorded in science notebooks, a few other groups created concept maps that looked like the one found in Figure 6.10. As the physics teacher strolled around the classroom, he was able to quickly assess who had read the assigned chapter from the night before, and who had not, because plasma had been featured at length in the textbook but not in his lecture!

We've reviewed types of graphic organizers and their uses, including construction of understanding, promotion of creative thinking processes, and assessment. These visual displays foster nonlinear thinking and reveal the relationship of parts to whole. Let's look at how teachers use graphic organizers in their content area classrooms.

Figure 6.9   States of Matter Concept Map

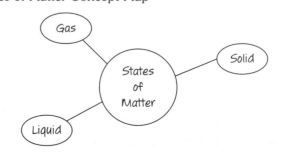

Figure 6.10   States of Matter Concept Map

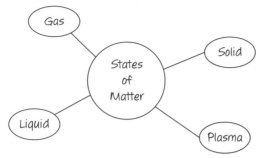

Strategies at Work

Graphic Organizers in English

This teacher's got her students going in circles—compare/contrast circles, that is. When Ms. Perez-Peters teaches tall tales in her ninth-grade English class, she knows that some of her students, who have come from all over the world, may not be familiar with these American folktales. She finds that Venn diagrams (Venn, 1894) are effective tools in the study of this genre. As her class reads folktales about Pecos Bill, John Henry, Paul Bunyan, Johnny Appleseed, and Tony Beaver, they use Venn diagrams to demonstrate the characteristics of tall tales that are properties of all literature, and those unique to the genre. As they read, they realize that most of the people in tall tales are working folks whose character traits have been exaggerated and made stronger and larger than life. The design of a Venn diagram lets students create a structure, and insert signal words and target vocabulary in an organized visual form, ready to process into paragraph form and class presentations. Later, students compared and contrasted characters featured in tall tales. Figure 6.11 contains one student's representation of the similarities and differences between Johnny Appleseed and Tony Beaver.

Ms. Perez-Peters scaffolded instruction on the use of Venn diagrams. She first demonstrated its use at the board, with students quickly joining in on the class discussion that allowed the ideas to take shape. She modeled some portions of it, beginning with the major headings. Then small groups worked together to contribute information. Within a few days of introducing this form of concept mapping, her students were developing their own Venn diagrams. Ms. Perez-Peters feels confident that her students can transfer this practice to other subject areas because they now use it independently, without direction from their teacher.

Down the hallway in Mr. Kounalis' English class, students are using graphic organizers as a post-reading activity. You see, in his class students don't just read short stories, they rebuild them from the foundation up. Students create flow diagrams that mirror the concept of construction. Mr. K., as they refer to their teacher, explains that these flow diagrams reflect the process used by the author. "One doesn't build a building haphazardly, without a plan or structure. To construct the building, frames and scaffolds are necessary. We can't build a story or produce a piece of writing without making use of a plan in an ordered and detailed process."

Students deconstructed Walter Dean Myer's short story, "The Fighter" (Myers, 2001) to analyze the writer's craft. Using the elements of story—setting, character, plot, conflict, climax, resolution, and theme—students worked in groups to record the building blocks of the tale. However, unlike the story mountain used by Ms. ElWardi's

Your students will invariably ask who "Venn" was, so here's the answer. John Venn was a mathematician specializing in the study of logic. According to William Dunham (1997) he was not really a very good mathematician, but he did manage to create one idea that made him really famous.

Metaphors such as the building used in this classroom assist students in constructing mental models.

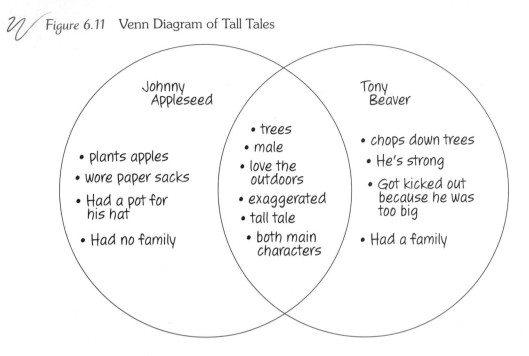

Figure 6.11   Venn Diagram of Tall Tales

Johnny Appleseed
- plants apples
- wore paper sacks
- Had a pot for his hat
- Had no family

- trees
- male
- love the outdoors
- exaggerated
- tall tale
- both main characters

Tony Beaver
- chops down trees
- He's strong
- Got kicked out because he was too big
- Had a family

students to identify literary devices, these students also looked for evidence of the author's use of sequence to reveal each element to the reader. As Mr. K. remarked, "Walter Dean Myers didn't just gather the building blocks; he placed each one carefully into the story. When an author assembles these elements artfully, the story hangs together."

Mr. K. observed that while building these maps, students made frequent connections back to the text as they manipulated and analyzed information. Their completed products depicted an understanding of not only what the story was about, but also a recognition of the care the author used to unfold the story. One group's map appears in Figure 6.12. The lively class discussions that followed this activity indicated that students were eager to explain their decisions and answer questions with evidence from the text.

Literary analysis can seem tedious to adolescents who may view a single reading of a story as sufficient. By using opportunities for creative expression, students can explore a text more deeply to examine the writer's craft. While graphic organizers are not the only means to accomplish this goal, these tools can prompt higher-order thinking.

See Bloom's taxonomy in chapter 2 for further discussion on higher-order thinking.

Graphic Organizers in Social Studies

With a little "Inspiration" and time in the computer lab, Marisol Acuna's World History class mapped out important concepts as they reviewed information on WWI. Within minutes at the computers, pages of information from both the text and their notes took on a visual form as students organized main ideas and supporting information. As a tool for review, concept mapping gave Ms. Acuna's students the opportunity to recall important concepts pertinent to an historical period, reproduce a structure that reflects the information, and then integrate targeted vocabulary essential to each concept.

Ms. Acuna modeled the use of Inspiration®, a computer program for students and teachers to design graphic organizers and outlines. She chose the Industrial Revolution, a topic covered weeks earlier in class, as the subject for the map. With the

Vintage High School Literacy Training
Sept. 20, 2005

VHS School-wide Literacy Strategies:

7. **Metacognitive Conversation: Talking to the Text and Each Other** (Fall 2005 Focus)
8. Participation Structures/Strategies
9. Pre-Reading/Activating Prior Knowledge
10. Vocabulary Development/Concept Mapping
11. Graphic Organizers/Cornell Notes
12. Summarization Strategies

I. **Overview/Orientation**
   ➤ Reading Apprenticeship
   ➤ Metacognitive Conversation
   ➤ *Improving Student Literacy*

IV. **Capturing Reading Processes with Reading Strategies Lists**

III. **Faculty Survey**

Figure 6.12   Student Flow Diagram in English Class

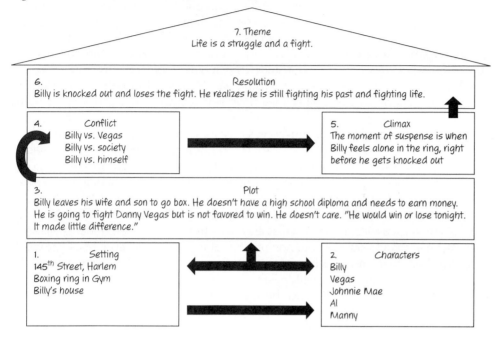

aid of her class, she designed a concept map of pertinent information following the directions from a pop-up menu on the screen. Students recalled chunks of information about the unit, and then watched as it was transformed into a graphic organizer.

Ms. Acuna further engaged her students by showing how they could use templates, including a tree diagram, flow diagram, and a cause and effect graphic organizer. She explained that the type of text or information can influence the template they might choose. All were clearly impressed with this feature, and when she clicked on a button that changed the completed concept map into a linear outline, the room filled with "oohs" and "ahhs!" At that point, students were very eager to create their own.

Ms. Acuna was also pleasantly surprised to watch her students weave the targeted vocabulary into their maps. As she circled the busy lab, she spotted words like *reparations, propaganda, ally, warfare, neutral, treaty,* and *policy* either in context or connected to a definition.

No student left the lab without a printout of their concept map and the corresponding linear outlines. Ms. Acuna commented on their value as an assessment tool as well. "When I spotted an error, I was able to question the student about it and clarify any misunderstandings right on the spot." These maps also served as perfect tools to structure expository writing. After the mapping session, Ms. Acuna's students wrote summaries that paraphrased information transferred from their graphic organizers. This new teacher learned an age-old lesson in education: teach strategies as well as content, and give your students the opportunity to use both.

> Text structures are explored in chapter 1.

> Students can use their graphic organizers as study guides for exam reviews.

Graphic Organizers in Mathematics

"Graphic organizers? My students don't leave mathematics class without them." Carol Chie uses an assortment of graphic organizers in geometry and pre-calculus, particularly at the beginning and end of units. She explains, "We use graphic organizers to bring in everything students already know, and relate it to current topics. Mathematics is taught unit by unit and very often students don't see any correlation between what we are learning now and what we've learned before. They'll ask, 'When am I going to use this? Why do I have to learn this?"' These questions are often heard in high school mathematics classes. Mathematics is a structure that builds on itself, and if students can build their own structures they will see that these theories interrelate. By using graphic organizers, they are more apt to see connections between what they have learned and what they are currently learning.

Ms. Chie introduces compare/contrast graphic organizers through classroom discussion. Her students identify similarities and differences between mathematical theories and she simply records it, rather than filling it in herself for them to copy. Her role is to ask questions that prompt connections and promote inquiry. As a class, they create a product that is more inclusive and complete than their individual graphic organizers will be initially because they are organizing collective knowledge. Ms. Chie sees this practice as vital in pre-calculus and calculus because these students will soon be working in study groups, a common practice at the university level. Ms. Chie wants more for them than simply using graphic organizers; she wants them to witness the benefits of collaborative study with peers.

> Research on collaboration suggests that students make meaning when they discuss content with classmates.

Eventually whole class practice becomes small group practice. This transition is vital to Ms. Chie because graphic organizers also serve as an assessment tool. At a glance, she has a clear picture of what each student has grasped. This is important because some similarities and differences are very minute, but critical. For example, in comparing an ellipse and a hyperbola, there is one sign difference between equations. If it's a minus, it creates a hyperbola; if it's a plus, it creates an ellipse. If students are going to have trouble determining whether the equation produces a hyperbola or an ellipse, the graphic organizer pinpoints the misunderstanding. If, on the other hand, the sign is correct, Ms. Chie knows that her students understand that a single sign is the determining factor. One student's organizer appears in Figure 6.13.

Graphic organizers like the one used in Ms. Chie's class are useful because they challenge students to see both analogous and disparate relationships among mathematical theories. In this way, she extends student understanding beyond memorization of algorithms to a deeper appreciation of how these formulas are woven together.

Graphic Organizers in Science

What a concept! Science teacher Larry Caudillo uses concept mapping to familiarize his biology students with scientific terminology and to construct schema. He often creates a concept map based on a piece of informational text his students will be reading. In this way, he can introduce a visual display to assist his students in learning new vocabulary. After the first reading of the text and further instruction by the teacher, students revisit the map in order to add new information. Mr. Caudillo then gives them responsibility for creating their own maps. He discovered that his students' concept maps are far more intricate and complex than those he has designed or taken from textbooks.

> Informational texts provide readers facts and details, unlike narrative texts that rely on a story structure.

Mr. Caudillo combines graphic organizers with other instructional strategies to engage his students in higher-order thinking. For example, he used a word sort activity to review before a unit exam in biochemistry. The review focused on macro-

Figure 6.13   Compare/Contrast in Pre-Calculus

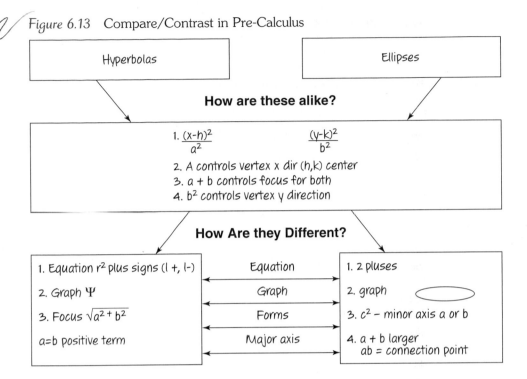

| Hyperbolas | Ellipses |

How are these alike?

1. $\dfrac{(x-h)^2}{a^2}$ $\dfrac{(y-k)^2}{b^2}$
2. A controls vertex x dir (h,k) center
3. a + b controls focus for both
4. b^2 controls vertex y direction

How Are they Different?

	Equation	
1. Equation r^2 plus signs (l +, l -)	Equation	1. 2 pluses
2. Graph Ψ	Graph	2. graph
3. Focus $\sqrt{a^2 + b^2}$	Forms	3. c^2 – minor axis a or b
a=b positive term	Major axis	4. a + b larger ab = connection point

molecules classified as lipids, proteins, carbohydrates, and nucleic acids. He chose terms as target vocabulary, then printed them on magnetized rectangular word cards. In addition, he gave the students blank cards so they could supply other terms they might want to use. When class began, students were asked to list and categorize the words. One group arranged the cards to look like the display in Figure 6.14.

See chapter 7 for further details on this activity.

Mr. Caudillo gave further directions. "Each table has ten minutes to design a concept map of all the target vocabulary you have just sorted. Remember, I expect you to label all the linkages to show the relationships. You'll transfer them to the white board and explain your reasoning. We'll decide which maps are most complete and accurate." As tables became hubs of activity, Mr. Caudillo circulated around the classroom of 40 students to assess their works in progress.

Ten minutes later, a table was selected to display their product on the white board. All eyes followed Ja'leel, who was chosen by his group to serve as reporter. He swiftly shuffled the magnetized word cards into a network depicting the complex relationships, then drew bubbles around words and labeled lines between words

Figure 6.14   Word Sort for Science Class

Nucleic Acids	Proteins	Carbohydrates	Lipids	Monomer
Nucleotide	Amino acid	saccharides	glycerol	polymer
	peptide	Simple sugars	Fatty acids	synthesis
	enzymes			

Figure 6.15   Student Concept Map in Science

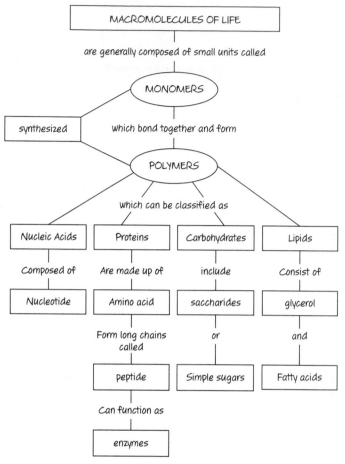

to symbolize theoretical connections. While students at each table watched the concept map take shape, many could be seen rereading and revising their own maps. When he was finished, his group's concept map looked like the one found in 6.15.

Graphic Organizers in Electives

Jeremy Merrill's students think their teacher gives the best lectures because he doesn't say anything! His students learn principles of art through their own discovery, and graphic organizers are a tool for clarifying this discovery process. For example, when Mr. Merrill's Studio Art students explored the similarities and differences between geometric and gestural drawings, they used the two interlocking circles of a Venn diagram to define the attributes of each one.

He introduced this activity by asking students to watch as he began to draw two still life forms on the whiteboard. He did not speak again until he had finished the drawings. After adding a large question mark above each drawing, he addressed the class:

> You all have copies of a reading at your table. I want you to look for anything that you think might relate to these two sketches. As a group, decide what is similar

about these two ways of sketching. Also, discuss what you find is different about them. Your job is to be able to compare and contrast these two forms of sketching.

Mr. Merrill then walked among the tables and listened in as his students read and discussed, paragraph by paragraph, what they were now discovering in print. They found that the written information matched what they had just seen their teacher render on the board.

After the reading and table discussions, Mr. Merrill asked, "Have you ever heard of a Venn diagram?"

"It looks like two circles that cross over in the middle," students at one table offered. "In the middle part, the two topics are the same, and the outside parts only show what is different." While the students spoke, he drew two large overlapping circles on another whiteboard.

"How should they be labeled?" he asked.

They immediately responded, "Geometric and Gestural."

The teacher then distributed chart paper for groups to develop a diagram that reflected both the differences and the similarities between the two drawing techniques. Students could be seen referring back to the text and posing questions of their group members. By putting information into a compare/contrast Venn diagram form, they could now connect what they had seen their teacher demonstrate to what they had then just read.

Within one lesson, Mr. Merrill used three modes of understanding—drawing, reading and mapping—as he led his students to discover the concepts integral to their next art project. With a clear understanding of the two sketching techniques, students then successfully used both approaches in their drawings of a still life. Just as important, these students moved between written and visual displays of information to construct their own schema of the subject.

Texts for independent reading should be selected on the basis of the content and ability of the students to comprehend with reduced teacher support.

Conclusion

Graphic organizers can be used throughout the curriculum to help students understand the relationships between ideas. Because they are tools for categorizing and storing information, visual displays can be useful in helping students understand complex information. In addition, they are particularly well-suited for representing non-linear information by showing the complexity of relationships between and among ideas, phrases, and words.

Graphic organizers are useful before students read, during their assigned reading, and after reading. While there is no one "ideal" time for using these visual displays, the most common application comes after the reading. However, the versatility of many graphic organizers make them flexible across instructional events. Common graphic organizers include concept maps, flow diagrams, tree diagrams, and matrices. Other choices include Venn diagrams and compare/contrast maps. While graphic organizers are popular with students and teachers, it is important to match the tool to the text.

As with other instructional strategies, it is essential to teach students how to use and construct graphic organizers. Without instruction, they cease to be tools and become fancy worksheets to be filled out for the teacher. Each tool should be introduced and scaffolded, and the growing cadre of organizers should be on hand for students to access when needed. Most importantly, students should be encouraged to construct their own unique organizers. When students are successful in accomplishing this goal, the teacher can be assured that the learners are employing higher-order thinking skills.

Regardless of when they are used, graphic organizers aid in comprehension. They have long been recognized as a metacomprehension tool, and students who successfully utilize graphic organizers are more likely to grasp the concepts discussed in the text. Further, graphic organizers can be used as an assessment tool providing teachers with an authentic glimpse into a student's thinking. Unlike traditional multiple-choice testing that restricts student responses, student-constructed graphic organizers can provide evidence of sophisticated levels of student knowledge.

References

Alvermann, D. E., & Boothby, P. R. (1982, September). *A strategy for making content reading successful: Grades 4-6.* Paper presented at the annual meeting of the Plains Regional Conference of the International Reading Association, Omaha, NE. [ED221853].

Alvermann, D. E., & Van Arnam, S. (1984, April). *Effects of spontaneous and induced lookbacks on self-perceived high and low ability comprehenders.* Paper presented at the annual meeting of the American Educational Research Association, New Orleans, LA. [ED246384].

Ausubel, D. P. (1960). The use of advance organizers in the learning and retention of meaningful verbal material. *Journal of Educational Psychology, 51,* 267–272.

Barron, R. F. (1969). The use of vocabulary as an advance organizer. In H. L. Herber & P. L. Sanders (Eds.), *Research in reading in the content areas: First year report* (pp. 29–39). Syracuse, NY: Syracuse University Reading and Language Arts Center.

Dunham, W. W. (1997). *The mathematical universe: An alphabetical journey through the great proofs, problems, and personalities.* New York: John Wiley and Sons.

Dye, G. A. (2000). Graphic organizers to the rescue! Helping students link—and remember—information. *Teaching Exceptional Children, 32*(3), 72–76.

Gordon, W. J. J. (1961). *Synectics: The development of creative capacity.* New York: Harper and Row.

Herber, H. L. (1970). *Teaching reading in the content areas.* Englewood Cliffs, NJ: Prentice Hall.

Howe, M. E., Grierson, S. T., & Richmond, M. G. (1997). A comparison of teachers' knowledge and use of content area reading strategies in the primary grades. *Reading Research and Instruction, 36,* 305–324.

Hyerle, D. (1996). *Visual tools for constructing knowledge.* Alexandria, VA: Association of Supervisors of Curriculum Development.

James, L. A., Abbott, M., & Greenwood, C. R. (2001). How Adam became a writer: Winning writing strategies for low-achieving students. *Teaching Exceptional Children, 33*(3), 30–37.

Jimenez, F. (1997). *The circuit: Stories from the life of a migrant child.* Albuquerque, NM: University of New Mexico.

Kiewra, K. A., Kauffman, D. F., Robinson, D. H., DuBois, N. F., & Staley, R. K. (1999). Supplementing floundering text with adjunct displays. *Instructional Science, 27,* 373–401.

Lewin, L., & Shoemaker, B. J. (1998). *Great performances: Creating classroom-based assessment tasks.* Alexandria, VA: Association for Supervision and Curriculum Development.

Lovitt, T. C., & Horton, S. V. (1994). Strategies for adapting science textbooks for youth with learning disabilities. *Remedial and Special Education, 15,* 105–116.

Myers, W. D. (2001). *145th Street: Short Stories.* New York: Bantam Doubleday Dell.

Robinson, D. H. (1998). Graphic organizers as aids to text learning. *Reading Research and Instruction, 37,* 85–105.

Shanahan, T. (1982, March). *Specific learning outcomes attributable to study procedures.* Paper presented at the annual meeting of the American Educational Research Association, New York, NY. [ED220536].

Stauffer, R. G. (1969). *Teaching reading as a thinking process.* New York: Harper Collins.

Vacca, R. T., & Vacca, J. L. (1998). *Content area reading: Literacy and learning across the curriculum* (6th ed.). New York: Longman.

Venn, J. (1894). *Symbolic logic* (2nd ed.). London, England: MacMillan.

Wood, K. D., Lapp, D., & Flood, J. (1992). *Guiding readers through text: A review of study guides.* Newark, DE: International Reading Association.

Woodward, J. (1994). The role of models in secondary science instruction. *Remedial and Special Education, 15,* 94–104.

Chapter 7

Word for Word: Vocabulary Development Across the Curriculum

NANCY FREY AND DOUGLAS FISHER

Konjit, a 10th-grade science student, is staring hard at the tiny slips of paper scattered across her desk. Her face is a mask of concentration as she carefully slides the papers, each containing a science term, into rows and columns. After several moves, she once again ponders her decisions about the order. Her teacher has given each student an envelope with 20 science vocabulary words written on 1" × 2" papers. Konjit's task is to arrange the words into a logical order, creating categories and groups. She now wonders whether to put *chlorine* with *chlorophyll*. After all, they begin with the same letters. She decides instead to put chlorine in the category of chemistry, while leaving *chlorophyll* in the column for biology. Satisfied, she signals the teacher that she is finished. The science teacher will confer with Konjit, who will explain her rationale for the categories and groups she created. "I'm finished!" she declares. "Word for word!"

The vocabulary demands on students skyrocket during the secondary school years, ballooning to an estimated 88,500 words (Nagy & Anderson, 1984). While academic language demands are high, it is estimated that everyday speech consists of only 5,000–7,000 words (Klein, 1988). Therefore, it is unlikely that conversation and discussion alone can compensate for a limited command of the academic vocabulary. Taken together, these two figures demonstrate what most secondary teachers already know—the vocabulary gap for many students is so large that it is difficult to identify where to begin.

The Importance of Word Knowledge

This gap in word knowledge is problematic because of its impact on content learning and reading comprehension (Flood, Lapp, & Fisher, 2003; Stahl & Fairbanks, 1986). Mastery of the technical language has long been recognized as a predictor of

121

success in any field. For example, in a study of 184 secondary students, Espin and Foegen (1996) found vocabulary to be an important predictor of content area performance. Vocabulary knowledge can also have a profound influence on reading comprehension, as evidenced in a 1992 study by Farley and Elmore. They examined the achievement of struggling college freshmen and discovered that vocabulary knowledge was a stronger predictor of reading comprehension than cognitive ability.

Given the academic vocabulary demands of the secondary school curriculum, it would seem logical to first identify and then explicitly teach the necessary words until the gap has been bridged. Indeed, vocabulary research through much of the twentieth century consisted of lists of words, such as *McGuffey's Eclectic Spelling-Book* (1879), Dolch's sight words (1936), and Thorndike and Lorge's (1944) *Teacher's Word Book of 30,000 Words.* In this stance, vocabulary was viewed as a subset of either comprehension or spelling, but was rarely examined closely in its own right. Instead, the emphasis at the instructional level was to teach individual words, and these lists guided teachers in making word selections. Instruction often relied on rote memorization of definitions followed by weekly vocabulary tests. These words were rarely derived from texts the students were reading.

Vocabulary Acquisition

Research in language acquisition in the 1980s had an important effect on trends in vocabulary instruction. Along with the studies about academic language demands and everyday usage, it was reported that students learn an average of 3,000 new words per year (Nagy & Herman, 1985), hardly an adequate pace for closing the vocabulary gap. Indeed, it appeared that teaching words in isolation exclusively was an inefficient way to foster word knowledge. At the same time, instructional approaches were influenced by a growing understanding of meaning as a component of vocabulary acquisition. Instructional practices shifted to culling vocabulary words from narrative and expository reading selections used in the classroom. Many teachers and educational researchers expressed dissatisfaction with this method as well, because of the hodgepodge nature of the word selection.

Vocabulary as Concepts or Labels.   The vexing issue in vocabulary word selection relates to the usefulness of the word and its relation to the curriculum. Some words are concepts, while others are labels. Given that students need to acquire a tremendous volume of vocabulary words each year, it seems careless to squander valuable instructional time on words that function only as labels in a particular reading. For example, in Lois Lowry's story *The Giver* (1994), a boy is faced with the challenge of confronting truth in his "perfect" community. The word *utopia* is a concept word, for it is central to the understanding of a society with no illness or poverty. On the other hand, the word *tunic* is a label describing the type of clothing worn by the characters. *Utopia* is well worth the instructional effort for students to think deeply about the complexities represented by this one word; *tunic* is a word that can be inferred through context clues and is not essential to comprehension. Students also benefit from instruction on the differences between concept and label words because it can prevent them getting bogged down in minutia at the expense of big ideas.

Self-Assessment of Current Knowledge.   Teaching vocabulary is further complicated by the varying word knowledge levels of individual students. Even when the core reading is held in common, students bring a range of word understanding to the text. Rather than apply a "one size fits all" approach to vocabulary instruction, it is wise to assess students before the reading. This awareness is valuable for the student as well because it highlights their understanding of what they know, as well as what they still need to learn in order to comprehend the reading. One method for accomplishing this is through *Vocabulary Self-Awareness* (Goodman, 2001). Words are introduced at the beginning of the reading or unit, and students complete a self-assessment of their knowledge of the words (see Figure 7.1). Each vocabulary word is rated according to the student's understanding, including an example and a definition. If they are very comfortable with the word, they give themselves a "+" (plus sign). If they think they know, but are unsure, they note the word with a "√" (check mark). If the word is new to them, they place a "−" (minus sign) next to the word. Over the course of the reading or unit, students add new information to the chart. The goal is to replace all the check marks and minus signs with a plus sign. Because students continually revisit their vocabulary charts to revise their entries, they have multiple opportunities to practice and extend their growing understanding of the terms. An excerpt of one student's vocabulary chart for *Civil Disobedience* (Thoreau, 1849/1965) can be found in Figure 7.2.

Vocabulary development is recursive. In order for a term to become part of a student's vocabulary, they need opportunities to revisit it.

Vocabulary Instruction

Current practices in vocabulary instruction seek to integrate these varied methods. Word selection is essential for content area language growth, and a growing number of teachers are identifying grade-level words for explicit instruction. However, reinforcement of understanding through meaning is also seen as critical to student learning. Blachowicz and Fisher (2000) identified four principles for effective vocabulary instruction. They advise that students should

- be actively involved in word learning,
- make personal connections,
- be immersed in vocabulary, and
- consolidate meaning through multiple information sources.

The authors note that while these principles apply to all learning, their experience has shown that these conditions are vital for vocabulary acquisition and retention.

Secondary teachers must also consider the type of vocabulary used in their instruction. Vacca and Vacca (1999) suggest that there are three types of vocabulary to consider—*general, specialized,* and *technical.* General vocabulary consists primarily of words used in everyday language, usually with widely agreed upon meanings. Examples of general vocabulary words include *pesky, bothersome,* and *vexing.* The meaning of these three words tends to be consistent across contexts, and the appearance of any one of these words would signal the reader that the subject of these adjectives would be annoying indeed! In contrast, specialized vocabulary is flexible and transportable across curricular disciplines—these words hold multiple meanings in different content areas. For example, the word *loom* has a common meaning— an impending event—as well as a more specialized definition in textile arts—a device for weaving thread or yarn into cloth. Finally, there are technical vocabulary words that are specific to only one field of study. *Concerto* in music, *meiosis* in science,

Figure 7.1 Vocabulary Self-Awareness Chart

Word	+	√	−	Example	Definition

Procedure:

1. Examine the list of words you have written in the first column.

2. Put a "+" next to each word you know well, and give an accurate example and definition of the word. Your definition and example must relate to the unit of study.

3. Place a "√" next to any words for which you can write only a definition or an example, but not both.

4. Put a "−" next to words that are new to you.

This chart will be used throughout the unit. By the end of the unit you should have the entire chart completed. Since you will be revising this chart, write in pencil.

Source: Goodman, L. (2001). A tool for learning: Vocabulary self-awareness. In C. Blanchfield (Ed.), *Creative vocabulary: Strategies for teaching vocabulary in grades K–12* (p. 46), Fresno, CA: San Joaquin Valley Writing Project. Used with permission.

Figure 7.2   Vocabulary Self-Awareness Example

Word	+	√	−	Example	Definition
prejudice	+			Not hiring a person because of their color, religion, or gender is a form of prejudice	A bias, usually not based in fact, against a person or group
Civil disobedience		√		Disobeying a law	
Transcendentalism			−		

and *abscissa* in mathematics are all examples of technical vocabulary specific to a content area. These words can be more difficult to teach because there is little association with previously known word meanings. In addition, they tend to be "dense" in meaning; that is, the level of knowledge necessary to fully understand the word is directly related to the content itself. Technical vocabulary, in particular, tends to be vexing for secondary content teachers because the fallback system for acquisition is often rote memorization.

Like other high school educators, the teachers in this chapter work at explicit instruction in general, specialized, and technical vocabulary that is grounded in the principles of effective word learning forwarded by Blachowicz and Fisher (2000). Let's look inside classrooms to see how teachers address vocabulary teaching and learning across the curriculum.

Content teachers must be aware of all three types of vocabulary in order to avoid teaching only the technical terms associated with the course.

Strategies at Work

Vocabulary Instruction in English

English classes are the primary location for teaching language skills and strategies that are transportable across the learning day. Therefore, vocabulary instruction sometimes focuses on analysis of familiar words through word study (Lapp, Jacobson, Fisher, & Flood, 2000). In many English classrooms, word walls are prominently displayed, and are particularly useful for English language learners.

Developing Familiarity Through Word Walls.   Word walls (Cunningham & Allington, 2003) are alphabetically arranged (by first letter) high-frequency words displayed in a manner to allow easy visual access to all students in the room. As Cunningham and Allington remind us, however, it is essential to "do" a word wall, not merely display one. Some teachers rely on a selection from the "500 Most Used Words List" (Harwell, 2001) of commonly used words in speaking and writing. Although they are relatively simple words, many are misapplied (*knew/new*) or misspelled (*friend, neighbor,* and *when*), leading to unclear communication. In addition to high frequency words, teachers also use word walls to highlight vocabulary that is

Similar lists are widely available, including Dolch sight words (*http://www.theschoolbell.com/ Links/Dolch/Dolch.html*), *Dr. Fry's 1000 Instant Words* (Fry, 1997), or the graded word lists in the Month by Month Phonics series (Cunningham & Hall, 1998).

The Internet has provided another important source of information on words and phrases. Teachers often bookmark websites like *http://www.rhymezone.com* for resources on rhyme schemes, *www.grammarbook.com* for help with punctuation and grammar, and *www.dictionary.com* for an all-purpose site for word definitions.

related to a unit of instruction. For example, during a study of *The Grapes of Wrath* (Steinbeck, 1939), a teacher may include words like *Dust Bowl, Okies, drought,* and *migrant* on the word wall. These English teachers "do" the word wall through brief (ten minutes or so) daily instruction around a particular set of words. Typically, five words are introduced and located on the word wall display. Novel games such as Guess the Covered Word (Cunningham & Allington, 2003), where a word is revealed one letter at a time, may be used. It is important that the words, once taught, remain in the same spot so students can reliably locate them.

Expanding Student Vocabulary.   Another popular method for expanding written vocabulary is through specialized word lists, thesauri, and dictionaries. Many English teachers have experienced the overuse of terms like "said" in their students' writing. This may occur because students have not explored how writers convey the way a character speaks a message to illuminate the action. Teachers can adopt the "said" word list to assist students in using more descriptive terms instead. Called "'Said' Is Dead" (Peterson, 1996), students in writing and drama courses post a list of words to help them use more interesting terms like *confided, quipped,* and *scoffed* in place of the aforementioned term when writing dialogue (see Table 7.1). Similarly, these same students also have a wealth of reference materials available to them to support their word choices. Student thesauri are useful for budding writers struggling to find the perfect word, but other specialized materials like a slang thesaurus, rhyming dictionary, and books of quotations are also popular with students.

Table 7.1   **Expanded Vocabulary Word List**

"Said" Is Dead

Enrich your dialogue writing with more descriptive terms like these:

added	moaned
advised	mumbled
allowed	objected
barked	parroted
babbled	pronounced
begged	protested
blurted	quipped
cajoled	reported
complained	scolded
confessed	scoffed
confided	simpered
demanded	snapped
dithered	swore
droned	stuttered
gasped	taunted
groaned	teased
howled	wailed
interjected	whimpered
interrupted	yammered
jabbed	yelled
jeered	yapped
leered	

Source: Peterson, A. (1996). *The writer's workout book: 113 stretches toward better prose.* Berkeley, CA: National Writing Project. Used with permission.

Developing Structural Word Analysis.   The ability to deconstruct words to ascertain meaning is directly related to a student's knowledge of root words and affixes. Root words are morphemes (units of meaning) that compose the foundation of all words. Affixes (prefixes and suffixes) are attached to the root word in order to modify the meaning. For example, the word *dictionary* comes from the Latin *dictum* meaning "to speak." Other root words are derived from Greek words, such as *phonogram* from *phono* meaning "sound." Still other root words are free morphemes, meaning that they can stand alone as a word. For example, *port, form,* and *act* are im**port**ant common root words that also serve as a plat**form** for **act**ivating word knowledge through the addition of a variety of affixes. By closely investigating the parts of a word, including root words, derivations, and affixes, students can acquire tools for use with unfamiliar words, thus expanding students' general and specialized vocabularies.

Word study often begins with free morphemes like *port* because their meaning is generally more accessible. After discussing the meaning of *port* as a Latin word for "carry," and the common definition of the word as "a place where ships can safely dock," word extensions become more apparent. *Porter* means a person who carries an object; *airport* means a safe place for airplanes, and *import* means to carry something into an area.

In addition to root word analysis, instruction about prefixes and suffixes also occurs regularly. Understanding of the morphological basis of affixes is critical to word knowledge. Cunningham (2002) estimates that "re-, dis-, un-, and in-/im- account for over half of all the prefixes readers will *ever see* . . . [and] -s/-es, -ed, and -ing account for 65% of all words with suffixes" (p. 4). Coupled with root word and derivational knowledge, students who understand common affixes possess a powerful set of skills for taking words apart and reassembling them to extract their meaning. This level of word analysis also appears to support reading as well because learners who can extract the morphological characteristics of the word will process and analyze across morphemes rather than syllables (Templeton, 1992).

Like context clues, these morphological characteristics contribute to a student's understanding of the term and the ways it might be used.

Focusing on Words With Multiple Meanings.   Confusion about words with multiple meanings can also confound English language learners. For example, the word *run* has 69 meanings, as defined by the *New Webster's Dictionary of the English Language* (1981)! This small word can refer to a rapid form of ambulation, entrance into a political contest, or a migration of fish, as well as dozens of other meanings. Interestingly, teachers report that it is often these humble words, not just those glamorous polysyllabic darlings strung like a necklace with multiple affixes, that interfere with reading comprehension. In order for students to correctly interpret which definition should be applied, instruction must include pointing out such words and then using them in a variety of texts. English language learners can build their specialized vocabulary through semantic instruction of multiple-meaning words like *run* and *bear.* By examining both the rules and the fluidity of meaning in language, students are positioned to make increasingly finer distinctions between words. After all, Mark Twain once said, "the difference between the right word and the almost right word is the difference between the lightning and the lightning bug!" (Twain, 1890).

Noticing Subtle Differences in Meaning.   Relationships between words can be particularly challenging when discussing synonyms. The difference between *annoyance* and *harassment* is a fine but distinct one. The ability to discern between this gradients of meaning is a skill tested on the Scholastic Aptitude Test and other college board exams. Truly "the difference between the right word and the almost right word" can impact the ability of the student to use precise language. These

Figure 7.3   Shades of Meaning

Shades of Meaning	Definitions and Sentences
fear	a feeling of anxiety because danger is nearby I have a fear of getting a shot at the doctor.
dread	a great fear mixed with awe or respect The girl dreaded moving to a new school.
terror	an intense fear and shock I saw terror in the driver's eyes right before he crashed.
panic	a sudden fear that might cause the person to collapse My mother panicked when she saw the cut on my face.
phobia	a fear that doesn't make sense My friend has a phobia about rollercoasters.

"shades of meaning" can be taught in an imaginative way using paint chip cards from the local hardware store (Blanchfield, 2001). Students attach a paint chip card containing shades of color to notebook paper to illustrate a string of synonyms. Definitions are written to the right of the paint chip card on which the word has been written. For example, Bridget created the card in Figure 7.3 to illustrate synonyms for the word *fear.*

Studying Multiple-Meaning Words.   Valerie Hansen's 10th-grade class studied multiple meanings through a series of activities. Using conversation about "crazy English," words like *hand, table, bill, change,* and *book* were first analyzed as multiple-meaning words. For instance, *hand* can mean the appendage at the end of the arm, or the indicator on a clock or dial. Students were then challenged to bring in ten other multiple-meaning words and present a lesson to the class on how the words can be used in a variety of contexts. These word challenges caused students to use on-line and traditional dictionaries and thesauri to locate novel examples. Ms. Hansen extended students' knowledge of multiple meanings through graphic organizers (see Figure 7.4) to assist students in making connections between multiple meanings. In the case of the multiple meanings for *run* discussed above, students could appreciate that all the meanings referred to the act of traveling rapidly. After many exposures to these words, she assessed their understanding of multiple meanings using a PowerPoint® presentation she created. Multiple choice questions were displayed, with possible answers appearing in red, blue, black, and green. Each student had similarly colored cards for responding to the questions. As each question appeared, students responded by holding up the color of the answer they chose. For example, they identified sentences that correctly used *table.* Ms. Hansen provided more support to students who needed it by programming the presentation to slowly dissolve each incorrect answer until only one remained. She shared, "By using the response cards, I am able to do a quick pan of the class to see who is getting it and who is not."

Learning Vocabulary as Parts of Speech.   Dana Kuhn's ninth-grade English class studied parts of speech as a method for understanding vocabulary in the context of

For more information on unique and surprising uses of English, see Richard Lederer's *Crazy English.*

Figure 7.4   Sample Multiple Meanings Organizer

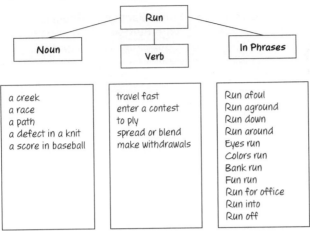

its appearance in a sentence. Mr. Kuhn used his own version of "Vocabulary Jeopardy" to engage students in cooperative learning activities while building their understanding of the language. Words were selected from a cross-matched list of vocabulary identified by the ninth-grade English department and readings that had been discussed and studied during recent lessons. He used the game as a formative assessment of student learning of words introduced the day before. Heterogeneous groups of four or five students competed as teams to provide questions that accurately matched the prompts displayed on the familiar game board constructed through a PowerPoint® display. The categories Mr. Kuhn used on a recent afternoon were Nouns, Adjectives, Verbs, and Spelling Required, a particularly challenging category for most students, especially his English language learners. The captain of each team chose the category and dollar amount while Mr. Kuhn read the prompt. Teams had ten seconds to consult before answering. The prompt "plentiful" appeared in the $400 Adjective slot. After consulting for a few moments, Haley's team rang in with "What is *abundant?*" Mr. Kuhn finds these team competitions to be useful because they "encourage students to teach other students." He does caution, however, to use games such as this judiciously—"have fun, but don't kill the game with overexposure!"

Game show formats provide a familiar frame for word exploration. Teachers can adapt "Wheel of Fortune," " $25,000 Pyramid," and "Password" to play with language in creative ways.

Vocabulary in Social Studies

A critical vocabulary skill for secondary learners is the ability to ascribe characteristics to technical vocabulary. Understanding the nuances of meaning behind terminology, for instance, the similarities and differences between the Bay of Pigs invasion and the Cuban Missile Crisis, is essential to the mastery of any content area. This ability to assign characteristics is also an important element in reading comprehension (Flood, Lapp, & Fisher, 2003) and builds connections between known and unknown concepts (Gipe, 1978-1979).

Semantic Feature Analysis.   A popular instructional strategy for categorizing terms by characteristics is semantic feature analysis (Anders & Bos, 1986). This procedure, also known as SFA, assists students in assigning characteristics, or features, in a grid pattern. Vocabulary terms comprise the rows, and the features make up the columns. Students place a "+" in each cell to indicate a relationship between the term and the

Figure 7.5   Semantic Feature Analysis Example

VOCABULARY WORD FEATURE	Peacekeeping effort	Built alliances with Europe	Effected by domestic policy	Escalated cold war
Joined United Nations (1945)	+	+	+	−
Berlin Blockade (1948)	−	+	+	+
Declaration of Human Rights (1948)	+	+	+	−
Signed NATO (1949) and SEATO (1954) treaties	+	+	+	+
Mutually assured destruction policy (1960)	+	+	+	−
US tests hydrogen bomb (1952)	−	−	+	+
Joined World Bank (1947)	+	+	+	−
Bay of Pigs invasion (1961)	−	−	+	+
Cuban Missile Crisis (1962)	−	+	+	+

SFA draws on what we know about visual display of information. SFA is an example of a matrix type of graphic organizer, as discussed in chapter 6.

feature, and a "−" when it is not a characteristic. Typically, students complete the grid in conjunction with a piece of assigned text. During a U.S. History class, students analyzed terms related to post-World War II U.S. foreign policy. The teacher created the grid in Figure 7.5 for students as they worked through a chapter in their textbook.

Many teachers attribute the power of SFA to its visual arrangement, particularly because it mimics the way the brain organizes information (Pittleman, Heimlich, Berglund, & French, 1991). Marco, a student in this classroom, seemed to confirm this observation when he said, "*Now* I get it! You can really see how these policies didn't all really help each other. No wonder it was so messed up."

Semantic feature analysis is an excellent example of a vocabulary strategy that taps into a student's visual learning modality. The use of multiple modalities of learning has been shown to support new learning (Armstrong, 1994). These modalities, or forms of expression, are frequently categorized as visual, auditory, and kinesthetic (movement) (Carbo, Dunn, & Dunn, 1991). While conventional wisdom cautions against attempting to categorize students according to a particular learning style, educators widely recognize the value of integrating these forms of expression into instruction. Certainly visual supports are widely used. As well, the auditory modality is represented in the chapter on questioning. However, learning through and with movement is often seen as more problematic, especially at the secondary level (Gage, 1995). It can be a challenge for the teacher to manage this type of expression in a busy classroom.

See chapter 4 for a detailed discussion of questioning by students and teachers.

Kinesthetics in Role Play.   An example of kinesthetic expression in vocabulary instruction is role playing. This practice of "acting out" vocabulary extends from Total Physical Response, a method of language instruction used with students who are English language learners (Asher, 1969) and those who are deaf (Marlatt, 1995). When students are invited to "act out" vocabulary, they engage in physical movement and gestures to portray a word. It is likely that these movements assist the performer in remembering the word because he or she is required to think critically about the features of the word.

The incorporation of role playing in social studies content has also been documented (Hillis & von Eschenbach, 1996). Marisol Acuna recently used vocabulary role play in her social studies class during a unit on health care decisions. The focus of the day's lesson was on the dangers associated with tobacco products. She identified relevant vocabulary and then invited students to study the words in an unconventional way—through drama. Students worked in small groups to research specialized vocabulary words and phrases like *advertisement, big tobacco company,* and *exposure.* After discussion and clarification about word meanings, each group then crafted a script using the identified vocabulary words. A requirement of the skit was that it must accurately convey the significance of the word or phrase.

Corita, Scott, and Kyle selected *tobacco subsidies* as one of the terms to demonstrate during vocabulary role play. Scott, as the tobacco farmer, tells his wife (Corita) that he'd like to replace his tobacco fields with spinach in order to contribute to the health of the nation. The two farmers then turn to Kyle, the farm management agent, to explain their decision. "We want to plant a new crop," explains Corita. Kyle, as the agent, replies, "You can plant what you want, but you'll lose your *tobacco subsidy* from the government." "You mean I won't get a check for each acre of tobacco I harvest? How can I afford to keep my farm?" says Scott. Ms. Acuna later uses the students' definitions from their skits to illustrate examples in their vocabulary journals.

Student-generated role plays can be further developed into Reader's Theatre scripts, as discussed in chapter 3.

Vocabulary in Mathematics

It has been a long-held tradition in secondary schooling that explicit vocabulary instruction is an essential prereading activity to support students' subsequent comprehension (Moore, Readence, & Rickelman, 1989; Tierney & Cunningham, 1984). However, many teachers have experienced the dilemma of pre-teaching the vocabulary to such an extent that the student has little opportunity to apply it, relying instead on rote memorization at the expense of deeper understanding (Johnson & Pearson, 1984). Therefore, a "chicken-and-egg" conundrum results—what comes first, the vocabulary or the connected text?

Vocabulary in Context.   Many content area teachers seek to resolve this argument by teaching both the vocabulary *and* the context for its use simultaneously. These teachers find success in timing the instruction of technical vocabulary using a sequence of "introduce, define, discuss, and apply." In this way, students are alerted to the necessity of a new word, provided a definition, given an opportunity to further refine their understanding through peer discussion, then invited to experience the word within connected text. This sequence is particularly valuable when teaching technical vocabulary.

Vacca and Vacca (1999) believe that "vocabulary is as unique to a content area as fingerprints are to a human being" (p. 314). Indeed, few content areas are more defined by their vocabulary than the field of mathematics. Complicating matters further is the importance of what the National Council for Teachers of Mathematics (2000) calls the "factual, procedural, and conceptual understandings that are inexorably woven together in the study of mathematics." This means that in mathematics students must learn the definition of a term, the algorithms associated with the

The National Council for Teachers of Mathematics website can be found at *www.nctm.org.*

Encouraging students to look for examples in magazines allows them to see the application of concepts in their own environment.

term, as well as the underlying principles that will allow them to apply a flexible understanding to solve unfamiliar problems.

Vocabulary Development Specific to a Content Area.   Constantina Burow, a geometry teacher, uses an innovative approach to building flexible technical vocabulary for her students. Through the use of mathematics journals, she encourages students to define and apply their knowledge of the language of geometry. She follows a sequence of instruction that begins with introducing and defining mathematical terms. Discussing real world examples and applying the vocabulary occurs at length in whole-class and small group activities. Students apply the new algorithms through guided practice, and then extend their understanding by applying these concepts to novel problems. Sounds familiar, right? This sequence is not uncommon in mathematics classes throughout U.S. high schools. However, Mrs. Burow's use of mathematics journals allows students to consolidate these instructional activities. Early in the semester, students are taught a two-page frame to use in their mathematics journals (see Figure 7.6). At the top of the left page, students assemble photos from magazines that mimic the geometric shape in question. On the lower half of the page, students write a summary in their own words. Diagrams, formulas, and theorems appear on the facing page.

Figure 7.6   Sample Page From Mathematics Journal

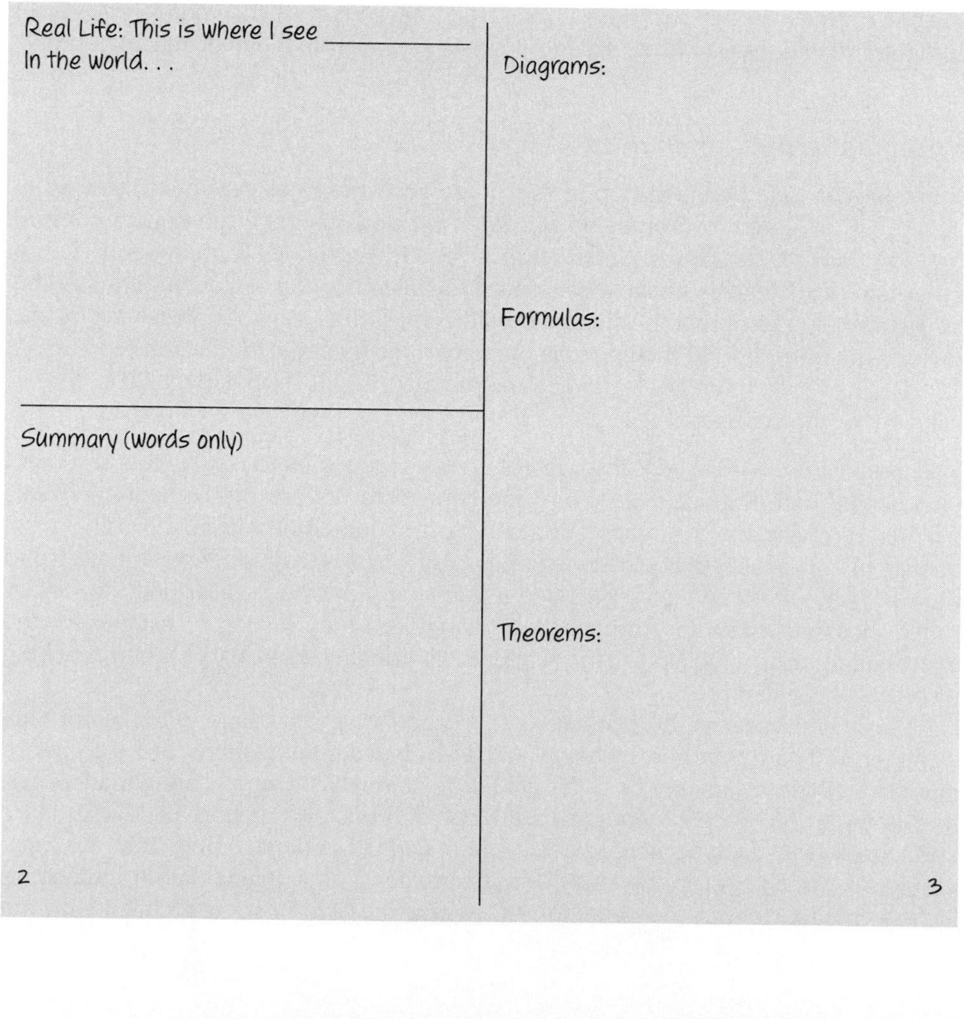

Real Life: This is where I see _____
In the world. . .

Diagrams:

Formulas:

Summary (words only)

Theorems:

2

3

By using this format, students are able to skim and scan a great deal of information as they read from the textbook and other source materials. These mathematics journals serve as more than a notebook. While another section is reserved for class notes, these pages are reserved for students' individual expressions of the meaning of geometric terms. Isabel, a student in Mrs. Burow's class, had diagrams of quadrilaterals (squares, rectangles, and parallelograms) on a page, along with their accompanying formulas and theorems. On the left, she had clipped an ad for a square Tommy Hilfiger™ watch as an example of a quadrilateral. The photograph represented another meaning as well for Isabel, who pointed out that the Hilfiger logo on the watch face was composed of rectangles, another form of parallelogram. Below the photo she wrote, "Finding the area of a quadrilateral you need to multiply the base of the figure times the true height of the figure (true height makes a 90° angle with base). To find the perimeter you add up all the sides."

Mrs. Burow has found that the use of a consistent frame for defining and extending geometry vocabulary has served as an excellent reference for students as well. When reading their textbook and other mathematics materials, students can use their own journals to remind them about the meaning of unfamiliar words, thus reinforcing their growing acquisition of mathematical vocabulary.

Vocabulary in Science

The ability to manipulate words can be an important device in acquiring vocabulary. Unfortunately, committing words to paper often seems permanent and intractable to many students, as if the act of writing terms down means they must remain fixed and static. Word sorts can provide students with a way to arrange and rearrange words in ways that mimic the critical thinking processes they use in applying known words to comprehending new text. Much like a key in search of a lock, readers try a variety of related words until they discover the one meaning that supports their ability to understand a passage.

Science Word Sorts.   Sorting words involves the manipulation of a set of words, usually written on individual slips of paper, into a series of categories or related concepts. More than 25 years ago, Gillet and Temple (1978) described a process for helping students study the relationships between words. Word sorts typically consist of 10 to 20 terms and can be closed or open. Closed sorting activities are performed using categories provided by the teacher. For example, the words *chromosome, chromium,* and *chromosphere* belong in the categories, respectively, of *biology, chemistry,* and *astronomy,* which were furnished by the teacher to help students organize their understanding. In fact, a similar closed sort was illustrated in the opening vignette for this chapter. An open sort is similar, but students create a set of categories to reflect their understanding of the relationships between and among a set of words. Both of these examples represent conceptual word sorts, because students are using their semantic knowledge of terms. Other word sorts may focus word patterns (e.g., -at and –ag words), or derivations (words with the Latin root *nomen* or *nominis*).

Science teacher Larry Caudillo uses word sorts to assist his biology students in preparing concept maps. During a review lesson on the molecules of life, Mr. Caudillo presented his students with the words *saccharides, DNA, glycerol, amino acid, fatty acids, carboxyl, RNA,* and *R-group* in an open sort. The class was instructed to work in small clusters to create categories and group accordingly. Group members engaged in a lively conversation about the meanings and relationships between and

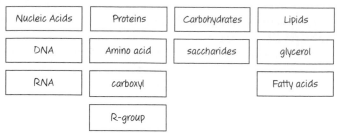

Figure 7.7 Word Sort in Science

See chapter 6 to find out what Mr. Caudillo did with the graphic organizers.

among the words in the set. After much debate, each group arrived at a arrangement. Using blank cards, Nalia, Maria, Terrence, and Carl created four categories and arranged their cards like those in Figure 7.7.

This correct arrangement reflected the students' knowledge of the four macromolecules that comprise all life forms. He further challenged them to supply a rationale for their decisions, and was particularly pleased to see them return to their textbook and class notes to justify their answers.

Vocabulary in Electives

An important element in mastering new vocabulary words is repetition and rehearsal with purpose (Baker, Simmons, & Kameenui, 1995). There is little evidence to show that students master vocabulary with traditional methods of rote memorization through oral and written drills (Anderson & Nagy, 1992; Gu & Johnson, 1996). Rather, it is repetition embedded in a meaningful context that supports vocabulary acquisition. This concept of meaningful repetition has its roots in Reader's Theatre, a technique for promoting reading fluency through public performance (Martinez, Roser, & Strecker, 1998–1999).

"With purpose" is a key phrase. Student learning is greatly enhanced when connected to meaningful activities.

Meaningful Repetition. Music teacher Debbie Nevin understands the importance of performance as a learning tool. Students in her band classes must become comfortable with public performance if they are to be successful in her course. She also recognizes that it is vital for her students, especially her English language learners, to get adequate time conversing with adults and other fluent language models (National Center on Education and the Economy, 2001). One technique she uses to accomplish this is Quiz Me vocabulary cards (see Figure 7.8). Students in Ms. Nevin's classes create vocabulary cards that are constructed from 1″ × 3″ cardstock. As vocabulary is introduced, a word is written on the card, along with the definition. On the back of each card is space for five signatures. A hole is punched in the corner and the cards are strung on a binder ring. Students are required to collect five signatures from adults on campus for each word. They are instructed to approach an adult, explain the assignment, and then request their assistance. The adult quizzes the student on each word, then signs the back of each correct response. In addition to creating a purposeful repetition and rehearsal, Ms. Nevin has also discovered a way for her students to interact with teachers and other adults around campus.

Activities like Quiz Me cards encourage students to initiate conversations with adults outside of the classroom.

Visual Representations to Understand Word Meanings. Vocabulary cards are used in a different "fashion" in Karen Tennen's clothing design class. Like other content areas, consumer science has its own unique set of vocabulary. Ms. Tennen remarks that "students need to read a guide sheet in order to construct a garment . . . and there are many terms the students need to understand before they can lay out

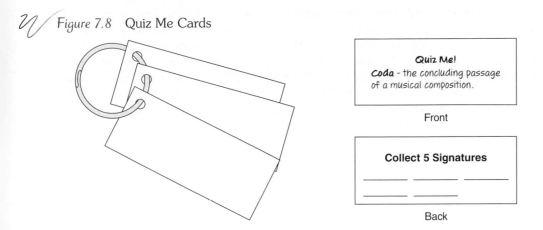

Figure 7.8   Quiz Me Cards

Quiz Me!
Coda - *the concluding passage of a musical composition.*

Front

Collect 5 Signatures

Back

Figure 7.9   Vocabulary Cards in Clothing Design Class

Template

Vocabulary word	definition in students own words
Graphic or picture	Sentence using word

Example

Bias	to cut on an angle to the straight grain
	A bias cut uses more fabric.

their pattern." When introducing the basics of pattern layout, Ms. Tennen taught specialized vocabulary words that would assist students in accurately cutting out their fabric pieces. They were given a set of 4″ × 6″ index cards and instructed to divide each into quadrants (see Figure 7.9). Terms such as *bias, bound edge, face, nap,* and *notch* were each written in the top left quadrant, and the definition, after class instruction, was recorded in the student's own words in the upper right quadrant of the card. A sentence using the term is written in the lower right quadrant, and a diagram or graphic symbol representing the term is drawn in the lower left quadrant.

Constructing vocabulary cards serves several uses in this class. First, when placed on a binder ring the cards become an easily accessible reference for the student, preventing costly errors to expensive fabric. The time involved in creating each card also provides an opportunity for students to concentrate on the meaning, use, and representation of the term, thereby increasing the likelihood that the term will become a part of their permanent vocabulary. Finally, the inclusion of a graphic piece in each card is particularly appropriate for Ms. Tennen's class, because many of these concepts are represented on the tissue pattern as a symbol, rather than a word. For instance, when a pattern needs to be cut on a bias, or angle to the fabric, it is denoted by an arrow (→) indicating the direction. A notch is often represented by ▲. These symbols are universally recognized as indicators of specific sewing concepts, and it is essential that students in this class are comfortable with the lexicon, both in word and symbol, of the field.

Conclusion

The number of words students need in their academic vocabulary skyrockets during their secondary schooling years. Isolated instruction in individual words is an ineffective use of instructional time, and is proven to be inadequate to keep pace with the content area needs. Instead, effective teachers rely on a battery of approaches to foster learning of general, specialized, and technical vocabulary.

Common vocabulary can be successfully taught through word walls constructed from any one of a number of sources for word lists. These visual glossaries can assist students in both usage and spelling. Interesting and innovative resource materials, such as rhyming dictionaries, thesauri, slang dictionaries, and web sites can expand students' knowledge and usage of words.

A particular challenge for English language learners is the array of multiple meaning words. Often Anglo-Saxon in origin, these small words can offer a broad number of meanings across varied grammatical structures. Explicit instruction in multiple meaning words can boost comprehension.

Specialized and technical vocabulary in the content area is also vital for learning. Vocabulary role play and word sorts can introduce novel ways for students to experience a deeper understanding of a word and its relationship to other words. Teachers have also found success with structuring activities to invite students to write about words. Examples of these strategies include vocabulary journals and cards.

Remember that each of the vocabulary development strategies in this chapter can be used across the curriculum, and not only in the content areas discussed here. For instance, word walls are used extensively in mathematics and science, and vocabulary cards are regularly featured in English classes.

References

Anders, P. L., & Bos, C. S. (1986). Semantic feature analysis: An interactive strategy for vocabulary development and text comprehension. *Journal of Reading, 29,* 610–616.

Anderson, R. C., & Nagy, W. E. (1992). The vocabulary conundrum. *American Educator: The Professional Journal of the American Federation of Teachers, 16*(4), 14–18, 44–47.

Armstrong, T. (1994). *Multiple intelligences in the classroom.* Alexandria, VA: Association for Supervisors of Curriculum Development.

Asher, J. J. (1969). The total physical response approach to second language learning. *Modern Language Journal, 53*(1), 3–17.

Baker, S. K., Simmons, D. C., & Kame'enui, E. J. (1995). *Vocabulary acquisition: Curricular and instructional implications for diverse learners.* Technical report no. 13. University of Oregon: National Center to Improve the Tools for Educators.

Blachowicz, C. L. Z., & Fisher, P. (2000). Vocabulary instruction. In M. L. Kamil, P. B. Mosenthal, P. D. Pearson, & R. Barr (Eds.), *Handbook of reading research* (Vol. III, pp. 503–523). Mahwah, NJ: Lawrence Erlbaum.

Blanchfield, C. (Ed.). (2001). *Creative vocabulary: Strategies for teaching vocabulary in grades K–12.* Fresno, CA: San Joaquin Valley Writing Project.

Carbo, M., Dunn, R., & Dunn, K. (1991). *Teaching students to read through their individual learning styles.* Boston: Allyn and Bacon.

Cunningham, P. M. (2002). *Prefixes and suffixes: Systematic sequential phonics and spelling.* Greensboro, NC: Carson-Dellosa.

Cunningham, P. M., & Allington, R. L. (2003). *Classrooms that work: They can all read and write* (3rd ed.). Boston: Allyn & Bacon.

Cunningham, P. M., & Hall, D. P. (1998). *Month-by-month phonics for the upper grades.* Greensboro, NC: Carson-Dellosa.

Dolch, E. W. (1936). A basic sight vocabulary. *The Elementary School Journal, 36,* 456–460.

Espin, C. A., & Foegen, A. (1996). Validity of general outcome measures for predicting secondary students' performance on content-area tasks. *Exceptional Children, 62,* 497–514.

Farley, M. J., & Elmore, P. B. (1992). The relationship of reading comprehension to critical thinking skills, cognitive ability, and vocabulary for a sample of underachieving college freshmen. *Educational and Psychological Measurement, 52,* 921–931.

Flood, J., Lapp, D., & Fisher, D. (2003). Reading comprehension instruction. In J. Flood, D. Lapp, J. M. Jensen, & J. R. Squire (Eds.), *Handbook of research on teaching the English language arts* (pp. 931–941). Mahwah, NJ: Lawrence Erlbaum.

Fry, E. B. (1997). *Dr. Fry's 1000 instant words: The most common words for teaching reading, writing, and spelling.* Westminister, CA: Teacher Created Materials.

Gage, R. (1995). Excuse me, you're cramping my style: Kinesthetics for the classroom. *English Journal, 84*(8), 52–55.

Gillet, J. W., & Temple, C. (1978). Word knowledge: A cognitive view. *Reading World, 18,* 132–140.

Gipe, J. (1978–1979). Investigation techniques for teaching word meanings. *Reading Research Quarterly, 4,* 624–644.

Goodman, L. (2001). A tool for learning: Vocabulary self-awareness. In C. Blanchfield (Ed.), *Creative vocabulary: Strategies for teaching vocabulary in grades K–12.* Fresno, CA: San Joaquin Valley Writing Project.

Gu, Y., & Johnson, R. K. (1996). Vocabulary learning strategies and language learning outcomes. *Language Learning, 46,* 643–679.

Harwell, J. M. (2001). *Complete learning disabilities handbook: Ready-to-use strategies and activities for teaching students with learning disabilities* (2nd ed.). Paramus, NJ: Center for Applied Research in Education.

Hillis, M. R., & von Eschenbach, J. F. (1996). Varying instructional strategies to accommodate diverse thinking skills: Curriculum concerns. *Social Studies and the Young Learner, 9*(2), 20–23.

Johnson, D. D., & Pearson, P. D. (1984). *Teaching reading vocabulary* (2nd ed.). New York: Holt, Rinehart, & Winston.

Klein, M. L. (1988). *Teaching reading comprehension and vocabulary: A guide for teachers.* Upper Saddle River, NJ: Prentice Hall.

Lapp, D., Jacobson, J., Fisher, D., & Flood, J. (2000). Tried and true word study and vocabulary practices. *The California Reader, 33*(2), 25–30.

Lederer, R. (1998). *Crazy English: The ultimate joyride through our language.* New York: Pocket Books.

Lowry, L. (1994). *The giver.* New York: Laurel Leaf.

Marlatt, E. A. (1995). Language through total physical response. *Perspectives in Education and Deafness, 13*(4), 18–20.

Martinez, M., Roser, N. L., & Strecker, S. (1998–1999). "I never thought I could be a star:" A reader's theatre ticket to fluency. *The Reading Teacher, 52,* 326–334.

McGuffey's Eclectic Spelling-Book. (1879). Rev. ed. New York: John Wiley and Sons. (Modern reproduction).

Moore, D. W., Readence, J. E., & Rickelman, R. J. (1989). *Prereading activities for content area reading and writing* (2nd ed.). Newark, DE: International Reading Association.

Nagy, W. E., & Anderson, R. C. (1984). How many words are there in printed school English? *Reading Research Quarterly, 19,* 304–330.

Nagy, W. E., & Herman, P. (1985). Incidental vs. instructional approaches to increasing reading vocabulary. *Educational Perspectives, 23,* 16–21.

National Center on Education and the Economy. (2001). *Speaking and listening.* Pittsburgh, PA: Author.

National Council for Teachers of Mathematics. (2000). *Principles and standards for school mathematics.* Reston, VA: NCTM.

New Webster's dictionary of the English language. (1981). New York: Delair.

Peterson, A. (1996). *The writer's workout book: 113 stretches toward better prose.* Berkeley, CA: National Writing Project. Used with permission.

Pittleman, S. D., Heimlich, J. E., Berglund, R. L., & French, M. P. (1991). *Semantic feature analysis: Classroom applications.* Newark, DE: International Reading Association.

Stahl, S. A., & Fairbanks, M. M. (1986). The effects of vocabulary instruction: A model-based meta-analysis. *Review of Educational Research, 56,* 72–110.

Steinbeck, J. (1939). *The grapes of wrath.* New York: Viking.

Templeton, S. (1992). Theory, nature and pedagogy of higher-order orthographic development in older children. In S. Templeton & D. Bear (Eds.), *Development of orthographic knowledge and the foundations of literacy: A memorial festschrift for Edmund H. Henderson* (pp. 253–278). Hillsdale, NJ: Lawrence Erlbaum.

Thoreau, H. D. (1849/1965). *Civil disobedience.* New York: HarperCollins.

Thorndike, E. L., & Lorge, I. (1944). *The teacher's word book of 30,000 words.* New York: Teachers College, Columbia University.

Tierney, R. J., & Cunningham, J. W. (1984). Research on reading comprehension. In P. D. Pearson, R. Barr, M. L. Kamil, & P. Mosenthal (Eds.), *Handbook of reading research* (pp. 609–655). Mahwah, NJ: Lawrence Erlbaum.

Twain, M. (1890). In G. Bainton (Ed.), *The art of authorship: Literary reminiscences, methods of work, and advice to young beginners, personally contributed by leading authors of the day* (pp. 85–88). New York: D. Appleton and Company.

Vacca, R. T., & Vacca, J. L. (1999). *Content area reading: Literacy and learning across the curriculum* (6th ed.). New York: Longman.

Chapter 8

The Power in the Pen: Writing to Learn

DOUGLAS FISHER, NANCY FREY, AND RITA ELWARDI

Walking into Mr. Hayden's geometry class, guests are often surprised to see students busily writing what looks like journal entry responses to a series of questions on the board. Mr. Hayden reminds them as he slowly walks up and down the aisles, "Don't solve the problem yet! Write down what you are thinking, and I don't mean who you want to ask out on a date. Look at the steps on the board. First, write what you see and recognize in the problem; second, what kind of problem it is; third, what it means you have to do; and fourth and only then, the first step you will take to solve it." As the students write, Mr. Hayden assesses their work, reading and commenting on the written accounts of their thinking processes.

He stops briefly at Kofi's desk, scrolls down the page, and says, "I like the way you thought that through. Now, how will you begin to solve it?"

Kofi explains what he thinks the first step is and waits for Mr. Hayden's response.

"O.K., write it down." As his teacher quickly moves on, the young man starts writing.

"So, Jessica, you wrote that it's a parabola. So, what does that mean?"

A young girl smiles, but says nothing.

"Can't explain it? Where will you look to find the explanation?"

The girl's hesitant response is just above a whisper.

"You're right, the glossary," and he waits for her to locate the word. "Found it? Good, now write down what a parabola is." Then Mr. Hayden moves on, leaving another student busy writing.

When asked why writing is part of his geometry curriculum, Mr. Hayden explains that students have to be specific in a written explanation, much more so than in speaking. "My students have to think through each step as they explain it in written form and I see what is missing or unclear to them. Then I know how best to guide them through the steps of a problem. It's a process that informs both me and my students."

Kofi says simply, "It just helps me see what I know."

Defining and Defending Writing to Learn

Before we examine the research and instructional strategies used in writing-to-learn, a few definitions are in order. Writing to learn differs from learning to write in several important ways. Students need to "learn to write" throughout their lives. When they are in elementary school, children learn to encode words, spell, construct sentences, figure out the mechanics of paragraphs, and develop understandings of grammar. As they get older, students refine and expand on these skills. Teachers who focus on learning to write typically use process writing as an instructional approach (Atwell, 1998; Graves, 1983). While the processes used by each writer differ and are usually quite recursive, Jenkinson (1988) asserts that student writers typically go "through some variation of these steps:

1. prewriting activities (jotting down ideas, listing thoughts, brainstorming, gathering information, and so on);
2. writing a draft;
3. peer review of the draft;
4. revising;
5. editing;
6. writing the final draft; and
7. publishing." (p. 714)

While most common in English classrooms, process writing can be used throughout the curriculum. For example, social studies teachers may wish to engage their students in persuasive essay writing about the causes of World War II or a rationale for democracy.

Getting Students Involved

Writing to learn differs from other types of writing because it is not a process piece that will go through multiple refinements toward an intended final product. Instead, it is meant to be a catalyst for further learning—an opportunity for students to recall, clarify, and question what they know and what they still wonder about. Writing to learn "involves getting students to think about and to find the words to explain what they are learning, how they understand that learning, and what their own processes of learning involve" (Mitchell, 1996, p. 93). As Jenkinson (1988) explains, "writing should be a process in which writers discover what they know and do not know about their topics, their language, themselves, and their ability to communicate with specific audiences" (p. 714). For example, a social studies teacher may ask students to respond to a writing to learn prompt such as "explain the bombing of Hiroshima to your younger brother or sister." Responding to this prompt requires that the student consider their prior knowledge about the bombing, the cognitive development of their younger siblings, what they have read or listened to about the topic, and how to best convey this information in writing.

Applying Three Kinds of Knowledge

Thus, writing to learn requires students to use different kinds of knowledge at different times. Cognitive scientists generally think of three kinds of knowledge—declara-

Try writing to learn for yourself. Take a few minutes to write about the types of knowledge you believe are necessary for academic learning. We'll discuss this further in the next section.

Prior knowledge refers to schemas a student has already created. These are influenced by experiences, topic knowledge, and cultural perspectives.

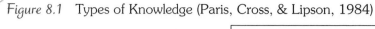

Figure 8.1   Types of Knowledge (Paris, Cross, & Lipson, 1984)

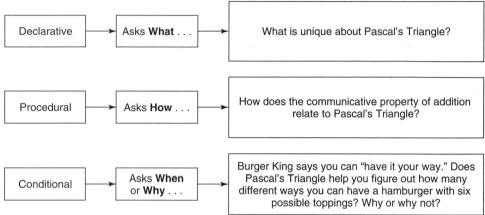

tive, procedural, and conditional (Paris, Cross, & Lipson, 1984; Sternberg & Williams, 2002). These types of knowledge are illustrated in Figure 8.1, using questions an algebra teacher might use.

Declarative Knowledge.   Declarative knowledge focuses on things that we "know" such as labels, names, facts, and lists. While often considered boring, declarative knowledge is an important part of what we know as adults. It is also the easiest kind of knowledge to impart in lectures and reading assignments. In school, students must have a number of experiences that develop their declarative knowledge. Some writing to learn prompts can be used to demonstrate this type of knowledge. For example, a teacher may ask students to explain the types of muscles in the body.

Procedural Knowledge.   In addition to declarative knowledge in which students recall specific information, students must demonstrate their understanding of procedural knowledge. This type of knowledge requires that students know how to do something; they must know how to apply their knowledge. This type of knowledge is more difficult to convey in a traditional lecture or reading—students need experience putting their knowledge into practice. Again, some writing to learn prompts can facilitate and assess this type of knowledge. For example, a teacher may ask students to describe the steps necessary to complete a science lab or solve a mathematics problem.

Conditional Knowledge.   Finally, conditional knowledge is concerned with when or why something is done–the various conditions that influence our decisions to use knowledge. Stated another way, conditional knowledge is about strategies and when to use them. Again, writing to learn can create prompts in which students are provided scenarios and are asked to use their knowledge in novel ways. For example, a biology teacher may ask students to consider the pros and cons of embryonic research.

In other words (and rather simply stated), "What" is declarative knowledge, "How" is procedural knowledge, and "When" or "Why" is conditional knowledge. Clearly, students need to develop their knowledge in each of these categories, and teachers can monitor this development with appropriate writing to learn activities.

Read your initial response to the writing to learn prompt about types of knowledge. Add new information and revise any statements to reflect your new understanding of academic knowledge demands.

Why Is Writing Neglected in Many Content Area Classes?

Unfortunately, many content teachers do not consider writing part of their curriculum. In too many content classrooms, writing is neglected because those teachers believe that writing is best left for the English department (Mitchell, 1996). We believe this is likely a result of over-emphasis on process writing and the confusion between learning to write and writing to learn. There exists considerable evidence across disciplines that writing builds and reinforces content learning. For example, McIntosh and Draper (2001) describe the ways in which writing can facilitate learning in mathematics. Miller and England (1989) provide data on improvement in algebra knowledge when writing to learn was used in the classroom. Beyond mathematics, writing to learn has been employed in English, social studies, science, and family and consumer sciences (Andrews, 1997; Holbrook, 1987; Keys, 1999a, 1999b; Lytton, Marshall-Baker, Benson, & Blieszner, 1996; Mitchell, 1996).

Using Writing Prompts

There are a number of ways that writing to learn can be implemented in content classrooms. Writing to learn is based on writing prompts that the teacher provides students. These prompts can range from very open-ended—"What did you think was confusing about this topic?"—to fairly specific—"Discuss the role of photosynthesis in plant life." The range of prompts can include (Andrews, 1997; Fisher, 2001; Mitchell, 1996):

- *Admit Slips.* Upon entering the classroom, students write on an assigned topic such as "What did you notice was important in yesterday's discussion?" or "Explain the difference between jazz and rock."
- *Crystal Ball.* Students describe what they think class will be about, what will happen next in the novel they are reading, or the next step in a lab.
- *Found Poems.* Students re-read an assigned text and find key phrases that "speak" to them, then arrange these into a poem structure without adding any of their own words.
- *Awards.* Students recommend someone or something for an award that the teacher has created such as "the best artist of the century, living or dead."
- *Cinquains.* A 5 line poem in which the first line is the topic (a noun), the second line is description of the topic in two words, the third line is three "ing" words, the fourth line is a description of the topic in four words, and the final line is a synonym of the topic word from line one.
- *Yesterday's News.* Students summarize the information presented the day before, either from a film, lecture, discussion, or reading.
- *"What If" Scenarios.* Students respond to prompts in which information is changed from what they know and they predict outcomes. For example, students may be asked to respond to "what would be different if the Civil War was fought in 1920?"
- *Take a Stand.* Students discuss their opinions about a controversial topic such as "just because we can, should we clone people?"

- *Letters.* Students write letters to others, including elected officials, family members, friends, people who made a difference, etc. For example, students may respond to the prompt, "write a letter to Dr. Martin Luther King informing him of the progress we have made on racism since his death."
- *Exit Slips.* Used as a closure activity at the end of the period, students write on an assigned prompt such as "The three best things I learned today are . . ."

The critical element that all of these writing to learn events have in common is that students do not correct or rewrite their pieces. Instead, each become a starting point for learning.

Perspective Writing Through RAFT.   Naturally, there are several hundred ways to structure writing to learn prompts. Those above are just a few. In addition to these general types of prompts, students can be taught perspective writing during writing to learn by using RAFT prompts (Santa & Havens, 1995).

RAFT stands for:

R = Role (who is the writer, what is role of the writer?)

A = Audience (to whom are you writing?)

F = Format (what format should the writing be in?)

T = Topic (what are you writing about?)

In perspective writing, there is rarely one "right" answer. Instead, it can serve as an excellent means of prompting discussion among students who can use their written pieces to support their viewpoint.

When students are first introduced to RAFT, everyone responds to the same prompt. For example, students may enter a social studies classroom and see the following written on the board:

R = a sailor at Pearl Harbor, December 7, 1941

A = people on the mainland

F = a telegram

T = We've been attacked!

Once students become familiar with the RAFT format, teachers can assign groups of students different components and then invite group conversations about the topic at hand. For example, in a social studies class, students may enter the room to find information like that in Table 8.1 written on the board.

As you can imagine, this type of writing provides students with an opportunity to use their knowledge and skills in writing and discussion as they share their responses to the RAFT exercise above. As you will see, teachers across the curriculum use writing to learn to facilitate learning within their content area.

Table 8.1   **Sample of RAFT Format**

	Last name A–M	**Last name N–Z**
R	King George	colonists
A	colonists	King George
F	Informational letter	Protest letter
T	Why the taxes?	Why the taxes?

Strategies at Work

Writing to Learn in English

"Look beyond the literal meaning of the words in the selection. When you write, go deeper." This is Ms. Penczar's gentle encouragement to her World Literature students as they write to learn in their learning logs (e.g., Mitchell, 1996). Although these students read volumes of literature in this course, they may not comprehend some of the inferences as they read through a selection the first time. Writing also makes the writer pay more attention—to what the character is saying, why the character is saying that, and who comprises the audience. These students can easily recall and recite the basic elements of literature, but until they give themselves time to reflect and write, they often do not identify implied meanings layered within the rich literature they study. Ms. Penczar schedules regular writing time as she knows that otherwise students may do only superficial reading, instead of thinking in depth about underlying themes and motives. Her learning logs are spiral bound notebooks that students maintain over the course of the term. She uses various prompts at different times in the school year to focus her students on texts.

> *Inferring is a comprehension strategy that requires students to draw conclusions that are not explicitly stated in the text.*

Learning Logs.   During her unit on short stories, Ms. Penczar's students respond in their learning logs to questions that she periodically posts on the board or shares orally. For example, in the short story *Bad Influence,* by Judith Ortiz Cofer (1996), a young girl is sent from her home in Patterson, New Jersey, to spend the summer with her grandparents in Puerto Rico. Much like the main character in the story, Ms. Penczar's students initially viewed the grandparents stereotypically. When the class responded to the question, "What does Rita know about her grandparents," their responses were literal—"They're old," "They got married at fifteen," "They loved Rita [their granddaughter]." In contrast, when they later responded in their learning logs to the question, "What did Rita learn about her grandparents?" their responses were more reflective, such as the student examples that follow:

> They [the grandparents] are very serious towards their religion and hold a great deal of respect towards each other. . . . her grandfather is a great spiritualist who's well respected by all. During the summer Rita learned the value of family and friends. (Omar)
>
> Originally, Rita thought her grandfather was a crazy old man. But when the richest woman on the island (who could afford anything she wanted) asked for his help, Rita realized that he was a very wise, spiritual man who the people of the town respected and went to for help. Her grandmother also received the respect of the town's people. From their example Rita learned about friendship—the fact that you can learn about and become friends with the most unexpected people. (Andrea)
>
> Rita thought her grandfather was loony. Later she learned that he had a special talent, which was that he could communicate with spirits, ask them for help. He could see into a person's heart, thoughts and dreams. (Eric)

As they read, Ms. Penczar also suggests that they choose three quotes, or "golden lines," from each chapter. These golden lines must stand out to them and they must explain their reasons for the choices, questions each choice brings to mind, or how it relates to either a character or the progression of the plot. Ms.

Penczar makes good use of her students' writing. As she reviews the learning logs, she is able to use her students' own insights to refer back to the important elements of the text. Their responses are also a source for quotes and analysis later in the course when they must compose a character analysis or thematic essay—thus she links writing to learn and process writing in a way that ensures her students are successful.

Writing to Learn in Mathematics

"Name That Math!" is what Mr. Hayden calls his writing to learn activity in the geometry classes he teaches. Used as an admit slip (e.g., Andrews, 1997), he asks his students to follow a series of steps, in writing, before they start to solve the problem of the day. The first time students see "Name That Math!" is when Mr. Hayden models his own thought process with a problem he has written on the white board:

"What is the volume of a cylinder with a height of 6 feet and a radius of 2 feet?"

Teaching Students to Ask Themselves Questions.   Mr. Hayden wants students to make a habit of asking themselves the following questions when he asks them to "Name That Math:"

1. What's the key word in the problem?
2. What's the rule?
3. What's the first step?

Mr. Hayden then reads the word problem on the board as he thinks aloud his response to question #1. "What key word can I identify in the problem that tells me what I need to know?" he asks himself. He tells the students that every word problem or mathematics question has a clue. "Look for that clue and you'll know what you have to do. It might be connected to surface area, or volume, or the Pythagorean theorem, but the first step is to find it." To illustrate this, Mr. Hayden then points to the key word "volume" in the above problem.

Next, Mr. Hayden explains how to think through question #2, "What's the rule?" by telling the students that rules can be formulas, definitions, theorems or proofs that are connected to that key word. He reminds them that until they know what the rule is, they can't do the first step. Mr. Hayden again models what he wants the student to do. He explains that the rule for the above problem is the formula for volume of a cylinder. He thinks aloud and says, "The formula for volume of a cylinder is $V = Bh$, where B is the base area and h is the height."

Students begin to see that they can attempt the first step of solving the problem only after finding the key word and identifying the rule. Mr. Hayden then tells his students the answer to question 3, "What is the first step?" when he informs them, "You must plug the values into the formula to solve the problem. Now, and only now, can you proceed to solve the problem with math."

Modeling Each Step.   Mr. Hayden understands the importance of modeling each step. As he explains, "I modeled for the students throughout the year so that whenever they see a problem they will immediately identify what kind of mathematics problem it is. They must be able to "Name That Math." After modeling this thinking process for a week, he lets the students begin the same process on their own. These

The teacher can use student samples from writing to learn events to assess what grammar structures or writing conventions need to be retaught.

A think aloud is an instructional technique for modeling how a fluent reader, in this case the teacher, uses comprehension strategies to understand text.

writing to learn steps clarify the thought process students need to solve mathematics problems. The students write the following on a sheet of paper:

1. The problem from the board is:
2. What am I thinking? (Students must think through "Name That Math" in the three steps they have seen their teacher model).

   - What is the key word in the problem?
   - What's the rule?
   - What's the first step?

3. Solve it with mathematics.
4. Solve it with words.

When students first attempt this writing to learn practice, Mr. Hayden does not tell the students what to write down for #2, "What am I thinking?" It is their turn to practice what their teacher has modeled; they must write what they are thinking when they see the problem. This written statement allows students to explain the thought process they go through to solve the problem. As students write, Mr. Hayden circulates and quickly reads each response. Depending on what they write, he can see whether or not they have understood the process. For example, Maria used writing to learn to solve a problem as follows:

Using writing to learn, Mr. Hayden can link assessment with instruction to determine what mathematics or problem-solving skills might need to be retaught.

1. Find the 1/16" scale volume of a square pyramid with a height of 75 feet and a base area of 2500 ft squared.
2. What am I thinking?

   The problem I have chosen is a volume problem. For this I need the volume of a pyramid with a square base. Another part of the problem tells me that I will need to find the similitude of the pyramid to a one-sixteenth scale. The rules for my problem are the formula for volume of a pyramid and finding the volume of the scale will be the volume of the model divided by the ratio cubed. The formula for volume of a pyramid is as follows: $V = 1/3\ Bh$, where B is base area and h is height. My problem gives me the height and the base area of the pyramid so the hard part of this question is going to be drawing it to scale. The first part of my process will be finding the volume of the model and then I will cube my ratio since this is a volume of the model to find the volume of the actual size.

When students get accustomed to implementing these steps on their own, the teacher can see that they are also independently incorporating the target vocabulary for this content area into their writing. In the student example above, Mr. Hayden saw just such a development. "Another part of the problem tells me that I will need to find the *similitude* of the pyramid, to a 1/16th scale," wrote Maria. Similitude is a term that Mr. Hayden taught in class and it has now become part of Maria's thought process. She used the target vocabulary, all the proper formulas, and all the terminology. She also used the sequenced steps the class has been working on all year. Mr. Hayden's modeling and the writing to learn prompts are beginning to pay off.

The next steps, #3, "Solve it with mathematics," and #4, "Solve it with words," requires that students solve the problem in numbers and then explain each step of the problem in written form.

Mr. Hayden knows the importance of #4 because it informs him, on the spot, of his students' thinking about mathematics. "It's truly authentic work. It can't be something that has been duplicated. They can't just copy an answer and be done with it," he notes.

Mr. Hayden also sees the improvement in the paragraphs the students are now writing. He reflects, "The first time we did this, I would get one-line statements such as the following. 'First I find the math. It's this. Then I do this.' They were very simplistic, one or two sentences. But, with practice, the responses became full-page written explanations using the proper vocabulary, terminology, and thought processes required. I can see how they thought the whole thing out and they haven't even started working on the problem yet. It's all just thought process."

Mr. Hayden, like many mathematics teachers, acknowledges the problem of decontextualized word problems—in other words, problems that are removed from student experiences. However, standardized tests are dominated by this type of question. Using "Name That Math" at the beginning of class allows Mr. Hayden to provide the necessary practice while lifting the experience beyond traditional multiple choice test items.

Writing to Learn in Social Studies

In Angie Swartz's U.S. history classes, students regularly practice writing to learn that is connected to her shared reading activity as well as partner discussions and individual student reflections on current events articles. Ms. Swartz uses questions that students can find in the text (right there) as well as questions that require them to think and search. She also is interested in her students' responses to texts, so she often includes a question that requires students to "think about their thinking" by listing the metacognitive strategies they applied.

Thinking About Thinking to Develop Questions.   During a community-wide discussion on the use of drug sniffing dogs in high schools, several articles appeared in the local newspapers. Ms. Swartz used these newspaper articles as part of her Newspapers in Education program (see nie.uniontribune.com) and asked students to consider the following questions:

1. What are the problems with using dogs to sniff out drugs in high schools?
2. What does the Supreme Court say about limiting students' rights?
3. What are the benefits of using drug testing and dog sniffing in the high schools?
4. Is the author biased? What is your evidence that she is or is not?
5. Take a stand—what do you think about this issue?

Ms. Swartz gave students time to write the questions down, consider the type of question, and decide what to look for as they read. They did not write yet. Instead, Ms. Swartz read aloud a newspaper article titled "Taking the Dog's Word Over the Kid's" while students follow along with a copy of their own. The class is not just sitting back and listening; students are busy highlighting, underlining, and marking up the text with marginalia as they keep the focus questions in mind.

Responding to Questions Through Sustained Writing.   After her shared reading, Ms. Swartz asked students to respond to the questions during 10 minutes of sustained silent writing. During this focused writing time, students revisit the text, looking again at the notes, highlighting, or underlining they made during their first reading. Their writing has purpose because they know that they will be sharing it with peers in a few minutes. Ms. Swartz circulates throughout the room coaxing any reluctant writers.

Shared reading is an instructional strategy where students have access to the text while the teacher leads the reading. See chapter 3 for a discussion of shared reading.

Ms. Swartz is applying a Question-Answer Relationship frame. See chapter 4 for more information on QAR.

Most communities have a Newspapers in Education program.

Arnold's responses to the questions included:

1. There is confusion such as the ones stated in the article where the dog sensed the smell of drugs on a student, but there was no proof that the student was in possession of any.
2. It's OK because they are doing it with the excuse that they want to keep schools safe.
3. Schools are able to identify or have a chance to investigate a potential drug user.
4. Yes, she does not agree with drug sniffing dogs on campus. She says it in the last sentence of the article. I can tell by the tone of the sentence.
5. I think that it is okay to use the dogs. We don't need drugs at our school. If kids have drugs, maybe they will keep them at home.

Using Questions and Responses in Paired Discussion Groups. After the students work individually to put their thoughts in writing, they move into paired discussion groups. They are directed to use the prompt questions and their written responses to aid in the discussion. To keep students focused and on task, Ms. Swartz asks students to add at least two additional points to their notes that are identified during the discussion. To hold students accountable, they switch from pen to pencil (or change ink colors) for this task. As students listen and write, they are revisiting the text a third time and are gaining insight from their partner's ideas or perspective. This step also ensures that students are active and responsible listeners. After talking with Olga, Arnold added the following notes to his paper:

This is a simple management technique to ensure that students are participating.

1. No problems because a dog's sense of smell is nine times better than humans, and dogs are trained to sniff out drugs.
2. Since the student is in a public place their rights may be limited.
3. A student would think twice about bringing drugs into school knowing that a dog could sniff personal belongings. But if a dog was wrong and that student got in trouble, that could cause a big problem.

Finalizing Ideas and Opinions. After the partner discussion, a lively class discussion ensues. Students refer to their written thoughts collected during sustained silent writing and partner discussions and once again add to them as they express their ideas and listen to others. To conclude this lesson, Ms. Swartz asks the students to write again. This time, the prompt is "what do you now want to know, what questions do you still have, or what opinion have you formed about this issue?" Olga, disagreeing with her partner, wrote:

> I learned that this safety technique presents a problem with invasion of privacy. People who do drugs outside of school should not be punished for something they do in private, not at school. Students have the right not to be searched without cause. What is the board of education doing to protect students' privacy rights?

Writing to Learn in Science

Step into Ms. Antoinette Linton's biology class with pen and paper in hand and be prepared for writing to learn every day. Ms. Linton uses writing to learn as a metacognitive strategy that leads her biology students to think critically about the content presented. Entry slips help her students clarify what they think, consider what they have learned, and reflect on how their learning may contribute to their personal lives as critical readers and thinkers. These daily prompts may elicit a summary of the previous day's lecture or require students to think about the organization of information pertinent to their individual research topics. As her students assume responsibility to prepare for, organize and document research, these writing prompts guide students' thinking processes and give relevance and structure to the unit.

Using Entry Slips as Writing Prompts.   During her cancer research project, Ms. Linton uses entry slips to focus her students on the topic at hand. She knows that her students have many things on their minds each day—from tests in other classes to dances and football games. The first entry slip for her cancer research project invites students to respond to the prompt, "Write down what you know about cancer. You can include topics from texts, lecture, other sources, and what you already know. Just write freely, getting your thoughts and ideas down on paper. If you have questions about cancer, write those down, too." Excerpts of these initial student entries include:

Entry slips are an effective management technique for getting students focused on the content at hand.

- I don't know much about cancer. I just know that it can spread and sometimes there can be a cure.
- Cancer is bad cells that ceased to recognize signals to stop the growing process.
- There are different types of cancer. Some people die from it.
- It occurs when there are problems with the enzymes that control cell division.
- It's a disease that can kill you, because of bad enzymes and damaged genes.

Some students asked questions in their entry slips:

- Which is the most common cancer?
- Can an infection cause cancer?
- Is cancer more common in men or women?

Informing Instruction Through Student Responses.   The students' responses provide Ms. Linton a view of what her students already know about the topic, and focus her subsequent lesson planning. Their responses inform instruction because Ms. Linton can clearly identify the students' background information that is missing or misleading, correct or incorrect. She now knows, for example, that she must provide specific information about cancer therapy and the absence of a cure.

Another day, Ms. Linton's entry slip prompt read, "What do I need to know about cancer in order to complete my research paper?" The students must now consider future lectures, readings and labs in the following way: The information that my teacher is about to give me will make me successful in my end product, which is a research paper or a presentation. So before she gets started, I need to set up a structure so that I can manipulate the materials she is about to present. Juan's entry illustrates how he is taking responsibility to organize information.

This presentation is also well-suited for Cornell notes. See chapter 5 on this type of notetaking.

What do I need to know about cancer in order to complete my research paper? I need to find answers to a lot of questions, like . . .

- How and why does it start?
- How many people have it?
- How can you prevent it?
- How can you tell if you're infected or not?
- What can result from an abnormal cycle of cell division?
- What are the causes and the current medications?

Another day, the entry slip prompt reads, "What cancer research are you most interested in doing?" Excerpts of student responses included:

- I found out that viruses can be causes of cancer. If I can do research, this is where I want to go. I would like to know more about HIV and AIDS.
- I would like to learn more about breast cancer. My mom had breast cancer, but I didn't know much about it.
- Cancer is the second leading cause of death in the U.S. The four most prevalent types of cancer are lung, colon, breast and prostate. What are the drugs used for these cancers and do they work?

Helping Students Connect Information Through Writing Prompts. Writing to learn prompts give students the opportunity to connect information gathered from class lectures, readings, and their own queries about the topic from their previous entry slips. Students then make choices that interest them, but at a point where these choices are informed, based on a growing bank of knowledge on the subject. However, Ms. Linton does not always focus her entry slip prompts on science. One day the students entered the classroom to find this prompt, "When writing a research paper, what steps should you follow?" Responding to this, Carolina wrote, "It should have an introduction, body paragraphs, and a conclusion. Before starting the paper, you must research first, then create an outline based on what you found out from your questions. That outline turns into a draft. We revise it and get a final product. Listing your references is also necessary."

In this case, the teacher is using writing to learn as a means of determining whether students understand the steps in a procedure and the directions she has given.

Writing to Learn in Electives

Brooke Stern, a teacher of English Language Development (ELD), weaves a number of literacy and language acquisition strategies including writing to learn into a unit of study she designed, titled, "Anne Frank and the Holocaust." During this unit, the students gain background knowledge on Nazi Germany from a variety of sources including pictures, film clips, timelines, and Internet searches. The following snapshot of one lesson captures her students engaged in both the content and the writing to learn activities.

Guiding Reading to Guide Writing. In the shared reading of a passage from *Anne Frank: The Diary of a Young Girl* (Frank, 1993), Ms. Stern reads aloud while students follow along with their own copies of the text. All the time spent front-loading students during her prereading and vocabulary development activities made this reading activity successful. Ms. Stern modeled self-questioning, clarifying, summarizing and predicting aloud. At midpoint in a passage, Ms. Stern asked her students, "What are the main events that have occurred so far?" She then guided her students to write a summary of what they had read, using signal words indicating the sequence of events they had previously studied. She cautioned them, "I don't want to see you copy the text; I want to see your own words in your writing." Jamal's summary of the reading thus far demonstrates both his emerging understanding of text structure and his confidence. His unconventional spelling and grammar is preserved here:

These are the steps in reciprocal teaching. See chapter 9 for more details.

First Anne Frank was born in June 12, 1929 in the country of Germany. Something bad was happening there because the people lost there jobs. Then in 1933 Adolf Hitler came to power and he told to the Germans that they were better immediately began to discriminated the Jews people. Next Anne father took his family to Amsterdam in the Netherlands because they want to be safe from the Nazis. After in 1930 Hitler declared war on Poland. Finally Anne in his family went to a secret annex.

Ms. Stern then asked her students to write once again, this time with the prompt, "What do you think will happen next?" Having provided such a wealth of background knowledge, her students were able to make the following predictions:

- I think Anne finally is going to be cabturd [captured].
- I think what would happen is that they are going to a camp and all are going to die.
- My predict I think the hiding of Anne and her family is great because they can hide from the German. I think the hiding play [place] will be discover by the German.
- I think that may be the solders will round them and will sent to a concentration camps.

Recognizing Growth in Literacy Development.   Upon the completion of this unit, Ms. Stern saw literacy growth in a number of areas. Her students were able to recognize errors in their work and correct them. Their fluency in writing increased, as did their use of conventional English spelling and grammar. Signal words and target vocabulary were beginning to appear in their writing. Writing to learn is a strong component of second language literacy scaffolding, one that affords English language learners daily opportunities to write what they think and know. It also provides them with an opportunity to rehearse the language and organize their ideas before discussions.

Conclusion

Writing to learn "is a tool we can use to see how students are thinking about and understanding what they are doing and learning in the classroom" (Mitchell, 1996, p. 93). It differs from learning to write in purpose. Process writing is used by students to refine their pieces through editing and rewriting. In contrast, writing to learn serves as a way to activate prior knowledge, recall newly learned information, make connections to other concepts, and promote reflective questioning.

This instructional strategy is useful across content areas, in part because what students write about can be easily tailored to the subject. Prompts can be constructed to ask about declarative, procedural, or conditional knowledge. First, write to learn allows students to think about the content at hand and to focus on the subject. Students are invited to compose their thoughts and take stock of their beliefs and opinions before engaging in discussion. This rehearsal of language is likely to be especially useful for English language learners, who benefit from the chance to order ideas before sharing them with others.

Second, writing to learn provides students with data that they can use later for essays or class assignments. Learning logs are especially useful for this because they create a record of previous learning, allowing students to see how the teacher assembled the conceptual framework of the unit. Finally, writing to learn provides teachers a glimpse inside the student's mind—a rare opportunity to assess a student's understanding of the content. These brief writing events can allow the teacher to witness each student's use of logic, reasoning, and information to arrive at solutions and apply concepts.

The strength of writing to learn lies in its intended audience. Process writing ultimately must find an outside audience to influence, persuade, and move, for that is "the power of the pen." Writing to learn has an audience of one—the writer. Teachers create a quiet space for students to engage in an internal dialogue that leads them on a journey of self-reflection. How often have you heard a writer remark that they didn't know what they thought about something until they read what they had written? And so it is with writing to learn. When students discover that these writing events illuminate their own understanding, they discover the power *in* the pen.

References

Andrews, S. E. (1997). Writing to learn in content area reading class. *Journal of Adolescent & Adult Literacy, 41,* 141–142.

Atwell, N. (1998). *In the middle: Writing, reading, and learning with adolescents* (2nd ed.). Upper Montclair, NJ: Boynton/Cook.

Cofer, J. O. (1996). *An island like you: Stories of the barrio.* New York: Puffin.

Fisher, D. (2001). "We're moving on up": Creating a schoolwide literacy effort in an urban high school. *Journal of Adolescent & Adult Literacy, 45,* 92–101.

Frank, A. (1993). *Anne Frank: The diary of a young girl.* New York: Prentice Hall.

Graves, D. H. (1983). *Writing: Teachers and children at work.* Portsmouth, NH: Heinemann.

Holbrook, H. T. (1987). Writing to learn in the social studies. *The Reading Teacher, 41,* 216–219.

Jenkinson, E. B. (1988). Learning to write/writing to learn. *Phi Delta Kappan, 69,* 712–717.

Keys, C. W. (1999a). Language as an indicator of meaning generation: An analysis of middle school students' written discourse about scientific investigations. *Journal of Research in Science Teaching, 36,* 1044–1061.

Keys, C. W. (1999b). Revitalizing instruction in scientific genres: Connecting knowledge production with writing to learn in science. *Science Education, 83,* 115–130.

Lytton, R. H., Marshall-Baker, A., Benson, M. J., & Blieszner, R. (1996, Spring). Writing to learn: Course examples in family and consumer sciences. *Journal of Family and Consumer Sciences, 88,* 35–41.

McIntosh, M. E., & Draper, R. J. (2001). Using learning logs in mathematics: Writing to learn. *Mathematics Teacher, 94,* 554–557.

Miller, L. D., & England, D. A. (1989). Writing to learn algebra. *School Science and Mathematics, 89,* 299–312.

Mitchell, D. (1996, September). Writing to learn across the curriculum and the English teacher. *English Journal, 85,* 93–97.

Paris, S. G., Cross, D. R., & Lipson, M. Y. (1984). Informed strategies for learning: A program to improve children's reading awareness and comprehension. *Journal of Educational Psychology, 76,* 1239–1252.

Santa, C., & Havens, L. (1995). *Creating independence through student-owned strategies: Project CRISS.* Dubuque, IA: Kendall-Hunt.

Sternberg, R. J., & Williams, W. M. (2002). *Educational psychology.* Boston: Allyn & Bacon.

Chapter 9

Reciprocal Teaching: Giving Responsibility to Students

DOUGLAS FISHER, NANCY FREY, AND TOM FEHRENBACHER

"What's going to happen next?" Tenth-grade world history students consider their teacher, Mr. Arco's question about Nazi Germany and WWII. "Do you think the Nazis are going to stop after their invasions of Austria and Czechoslovakia?"

"It's not likely. The Nazis aren't going to stop," Kelly responds eagerly.

"Will they start to use violence?" As Kelly considers his question, Mr. Arco starts to wind down the shared reading portion of the lesson. "I think Kelly is right. The Nazis have a very aggressive attitude. But we will have to read more to find out just what happens."

Through the questions he has already asked in shared reading, Mr. Arco models the process of reciprocal teaching the students will soon be using in groups.

"At this point, I'd like to continue with our reading using a fish bowl group. Could I get some volunteers?" By asking a group of students to model the procedure in front of their peers, Mr. Arco takes the next step in his "gradual release of responsibility."

Several of Mr. Arco's more vocal students raise their hands and take seats in the front of the room. Geoffrey is appointed by Mr. Arco as the teacher leader. Serina, Sophiny, and Roberto join him in the middle of the room. Mr. Arco refers Geoffrey and the class to four questions he has posted on the board:

1. What was that about?

2. What don't you understand?

3. How can you summarize this?

4. What is going to happen next?

While the rest of the class listens, Geoffrey is asked to start the process. He begins by asking Serina to read a passage regarding the nonaggression pact signed between the Soviet Union and Germany.

Following the outline on the board, Geoffrey then asks another student in the group, "Sorphiny, what was that about?"

"Something about how they signed a nonaggression pact or something like that."

"What don't you understand, Serina?" Geoffrey continues with the process.

"I didn't understand why the governments, the Soviet and German governments, signed the Molotov-Rarimtoff (sic) nonaggression pact."

"Okay. . . ." Geoffrey responds, "let's go ahead and take down a summary bullet."

"Something about how they signed a nonaggression pact?" Sorphiny wonders aloud.

"Let me ask you guys a question," Geoffrey continues. "Why did Germany sign the nonaggression pact, if they were just going to break it anyway?" He pauses. "I think I know the answer."

"Why?" asks Sorphiny.

"Because that puts the other countries thinking that Germany is not going to do any damage."

The fourth student, Roberto, enters the conversation, "Also, I kind of think that Germany didn't care about breaking the pact because they knew they weren't going to be a part of the League of Nations or anything anyway, so why not break it. Germany would just use the pact to get the trust of the other countries and then break it."

"Okay." Geoffrey says.

Before he can continue, Serina adds, "I also think the pact was signed because Germany knew that they were an aggressive country and that they weren't going to be a part of a peaceful, unified, you know, ahh, company such as the United Nations."

"What is our bullet going to be, again?" Geoffrey asks, bringing the group back to the task.

"Okay," Serina continues, "the bullet should be that the pact was signed by the German government as a plan to divide up Eastern Europe so that after they decided not to be a peaceful country that they would already have Europe because it was already divided. They would be taking advantage of what they already had, not because they wanted to be a peaceful country."

"Do you agree?" Geoffrey asks the others.

"Yeah," says Sorphiny.

"I know but we have to find a way to paraphrase it," Geoffrey continues.

"Why don't we say that Germany planned to break the nonaggression pact," Roberto adds.

"Good that's our bullet. Write it down." Geoffrey says. Mr. Arco concurs with the group and asks that the entire class write down the fish bowl group's bullet. To continue the process, Geoffrey asks Roberto, "What is going to happen next?"

"War."

"Are they going to invade Poland or anything?" Geoffrey wonders out loud.

"Oh yeah, they are going to do that."

"Okay, so let's go on. Sorphiny can you read next?"

Mr. Arco allows the fish bowl group to continue through another cycle of reciprocal teaching, reminding the class to write down the group's next bullet. Upon completion, he calls for questions about the reciprocal teaching process from the class. "Does everyone understand how a reciprocal teaching group operates?"

"What if we understand everything in the paragraph?" Aneth asks.

"That is not likely to happen. Consider vocabulary words. Ask yourself what the author might not be telling you. There is usually always something to ask or wonder about." Mr. Arco responds.

"What if we can't agree on the bullet or something?" another asks.

"That is why you have a leader. It is up to her or him to settle the disputes and keep the group moving." Mr. Arco answers a few more questions, then decides to move on. "Let's give the process a try. I will come around the room and help those of you who might have more questions. Let's get into groups of four. Today you may pick your own leader." By moving into groups and starting the process outlined on the board (see Figure 9.1), Mr. Arco's students take their first step into the exciting world of reciprocal teaching.

As Mr. Arco moves from group to group, he not only provides assistance, he learns more about his student's understanding of the material. Already from the fish bowl group, Mr. Arco knows he will need to address Germany's position regarding the League of Nations. As the United Nations did not form until after WWII, Mr. Arco will have to address the misunderstanding discussed in the fish bowl. Other teaching points will arise, as Mr. Arco listens and assists the students now earnestly engaged in reading the text and discussing it.

In the scenario described above, Mr. Arco took several steps to implement reciprocal teaching. The first step entailed a shared reading in which the teacher used reciprocal teaching questions to model the process with the entire class. A discussion then ensued with a fish bowl of students observed by the rest of the class. Finally, the students moved into groups to practice the activity and the teacher assisted and monitored the process.

> Shared reading is the instructional practice of reading a text passage with students who have access to it on an overhead or with individual copies. The teacher uses the shared reading to model comprehension strategies, discuss text structure, or highlight content.

Reciprocal Teaching: Comprehension at Work

What Does the Research Say About Reciprocal Teaching?

If teachers wish to move instruction from delivery to discovery, reciprocal teaching is an essential strategy to consider. As an approach that allows students to directly assist with the discovery of material and the subsequent construction of meaning, the strategy is ideally suited for the classroom intent on putting learning in the hands of the learner (e.g., Little & Richards, 2000). As an engaging, student-centered process, reciprocal teaching appeals to students. In addition, as a captivating strategy, reciprocal teaching is an important (and highly effective) strategy for students who are at risk in the traditional classroom either through disaffection or even oppositional attitudes to direct instruction (e.g., Carter, 1997; Palincsar & Herrenkohl, 2002). In fact, a review of 16 studies on reciprocal teaching suggests that this strategy increases standardized test scores for all students (Rosenshine & Meister, 1994). Reciprocal teaching has also been an effective strategy to students who struggle to read (Alfassi, 1998). Finally, reciprocal teaching is a powerful strategy to consider in the multi-cultural classrooms, as diverse viewpoints are considered and made part of the discovery of the text (e.g., King & Parent Johnson, 1999; Palincsar & Herrenkohl, 2002).

Defining Reciprocal Teaching

What exactly is reciprocal teaching and why is it so effective? Reciprocal teaching can be defined as a strategy in which students use *prediction, questioning, clarifying*, and *summarization* to help each other in the understanding of a text (Palincsar & Brown, 1984). While there are many variations of reciprocal teaching, each is centered upon these four comprehension skills requiring students to monitor their progress as they read the text. Fluent readers use these same behaviors to support their comprehension. Many believe that the effectiveness of reciprocal teaching

Figure 9.1   Class Guidelines for Reciprocal Teaching Groups

Prediction

We look and listen for clues that will tell us what may happen next or what we will learn from the text.

Good predictions are based on. . .

* what we already know

* what we understand from the text

* what pictures, charts, or graphs tell us

I think. . .

I predict. . .

I bet. . .

I wonder. . .

Question

We test ourselves about what we just read by asking ourselves questions.

We see if we really understand and can identify what is important.

We ask different kinds of questions:

* Factual questions:

   Who, what, when, where?

* Interpretive questions:

   How, why?

* Beyond the text questions:

   I wonder if. . .

   I'm curious about. . .

Clarify

We clear up confusion and find the meaning of unfamiliar words, sentences, ideas, or concepts.

This is confusing to me. . .

I need to reread, slow down, look at the graphs or illustrations, or break the word apart.

When I began reading this, I thought. . .

Then, when I read this part, I realized. . .

It didn't make sense until I. . .

Summarize

We restate the main ideas, events, or points.

A good summary includes. . .

* key people, items, or places

* key words and synonyms

* key ideas and concepts

The main point is. . .

If I put the ideas together, I now understand that. . .

The most important thing I read was. . .

comes from the metacognition required of the reader. "Without good metacognitive abilities, readers have little facility to understand what they read simply because, for them, the process of constructing meaning will not take place" (Carter, 1997, p. 65).

Each of the four components of reciprocal teaching is based on current knowledge of comprehension instruction (e.g., Flood, Lapp, & Fisher, 2003; Harvey & Goudvis, 2000; Keene & Zimmermann, 1997). When students *predict*, they use their background (or prior) knowledge and make an educated guess about the text and its resolution. In addition, predicting provides students with a purpose for reading the text as well as a motivator (to see if their predictions are correct). Harvey and Goudvis (2000) provide students with a prediction form that allows them to record their predictions and then determine if those predictions were correct or not.

The second phase of reciprocal teaching, *questioning*, ensures that students are focusing on the main ideas of the text. "This, in essence, is a time for students to test what the other students know about the reading" (Little & Richards, 2000, p. 191). In other words, students use their skills in determining main ideas and form those ideas into questions. Students are encouraged to vary the types of questions they ask and not limit their questioning to literal information. A side benefit of the questioning phase of reciprocal teaching is that students learn the difference between questions that provide them access to information and those that do not. As Keene and Zimmerman (1997) note, "proficient readers use questions to focus their attention on important components of the text; they understand that they can pose questions critically" (p. 119).

Once students have used their prediction and questioning skills, they are encouraged to *clarify* their understanding of the text with their peers. Clarifying encourages students to monitor their own comprehension–a strategy that good readers use regularly (Flood, Lapp, & Fisher, 2003). In addition, clarifying allows students to ask all kinds of questions about things they may not have understood including vocabulary words, references to unknown events, or connections the text has to other texts or the world (Harvey & Goudvis, 2000).

Finally, students are asked to *summarize* the information they have just read and talked about. This final phase is based on the idea that comprehension is increased when readings are discussed and written about (e.g., Daniels, 1994; Palincsar, 1987). Teachers (and group members) also use summarization to assess comprehension. Teachers often ask themselves, "Did the group get the main idea of the reading passage?" Group members often ask each other to share key points and then discuss those points until they can form a summary in their own words.

Implementing Reciprocal Teaching

While we have presented reciprocal teaching as a linear process, it is much more dynamic in practice. Students who understand the ground rules for reciprocal teaching will vary the process to fit the text and the group members' needs. As with other classroom structures, students will need practice in working in reciprocal teaching groups. Teachers may want to introduce reciprocal teaching slowly, one component at a time, or as Mr. Fehrenbacher does (see social studies below), introduce reciprocal teaching using a "fish bowl." It should also be noted that reciprocal teaching is cyclical. Once students have summarized a section of the text, they can use those summaries to predict information about the next section, and so on. Having said that, let's look inside a few classrooms and learn about the various ways that reciprocal teaching is used across content areas.

Students can use these skills individually and in concert during many aspects of the academic day.

This is a good opportunity to teach about questioning, such as with Question the Author. See chapter 4 for more information on student questioning.

A fish bowl is a modeling technique using students as participants. A small group of students are invited to the front of the room while the teacher guides their discussion and simultaneously instructs the rest of the class on the process being observed.

Strategies at Work

Reciprocal Teaching in the English Classroom

Groups of four students band together across Lisa Douglas' American literature class-room. Each student in the group has a role to play. Brightly colored cards of different hues sit on desks, each indicating a distinct role for their student owners. Today, Audrey will be the predictor, José the questioner, Beth the clarifier, and Ben the summarizer. Before Mrs. Douglas has finished moving through the room, Audrey starts her group.

"Do you guys remember where we were?"

"Look at the wall, Audrey. We've already summarized three parts." Beth refers the group leader to the wall behind her where the class has posted summaries from yesterday.

"Yeah. Okay. So we are here on page six. Right? So, Ben, could you please read for us?"

Ben reads a passage from *The Yellow Wallpaper* by Charlotte Perkins Gilman (1989). The short story tells of a woman in the late 1800's who has a mental illness and becomes more obsessed each day with her bedroom wallpaper.

As Ben concludes his passage, Audrey quickly inserts her opening remark, "Boy, I feel so sorry for that woman. No one seems to be able to help her. I predict that she is going to get worse and worse. They may even have to move her away somewhere to a hospital or mental person's home."

"No. I think she is going to get better. All she has to do is get rid of that ugly wallpaper."

"You've gotta be kidding, José. No way. I agree with Audrey."

"Me, too. Except maybe she will attack her husband or do some other crazy thing before they take her away." Each of the group members contributes a prediction to the discussion. Audrey moves her group along.

"Okay. I'm the predictor, so I want you to write my prediction down."

"And, that is?" remarks Ben.

"She is going to get worse." Audrey states with authority. She continues, "Lets see, José you are the questioner. So what question do you have?"

"What's her problem? I mean is she suffering from depression or what?"

The discussion continues around different questions posed by the group members. In the end, José determines the question to be used. The group work in Mrs. Douglas' room continues through the next step of reciprocal teaching, clarification, in much same way as predicting and questioning steps were accomplished. However, when her students reach the summarizing stage, each is asked to write a summary sentence that is shortened several times when the students pass their statements around the group. Then, the shortened versions are discussed and compared; a final product is produced using the best from all the versions. After this final summary is written down, students rotate their role-indicator card. Each group member has a new role to play in the reciprocal teaching process, a new passage of text is read, and the cycle continues.

Mrs. Douglas uses assigned roles when her students are learning about the reciprocal teaching process. As they become more proficient, the student roles will expand to facilitate the assigned component rather than serve as the sole individual responsible. For example, the student assigned to questioning will not have to contribute all the questions, but will facilitate a discussion in which questions are generated.

Students' roles change regularly, either daily or with the introduction of a new text.

This is especially useful as students are often required to write summaries for standardized tests.

Implementation Tips for the English Classroom

Based on the experiences in Mrs. Douglas' class and other English teachers, here are some recommendations for using reciprocal teaching in the secondary English classroom:

1. Divide the reading selection into logical parts.

2. Group the class heterogeneously (mixed ability) and distribute role-indicator cards.

3. Read a section aloud to the groups, and model each of the following four steps to the class:

- *Predict:* Based on what happened in this section, what are your predictions for the next section?

- *Question:* What questions do you have? Consider questions that have answers "right there" in the text, questions that require "thinking and searching" or that require your "opinion" to answer.

- *Clarify:* What words, ideas, or parts of the text are unclear to you?

- *Summarize:* Implement a process to arrive at a clear and concise summary. For example, each group member could write his or her own summary. These could then be passed around and shortened several times. The shortened versions could be shared or recorded in journals.

These are examples of Question-Answer Relationships. To read more about QAR, see chapter 4.

4. Distribute language charts for students to record their conversations. (To include more response sections the pattern may be repeated) (see Figure 9.2).

5. Allow each group to determine a leader to guide students through the four steps outlined above. Indicate to students that while it is the leader's responsibility to keep the students on task, it is the role-indicator cardholder's final determination regarding their section's notation in the R.T. Language Chart.

6. Enrichments and Assessment: Each group of students can create a visual storyboard or performance depicting critical points from the text. These can enhance traditional assessments.

Reciprocal Teaching in the Mathematics Classroom

Mr. Todd Kupras' students are on their hands and knees. Yardsticks clap down the sides of the algebra classroom. Groups of students huddle together over graph paper strewn across the floor of their trapezoid-shaped classroom. Today, students are assigned the task of measuring the classroom and calculating the cost of new carpet.

"How many of these little graph squares equals a foot?" demands Nakita.

"One square. One foot." David has answered the question before.

"How many feet long did you think this wall was going to be?"

"A lot more than 26 feet," admits David.

Working in groups of three or four, Mr. Kupras' students are completing the first of a four-step mathematics inquiry project. At each step, they use reciprocal teaching to help arrive at their solution. Of course they also refer to mathematics formulas and their textbook. Finishing with their first step of putting the room's layout on paper, the students are ready to start the next.

Predictions keep students engaged in the lesson and focused on the task at hand.

"So, we are supposed to come up with a possible answer first." Nakita is anxious to move on with the project.

"Well, the room looks like it's got a lot of square feet," Saram joins the discussion.

"And, what's a lot?"

Figure 9.2 Language Chart of English Class Reciprocal Teaching

Reading: _____ Section #: _____ Date: _____

Prediction:

_____

Question:

_____

Clarification:

_____

Summary Statement:

_____

Was the prediction confirmed: YES   NO

_____

Details:

"I'll say 200," decides Saram.

"You've got to be kidding. This room is bigger than that." Nakita argues.

"Okay, 400."

"Try doubling that. I bet it's 800 square feet," informs David.

The debate continues, as each member of the group makes or adjusts his or her estimate. Upon completion, the students continue the process using reciprocal teaching's next question: How do you go about finding an answer to the question?

"How do we find out?" Nakita continues.

"Beats me." Saram waits for the others to help.

"Are you so sure? What was Mr. Kupras talking about? We gotta find squares and triangles on our grid paper."

"Then what?" Saram continues his challenge.

"Are you saying you forgot already? Then we use the area formula to figure out the square foot of the shape," concludes David.

The group continues their discussion using Mr. Kupras' reciprocal teaching questions as their guide. Before moving to the next step of the process, they will arrive at an answer to the room's square footage and clarify that answer by rechecking their calculations or by formulating the problem in a different way to arrive at the same answer. In this algebra classroom, Mr. Kupras uses reciprocal teaching to frame the means to the problem's solution, gather information, complete computations and to share out the entire process through a presentation.

Implementation Tips for the Mathematics Classroom

Based on the experiences in Mr. Kupras' class and those of other mathematics teachers, here are some recommendations for using reciprocal teaching in the secondary mathematics classroom:

1. Review and discuss with students all mathematical principles, concepts, and formulas to be used in arriving at the solution to the problem.

2. The solution to the problem should require application of several sequential mathematical operations. The problem should be authentic and of importance to your students.

3. Place students into heterogeneous groups and share the Mathematical Inquiry Process (see Figure 9.3).

4. Manage by walking around the classroom; answer student questions and provide individual and small group instruction as needed.

5. Provide a forum for groups to share their answers and the ways in which they arrived at their answers. Groups not presenting should take notes and add them to their findings.

Reciprocal Teaching in the Social Studies Classroom

"Do police stop some people more often than others? Does a person's racial identity, clothes, gender, or age make him or her more likely to be questioned by police?" U.S. history students in Mr. Fehrenbacher's class begin to share the answers they have written to the question posted on the board.

"Of course they do. You can get in trouble just for 'driving while black.'" Melissa responds. The class laughs.

"So, you believe that African Americans get stopped by the police more often than others do." Mr. Fehrenbacher rephrases Melissa's remark, while posing another. "Is that the only group?"

"No. So do Mexican kids."

"Asians, too."

"So we can say that different ethnic and racial groups can be profiled. Is that right? Do clothes make a difference? Does the person's age or gender matter?" Mr. Fehrenbacher continues.

"Sure. If you're young they're going to pick on you."

In addition to popular culture, current events can illuminate the connections between events of the past and today's news.

Problem Framing: Deciding on the steps to be taken

- Prediction: What would be a reasonable answer to the problem?

- Question: What is being asked and how might you go about finding out the answer? (Please Note: If students are to demonstrate the practical ability to solve mathematical problems, the cultivation of such inquiry is essential. However, the development and employment of appropriate steps is required for the successful completion of this activity. Should groups of students not arrive at the correct strategy, please assist as necessary.)

Data Collection: Gathering information to use

- Prediction: What would be a reasonable answer to this step? What might the collection of data look like after you are done?

- Question: What is being asked in this first step? How do you go about finding the answer at this point?

- Summary: Have you recorded or charted the data?

- Clarification: Is your data correct? How can you check your data? What results do you get when you checked or repeated the process?

Mathematical Applications: Applying mathematics to the data

- Prediction: What would be a reasonable answer to the application of this formula?

- Question: What are the steps of the formula or application? How do you go about its application?

- Summary: What answers do your calculations provide?

- Clarification: How do you know your answer is right? What answer do you get upon checking or using another method? (Please note: The mathematical applications part of this process may take several consecutive operations. Students may wish to refer to their textbooks, handouts, and other written materials to assist in arriving at the solution. Reciprocal teaching questions may be used more than once, during this part of the process.)

Verification of Solution: Reflecting on the process

- Prediction: Was your prediction accurate? How close was your approximation to the actual solution?

- Question: How successful were the steps you took to complete the problem? Did you choose the best ones?

- Summary: Is your answer the correct one?

- Clarification: Have you checked your math? Could the problem be answered a different way? If so, can you arrive at the same solution?

Presentation of Problem's Solution: Sharing with your peers

- Prediction: Before you started any work, what did your group think the answer would be to the problem? Why did you think this answer was a reasonable one?

- Question: What steps did your group take to arrive at the solution to the problem?

- Summary: What answer did you arrive at? How does this answer compare to the predicted answer?

- Clarification: How do you know this answer is the correct one? How did you check your answer? Where you able to find other ways to arrive at the same answer during the process?

"Yah. Just cuz you're young, everyone is always thinking you're trouble." Others in the room join in agreement. Mr. Fehrenbacher brings the class back to a focus. "Is that all?"

"Well, they might pick on guys more."

"Anything else?"

The class pauses; the reasons for police profiling, for the moment, exhausted.

"How about the way you are dressed? Can that make a difference? If you are wearing baggy clothes, got a couple of tattoos, decked out in jewelry, would that attract the police's attention?" Accountable talk around the students' writing continues in the classroom. As it does, Mr. Fehrenbacher moves the lesson closer to the selected text—an editorial taken from the local newspaper entitled "A Case of Racial Profiling."

"Today we are going to look at the case of an MTV rap star who got some serious questioning from our local police. To do this we are going to use reciprocal teaching. I'll start by reading the first paragraph and discussing with you the four reciprocal teaching questions posted on the board. Then, I'd like to get some volunteers to come forward to do the next paragraph as a fish bowl for the class. After that, I'd like the entire class to get into groups to try it on their own."

As Mr. Fehrenbacher reads the first paragraph, the students follow handouts of the text. After finishing the passage, Mr. Fehrenbacher refers to his first reciprocal teaching question, "What's that about?" Students provide their views as Mr. Fehrenbacher guides and confirms. When the shared reading portion is done, four volunteers come to the front of the room. They repeat and model the process before the rest of the class. Soon everyone is placed into a group and leaders are appointed. With everyone reminded of the task ahead, Mr. Fehrenbacher's classroom goes to work.

At the end of the reading, Mr. Fehrenbacher's students write "zinger questions." These questions are based on the reading and are thrown at another group during the whole class discussion. Groups receive points if they can stump another group or the teacher with a question on the reading. Of course Mr. Fehrenbacher has guidelines for the zinger questions that ensure the questions are fair, thought-provoking, and are based on the reading. He also requires that the groups write their question and the answer in advance.

Implementation Tips for the Social Studies Classroom

Based on the experiences in Mr. Fehrenbacher's class and those of other social studies teachers, here are some recommendations for using reciprocal teaching in the secondary social studies classroom:

1. Begin reciprocal teaching with a shared reading. This ensures that students understand the purpose for the reading and know that the teacher cares about the material to be covered.

2. Establish clear group work expectations. Reciprocal teaching is best accomplished in classrooms that regularly practice effective group work. Students should be used to working with a group leader and participating in different roles within their group. Classroom management procedures will need to be in place to move students effectively into their groups, provide ongoing instruction to working groups, to ensure students complete the task, and to check for understanding through report outs or written work after completion of group work time.

Margin notes:

Newspaper articles are a useful source of reciprocal teaching and shared reading texts. As students often have questions that cannot be answered solely through the text, continuing coverage in the following days and weeks sheds new light on the topic. Thus, students are able to witness information that evolves.

Zinger questions increase motivation among groups as they are challenged to go deeper into the text instead of relying on 'right there' queries.

Beginning a reciprocal teaching event with a shared reading provides students with vocabulary and background knowledge for use in the peer group discussions.

3. Provide a model for the type of group work that is to be done. Regular use of a "fish bowl" in which the whole class (and the teacher) observes the group will help ensure that group work is effective and efficient. Fish bowls also allow the teacher to gauge if the text is too difficult or not interesting. If this is the case, the teacher may have to provide additional scaffolding of the text to ensure comprehension.

4. Consistently implement the Reciprocal Teaching cycle. The following steps encapsulate the basic concepts of reciprocal teaching into a simplified process that students can easily accomplish.

- Read.
- What's that about? (Question)
- What don't you understand? (Clarify)
- What is our summary bullet? (Summarize)
- What's going to happen next? (Predict)
- Read.

5. Use "zinger questions" to keep students motivated in their reading. An expectation is that groups write both the question and the answer in advance, before posing it to another group.

Reciprocal Teaching in the Science Classroom

Students huddle around the glow of computers in Dr. Lauren Birney's biology class. In each group, one student appears to be in charge of heated discussions and nervous arguments. In the corner of the room, three girls and two boys call upon their teacher to settle a dispute. In the middle of the room, a young man maintains control of the computer by keeping his hand firmly on the mouse. He works quickly to keep his peers happy by getting their ideas quickly on the screen. Nevertheless, the "computer expert's" efforts are closely monitored by the rest, the slightest misstep quickly criticized. Student PowerPoint® presentations are due tomorrow in Dr. Birney's class. A level of activity and anxiousness rises to meet the deadline.

Peer group cooperative work can translate to skills for mediating disputes outside of the classroom.

"Make sure you include a slide introducing each of the four skills," Dr. Birney turns to repeat loudly enough so that rest of the class overhears her advice to the inquiring corner group.

"Oh, yeah," a couple of group members murmur and poke each other about their need for adjustment. Others groups move ahead confidently; they have already taken care of that detail.

Dr. Lauren Birney and her students are in the last step of an extended project based on reciprocal teaching. Dr. Birney uses reciprocal teaching both as a basis for student group research and as a format for student presentations. Using the content standards in biology as a guide, groups of three or four students consider the relationship between biology and society. Dr. Birney's students select topics about the environment and health, including smoking and disease, the impact of pollution, global climate change, natural resource management, deforestation, or species endangerment.

In their research phase, Dr. Birney's students use reciprocal teaching as a group work strategy in the discovery and comprehension of texts. Using reciprocal teaching's four basic questions, students work together with text from the Internet, their biology textbook, and other classroom materials. The students first summarize their research, provide their classmates with essential questions about the topic, make points of clarification, and predict or make recommendations regarding the future of their topic.

Upon completion of their research, Dr. Birney's students present their findings using a PowerPoint® slide show and an LCD projector. The slide show is divided into four parts based on the reciprocal teaching model: Research Summary, Essential Questions, Points of Clarification and Future Impact. Thus, through the use of reciprocal teaching, the students engage with performance standards such as the need to "discuss and evaluate conclusions regarding personal and societal issues, taking into account principles of biology and related technology to present a report on a current issue."

The Internet provides a renewable source of information for use in classrooms. In science, new discoveries are announced on the Internet long before they appear in textbooks.

Implementation Tips for the Science Classroom

1. Explain to students the concept of reciprocal teaching—that we learn best when we teach.

2. Identify each of the four skills or strategies students will learn in order to help their classmates comprehend and remember what they read. Point out that learning these skills will also help improve their own reading comprehension. The skills include:

- *Summarizing.* Identifying and condensing the most important points in the text.
- *Questioning.* Formulating questions about what you don't know, what you need to know, or what you would like to know concerning the subject.
- *Clarifying.* Making sense of confusing text and potential barriers to comprehension such as new vocabulary terms, unclear referents, or difficult concepts.
- *Predicting.* Using information already given in the text, text structure, graphic aids, and background knowledge.

3. Model for students how to summarize, generate questions, clarify confusing text, and predict. Give students one day of practice for each of these skills.

4. After practice sessions, shift responsibility for the direction of discussion to student leaders working in small groups. Select different student leaders each day to practice each of the skills.

5. With greater proficiency, increase leader and group responsibility by sequencing the skills: summarizing, questioning, clarifying, and predicting. Instruct the leader to direct the group in a discussion using each of the skills in order at appropriate points in the text.

6. Each group is to gather information in each of the four areas. Allow time for students to discuss and select important points for each. Stress to students that their predictions about the research should also serve as a potential solution to the issue. Groups might be asked at this point: Now that you know what you do, what can be done to make things better?

7. Provide instruction about PowerPoint® slide shows. Provide an outline of the upcoming presentation: Summary, Essential Questions, Points of Clarification, Future Impact. Provide time for students to select, organize, and compose their slide show.

Reciprocal Teaching in the Physical Education Class

After Mr. Danny Timothy's students complete warm-up exercises in the courtyard, they clamor inside to take seats on the gym floor. As they do so, they are divided into six groups and provided a handout on the rules of volleyball.

Jigsawing is a student-directed learning activity for reading longer texts. Students work in small groups to read and discuss a smaller passage, then meet with a second small group composed of members who have read each of the other passages. The new group teaches and learns about the overall content of the reading from one another.

"Notice that you have been placed into six groups." As the students look around, Mr. Timothy continues, "the text on volleyball has also been divided into six sections. I am going to ask each group to read and discuss a different section of the text." Mr. Timothy uses a jigsaw procedure to provide each group with a section of the reading. While they may read the entire article later, at this point, they are only responsible for their assigned section.

Mr. Timothy numbers each group and refers them to their assigned section. Moving across the gym floor, he helps a few groups get started and assists others with questions as they arise. A purposeful murmur settles across the room as the students complete their assigned reading. He provides groups time to discuss their section of the reading before continuing. After several minutes, he asks, "Do any groups need more time?"

"No," most of the students respond.

"Then let's move on. While you were reading, I gave everyone a number. If you look at the gym walls I've placed some pieces of paper with different numbers written on them. Find the number you have been given on the wall and go over to that number."

Noise and clamor replace the calm of the room as students depart to find their new places in the gym. Mr. Timothy quickly calls his students back to order, making his next assignment in the jigsaw. "Everyone have a seat in a circle in your new group. We are going to call these groups your home number group. Now, if everyone will take a look at the volleyball text again. Could I have the people who read the first section raise their hands?"

As the students look around the room, they notice each group has someone who has read the first section. Mr. Timothy asks those who have read the next section to raise their hands. Thus he ensures that each group has at least one person responsible for each section of the volleyball text.

"I'd like to ask each of the experts to review with their new group the section they read. Let's start with those that did the first part." An animated conference ensues as students inform their peers about the first part of the reading.

Literal questions are important to grasp the details of a reading, while inferential questions encourage a deeper understanding of the nuances in the text. Remember to ask a variety of questions each time.

"The reciprocal teaching process will help us in our next step," Mr. Timothy states as he distributes handouts to the class. "You will notice that these questions ask you to define or clarify vocabulary words. Other questions ask that you summarize each of the sections together. I have included a few "right there" questions that can be answered by referring back to the text. There are also a few questions that ask you to apply or predict how these rules will be used when we play our first volleyball game. If the question has to do with your section, you are most likely to be the one with the answer. It will be your job to help your group members."

Sprawled over their texts and handouts, students work together to complete their work. They know that soon Mr. Timothy will ask them to share their answers. They also know that they will soon apply their knowledge of the rules on the volleyball court.

Implementation Tips for the Physical Education Class

1. Divide students into heterogeneous groups. Provide each group with a different section of a selected text. Appropriate texts for this exercise might include the rules for games, exercise guidelines, physical fitness charts, or dietary plans.

2. Allow students in each group time to read and discuss their assigned section. You may wish to provide students with a discussion guide or questions about key points of the section.

3. Arrange jigsaw groups. This can be easily accomplished by giving students in each group a different number (make sure there are as many numbers as there are reading sections).

4. Ask students to go to separate locations, posted with numbers, in your gym, field, or physical activities area.

5. Call upon students to raise their hands to identify their assigned text section to their new group. This will identify the students responsible for each section to their group.

6. Distribute handouts for completion. These handouts should be based upon the key components of reciprocal teaching (clarifier, summarizer, questioner, and predictor) and include:

- vocabulary clarifying questions,
- questions based upon each section of the text,
- questions that are essential to understanding, and
- questions that ask students to apply or predict how the text will be used in the game or other physical fitness activity.

7. Ensure that each student is responsible for teaching or helping the other group members with the section assigned to him or her. You may wish to do this by indicating the section number of the reading before each question.

8. Complete this exercise by having students return to their original groups (initial text expert groups) to review and correct answers to their section's questions. Sharing their answers with the whole class will serve as a check for understanding for the entire class.

9. In physical education, a natural application of this activity results when the students practice the physical activity, keep logs or journals of their diet, or play the game for which the text was intended. Discussion and reflections may refer back to the text, worksheets, or reciprocal teaching discussions.

Conclusion

Reciprocal teaching is an instructional strategy used to ensure that students comprehend texts. Reciprocal teaching provides teachers with a planned way for students to assume responsibility for their learning and the learning of their peers. Again, students will require time to practice this approach and teachers will need time to implement this classroom structure. This strategy reflects the metacognitive strategies used by fluent readers. Ultimately, reciprocal teaching will become fluid and dynamic. The specific order to the four components will vary based on students' interests, the selected text, the students' background knowledge, and who is in the group at any given time.

Having said that, we would like to reinforce the use of this instructional strategy. Reciprocal teaching draws on the comprehension research of good readers, it allows students authentic opportunities to use their vocabulary, it provides students experience with questions, and graphic organizers can be implemented within the instructional frame.

References

Alfassi, M. (1998). Reading for meaning: The efficacy of reciprocal teaching in fostering reading comprehension in high school students in remedial reading classes. *American Educational Research Journal, 35*, 309–332.

Carter, C. J. (1997). Why reciprocal teaching? *Educational Leadership, 54*(6), 64–68.

Daniels, H. (1994). *Literature circles: Voice and choice in the student-centered classroom*. York, ME: Stenhouse.

Flood, J., Lapp, D., & Fisher, D. (2003). Reading comprehension instruction. In J. Flood, D. Lapp, J. Jensen, & J. Squire (Eds.), *Handbook of research on teaching the English language arts* (2nd ed.) (pp. 931–941). Mahwah, NJ: Lawrence Erlbaum.

Gilman, C. P. (1989). *The yellow wallpaper*. New York: Bantam.

Harvey, S., & Goudvis, A. (2000). *Strategies that work: Teaching comprehension to enhance understanding.* York, ME: Stenhouse.

Keene, E. O., & Zimmermann, S. (1997). *Mosaic of thought: Teaching comprehension in a reader's workshop*. Portsmouth, NH: Heinemann.

King, C. M., & Parent Johnson, L. M. (1999). Constructing meaning via reciprocal teaching. *Reading Research and Instruction, 38*, 169–186.

Little, Q., & Richards, R. T. (2000). Teaching learners–learners teaching: Using reciprocal teaching to improve comprehension strategies in challenged readers. *Reading Improvement, 37*, 190–194.

Palincsar, A. S. (1987). Reciprocal teaching: Can student discussion boost comprehension? *Instructor, 96*(5), 56–58, 60.

Palincsar, A. S., & Brown, A. L. (1984). Reciprocal teaching of comprehension-fostering and comprehension-monitoring activities. *Cognition and Instruction, 1*, 117–175.

Palincsar, A. S., & Herrenkohl, L. R. (2002). Designing collaborative learning contexts. *Theory Into Practice, 41*(1), 26–32.

Rosenshine, B., & Meister, C. (1994). Reciprocal teaching: A review of the research. *Review of Educational Research, 64*, 479–530.

Chapter 10

...And in the Center Ring, High-Stakes Tests

DOUGLAS FISHER, NANCY FREY, AND TOM FEHRENBACHER

How will you know if your students have learned anything? How will you know if your students can use the strategies you have taught them? How will you know if the students in the classes you teach do well compared with other students in the state? Naturally, you will assess them. We are reminded that assessment is that which distinguishes between teaching and learning, because it is the teacher's way of ascertaining whether learning has taken place. Of course there are many types of assessments. Table 10.1 provides an overview of the various types of assessments that teachers use. As you can see, some of these assessments are more formal than others. Some of them are used to inform the teacher and his or her instruction while others are used for accountability purposes at the local, state, or national level. Students can be assessed for a variety of reasons, including:

The Eisenhower Clearinghouse has a large collection of classroom-based assessments that can be viewed at *www.enc.org/topics/assessment*

- diagnosing individual student needs (e.g., assessing developmental status, monitoring and communicating student progress, certifying competency, determining needs);
- informing instruction (e.g., evaluating instruction, modifying instructional strategies, identifying instructional needs);
- evaluation programs; and
- providing accountability information. (Lapp, Fisher, Flood, & Cabello, 2001, p. 7)

Standards and Assessment

Legislative Support for Testing

Educational reform over the past decade has focused on this fourth point–standards, assessments, and accountability. In 1994, the standards and assessment movement received significant and tangible support through the *Goals 2000: Educate America Act.* This Federal Act provided fiscal resources and other incentives

Table 10.1   **Guide to Formal and Informal Assessments.**

Formal Assessments

Type of Test	Purpose	Administration
Standardized	Yields a student's academic performance ranking compared to a normed sample of students	• Schedule determined by state and local agencies; often yearly. • Tests are usually timed and have strict protocols.
Criterion-Referenced	Measures a student's performance compared to a set of academic skills or objectives. Scores are reported as the proportion of correct answers.	• Tests may be untimed or timed. • May be administered annually or more frequently.

Informal Assessments

Type	Purpose	Administration
Observation	Gathers information about a student's academic, behavioral or social skills used in an authentic setting	Teacher records observational data in anecdotal notes, journals or daily logs.
Portfolio	Provides evidence of a student's academic growth through the collection of work samples	Student and teacher select representative samples of student work for display in a binder or other organizer.
Inventory	Documents student use of specified skills during a single observation	A commercially or teacher-produced form of observable behaviors is completed by the teacher.
Conference	Involves the student in direct feedback to the teacher in a one-to-one discussion	Often scheduled by teacher at regular intervals to gauge progress on more complex academic behaviors such as reading comprehension
Self-Assessment	Allows student to engage in reflective learning	Students assess their own academic performance using an age-appropriate checklist of indicators.
Survey	Collects student feedback about their interests, prior knowledge, or motivation about a topic	Student completes a commercially or teacher-produced survey of items.

You can find important information about your state education system at your state's department of education web site.

for the development of standards and assessments across the nation. At this point, every state in the nation except Iowa has state approved content standards.

Another Goals 2000 expectation has received increased attention recently. The development of assessments or tests that are aligned to the approved state standards will soon be in place across the nation. These assessments are supposed to help educators, parents, and community members understand student performance and hold schools accountable for this performance. To ensure that schools are moving in the desired direction, "valid, nondiscriminatory and reliable state assessments that are aligned to State standards, involve multiple measure of student performance and include all students, must be developed" [Goals 2000 Sec. 306 (c) (1) (B)].

Once standards were aligned with assessments, the third element of educational reform, accountability, could then take place. Accountability measures are commonly seen as standardized testing results, but may also include school satisfaction measures, graduation and grade retention rates, and attendance. In January of 2002, another Federal Act, *No Child Left Behind,* was signed into law. Seen as one of the most sweeping reforms of K–12 education in decades, the act proposes stronger accountability for student performance results. Districts and schools that fail to make adequate achievements in student performance will be subject to sanctions, corrective actions, and restructuring measures. Schools that meet or exceed their goals will be eligible for awards and financial incentives. Thus, teachers today must not only use strategies that help their students understand the content, they must also provide students with information about testing and assessment systems.

Accountability is a term used to refer to a broad range of goals and measures of those goals.

Financial rewards and sanctions are often described as the "carrot and stick" approach to school reform.

Concerns About Testing

This approach to school reform through high-stakes accountability is not without its critics. Numerous educators have expressed dismay at the efficacy of achieving higher levels of student achievement through these means (Meier, Kozol, & Cohen, 2000; Ohanian, 1999). Alfie Kohn, a psychologist long involved with issues of education, has criticized the emphasis on accountability measures as a method that is ineffective for promoting reform and harmful to students and teachers whose anxiety about test results may actually impede performance (Kohn, 2000). These controversies are likely to remain throughout the next decade, and, as educators, we believe it is important to consider opposing viewpoints on matters of such importance. But we are also cognizant of the present realities faced by today's teachers. Students will be tested; teachers and schools will be evaluated according to student performance on these tests. Therefore, the remainder of this chapter will provide guidance for ensuring that students perform well on these accountability measures.

Addressing High-Stakes Tests

At this point in time standardized tests, with significant rewards or consequences attached to them, are a part of the educational landscape. With the arrival of these high-stakes tests, teachers and schools are called upon to immediately improve student performance. To address the newly arriving expectations, several steps can be taken both in the short- and long-term. First and foremost, students must be motivated to do well on assessments. Consider the following scenario:

For more information on motivating students, see Harry K. Wong's (1992) *The first days of school.*

In the spring, two months before statewide testing, principal Doug Williams and librarian Dennis Donley schedule time to speak to every 9th through 11th grader concerning the upcoming state assessments and each student's most recent testing results. The ripple effect of these brief but positive conversations spreads across campus.

The principal and a 10th-grade student huddle next to each other on folding chairs in the hallway outside of room 1205, heads together, eyes on a sheet of computer printouts. Doug Williams points out indications of academic strength that come as a surprise to this young man.

"You must like math, your scores are high."

"Ah, no, I don't like math class much."

"That surprises me, you have real strength in that area."

"I do?"

"Yeah, your grades in math must be high."

"Well, no, not really, I just get 'C's, mostly."

"But, look at your scores. You could get 'A's."

"Hmm, well, yeah, maybe I can."

Mr. Williams catches the student's eye and, as they both exchange a thoughtful glance, expectations are raised.

Another day, sitting in a slice of sunlight between a row of bungalows, Mr. Williams meets with an English language learner and ends their conference by talking about the five minutes of test prep practice that begins each class period.

"Now, the day of the test, remember that when you see a reading comprehension passage, the first. . . "

"Yeah, the first thing I do is read the questions, so I can get a good idea about what to pay attention to when I read."

"Right! So, what else do you know a good test taker does?"

"Well, as soon as the time begins, I want to look quickly at all the pages so that I know what I have to do, and then I can choose the easy ones first. But I have to be careful, because if I skip and mark the wrong number. . . "

They regard each other with knowing smiles and growing confidence while she tells her principal what she knows, and he listens, nodding his head in silent affirmation.

The principal takes these student conversations a step further. At staff meetings, he relates what he's learned from students and uses it as a natural springboard for discussion and reflection across content areas. He asks teachers if they are surprised that a student, one who scores high on a standardized test, is just passing that class with a "C" and doesn't even realize he has strength in that academic area. He tells us how students are finishing his statements on test-taking tips.

Don't forget to include testing information in parent involvement activities. Family Nights, open house, and newsletters can be used to increase awareness of high-stakes testing and its ramifications.

As this scenario illustrates, the student's own perception, attitude, and positive disposition toward the test is essential. If students are to succeed on these assessments, they must view them as worthwhile, important, and achievable. To bring such a positive outlook about, it is essential that all school community members, especially the faculty, see the test as worthwhile, important and achievable. Should the teachers discount, disparage, or exhibit significant anxiety over the tests, the impact upon student performance will be quite negative. Such teachers have, in effect, told students these tests are not important or that success with such tests is not possible. Given such an outlook by the teacher, students are not likely to put forward any significant effort into test taking, and will instead assume failure before beginning.

To create a positive and successful test-taking climate, the entire school should engage in a long-term campaign that addresses three major areas:

1. test format practice,

2. reading strategies instruction, and

3. student engagement in reading (Guthrie, 2002).

As we look more closely at each of these areas in the remainder of this chapter, we must be careful not to allow the test practice to become the curriculum (Santman, 2002). In other words, we are not advocating that schools "teach to the test." Rather, we believe in teaching to the standards that are tested. When students are well-versed in standards-based content, they are more likely to do well on the test. School is still about creating citizens who can participate in the democracy.

Area #1: Test Format Practice

The worthiness of test format preparation depends upon how well it is infused into the curriculum, how connected it is to good general learning, and how it connects with effective literacy strategies (e.g., Duke & Ritchart, 1997). It is not enough, and may even be harmful to learning, if teachers simply find test items for their students to practice. Popham (2001) calls this type of practice "item-teaching" and believes that while it may improve student's scores, teachers cannot "infer that students can satisfactorily do other problems of that ilk" (p. 17). In other words, when teachers practice "item-teaching" they are preparing students only for specific test questions; little hope is provided that the learner has any fundamental understanding or can apply the concept to other areas.

Have you ever crammed for a test? How much did you remember six months later?

Popham suggests that teachers instead be involved in "curriculum-teaching," whereby they focus upon specific content or skills that will later be tested, or as he states, "test-represented." According to Popham, curriculum-teaching "will elevate students' scores on high stakes tests and, more importantly, will elevate students' mastery of the knowledge or skills on which the test items are based" (2001, p. 17).

Langer (2001) makes a similar point in her study of characteristics of literacy instruction in "beating the odds" schools. Langer identifies two quite different approaches to test preparation commonly practiced by teachers: separated or integrated. Test preparation can be either treated as a separate approach involving test practice and test hints or it can be directly integrated into the regular curriculum.

Schools that out-perform their demographic counterparts often use integrated test preparation. In an integrated approach, teachers spend time "carefully analyzing test demands and reformulating curriculum as necessary to be sure that students would, over time, develop the knowledge and skills necessary for accomplished performance" (p. 860). This stands in contrast to Popham's item-teaching approach that is predicated on how well the teacher matches his or her direct teaching to the test questions featured on this year's exam.

In high-performing schools, teachers see tests as an opportunity to "revise and reformulate their literacy curriculum" (Langer, 2001, p. 860). Such teachers provide their students enriched course work by using the tests to go deeper into an understanding of literacy skills, strategies, and content. In the process, test preparation is not seen as an additional activity, but one of many that ensure overall literacy learning (Langer, 2001).

To ensure that test format practice is integrated into the curriculum, we suggest that teachers focus on: attitude, general test-taking skills, direction words, multiple-choice questions, and skills for reading passages. Each of these areas is explored further.

Testing-Taking Attitude.   As we have noted, students' attitudes toward the test may be one of the most important factors for success. We have all seen students use the answer sheet to make designs, clearly not paying attention to the test questions. Students sometimes refer to this as "Christmas treeing" the score sheet because the

Figure 10.1   Classroom Poster

You too could become the next High SCORER!

S – Schedule your time while taking the test.

C – Use Clue words to help answer questions.

O – Omit difficult questions at first.

R – Read questions carefully.

E – Eliminate unreasonable choices.

R – Review your responses.

A mnemonic is a strategy for remembering a string of information, based on the first letter of each word. For example, a mnemonic device for remembering the Great lakes is HOMES: Huron, Ontario, Michigan, Erie, and Superior.

arrangement of bubbles on the scantron can be easily transformed into this holiday symbol. One schoolwide strategy is to use a mnemonic that the students can learn. The "High Scorer" (see Figure 10.1) posters remind students that the test is important and provides them with general information about test taking. These posters should be reviewed on a regular basis across content areas. Additionally, students should be asked to think about the following:

1. Be prepared. Get a good night's sleep the night before test days. Eat a good breakfast on the mornings of test days.
2. Relax. It's normal to feel a little nervous. Some questions will be easy, others hard. Very few people get all of the answers right. Don't worry about information you don't know, just do your best.
3. Think positively. Tell yourself, "I'm going to do the best I can." Then do it.
4. Practice your skills. They really will help you do your best work.

Regarding the aforementioned answer sheet transformations that become works of art for some students: as the test sheets are collected and secured at the end of each test day, those with designs are noted. These budding Picassos are invited to meet with Mr. Williams, the principal, to discuss the importance of test performance for the student.

General Test-Taking Skills.   The following items comprise an overall approach from the start of testing when directions are read and questions can be asked, to the last few minutes of testing—when stray marks can be erased. The points suggest that the test taker begin the test with confidence and curiosity, tackle the questions systematically, and finish the test with diligence and attention to detail. Again, many of these are things that students have not been taught. These skills should be reinforced in each class, especially when students complete teacher created tests throughout the year.

Some students have difficulty with test stamina—the ability to focus in a testing situation for prolonged periods of time.

1. Listen and read along with the teacher as he or she reads the directions to the test. Ask questions if you do not understand.

2. At the start of the test, quickly scan the pages and notice the types and number of questions—what's easy and what's hard. This will help you to make the best use of your time.

3. Budget your time, making sure you allow enough time to answer all of the questions. Pace yourself. Watch the time. If you don't know the answer to a question, move on and come back to it later.

4. Answer the questions you know first. You will have time to read the others more closely the second time you go over the test. When you skip a question, mark your answer sheet so you won't use that space to answer another question. Keep an eye on the answer sheet to be sure you're marking the right space.

5. When you skip a question, be alert for answers or clues in other questions. Answers often pop up in other questions. In addition, as you take the test your background knowledge about the subject will become more active and make it more likely you will be able to figure out the harder questions later.

6. When you get to the end of the test, start over with the first question you skipped. Be sure to erase stray marks when you go back over the test. Complete the answer sheet correctly by filling in the bubbles completely and erasing any other pencil marks.

7. Do not change an answer unless you can prove your first answer is wrong. Your first instinct is usually correct.

8. During the last two minutes of the test, go back and fill in all blank answers with the same letter. If you leave an answer blank, you're guaranteed to get it wrong!

Direction Words. The next important step in developing test format proficiency requires the students' careful consideration of the question or question stem itself. Success on each particular test item is dependent upon the clear understanding of exactly what the question is asking. If students do not take time to consider or do not know what the words mean in the question stem, there is little chance of success. Like the signal words associated with specific text structures these direction words signal the test taker to the task at hand. Extensive practice with these stems as part of the classroom's general pattern of instruction is essential. Teachers must teach students to read the questions carefully and look for important direction words such as:

You'll remember from chapter 1 that teaching about text structures provides students with an important comprehension strategy.

first step is	best answer is	the same as	refers to
the function of	except for	most likely to	a fact
opinion	the purpose of	infer from	

Practice with questions using these stems will allow students to arrive at, and become familiar with, the type of answer each stem is likely to require.

Additionally, there are common terms used on tests that students should understand. The following terms comprise a good start at understanding direction words:

These terms can be incorporated into your vocabulary instruction.

- *Analyze.* Break the subject into parts and discuss the parts.
- *Approximate, estimate.* Make a reasonable guess.
- *Characterize, identify, explain, describe.* Name the characteristics that make something special.
- *Choose the best answer.* Select the answer that is most correct.
- *Examine.* Look carefully at similar answers as one will be a better choice.
- *Chronological order.* Time order.
- *Comment.* Give your opinion and support it with facts and examples.
- *Compare.* Tell how two or more things are similar and how they are different.
- *Contrast.* Tell how two or more things are different.
- *Criticize, evaluate.* Give evidence on each side of an issue, draw a conclusion from the evidence, and make a judgment about the topic.
- *Discuss.* Tell all you can about the topic in the time available.

- *Fill in the blank, complete the sentence.* If a list of possible answers is given, use the best word from the list. If not, use the word you know that best fits the meaning of the sentence.
- *Interpret.* Explain the meaning.
- *Justify.* Furnish evidence to support your answer.
- *Name, list, mention.* List the information that is asked for.
- *Put in your own words.* Rewrite complicated language in everyday English.
- *Rank.* List the information that is asked for in some special order, such as order of occurrence or chronological order.
- *Skim.* Glance through passage quickly, looking for answers to specific questions.
- *State.* Give a short, simple answer. No discussion is necessary.
- *Summarize.* Briefly restate the passage, being sure to include the main points. Leave out small details. Your answer should be shorter than the original passage.
- *Trace.* Give major points in chronological order.

Multiple-Choice Questions.   In addition to specific vocabulary suggestions for the words in the test directions, teachers should also address effective test-taking skills for multiple-choice questions themselves. The following considerations examine the choices the test taker must make between a variety of potential answers to discover which is the correct answer. Making choices between the correct answer and the attractive "distracters" is a matter of both knowledge about the question and knowledge about test taking.

> Distracter items are constructed to fool test takers. They often use words and phrases that appear in the text passage but also contain a phrase that makes the response incorrect.

1. Read all of the choices carefully. The people who write tests know that many people will not read carefully. Even if you are sure you see the right answer, read them all to be sure there is no surprise hiding at the end.

2. Don't get fooled by answers that seem to contain the exact words that appeared in the passage. Read those carefully to see if the context is correct.

3. Most of the time, there will be one or two obviously wrong choices. Ignore these and concentrate on the ones that might be right.

4. If you are sure that two of the answer choices are correct, the correct answer is usually "all of the above." Do not choose this answer unless you are sure that at least two of the choices are correct.

5. Watch for negative words in the instructions such as *no* or *not.* Watch out for trick questions! Some tests use the word "not" to fool you; stop and ask yourself what the question is really asking.

6. Absolute words, such as *none, all, never,* or *always* usually indicate an incorrect choice. Very few things are absolute. Statements with words like *generally, some, often, usually,* or *most often* are more likely to be correct. Please note: Statements must be completely true to count as true. Statements with absolute words are often false.

Test Skills for Reading Passages.   Just as the heart of a successful education is literacy instruction, the heart of successful test performance is reading comprehension. Strategies for effective adolescent reading comprehension have been the focus of this book. When testing is the issue, nothing can substitute for proven and engaging literacy instruction if students are to demonstrate test achievement. More will be said about the important subject of literacy instruction itself as it relates to test taking in the next section of this chapter. Teachers should instruct students to do the following.

1. If the questions are based on a reading passage, read the questions first. Then you will know what to look for as you read. Don't read the choices yet; they will distract you.

2. After you have read the passage, read each question and answer the question in your head before you read the choices. If you know what kind of answer you are looking for, it will be easier to choose the right one.

Remember that these suggestions were not intended to be used six weeks or so before the test is given. The likelihood of successfully boosting achievement scores is diminished because without multiple opportunities to practice these techniques, students must rely on a confusing list of memorized, but not internalized, tips. For example, a student may ask, "Do I read the questions and the answers before the passage, or just the questions?" Instead they should be introduced and modeled starting at the beginning of the school year. Students should be expected to use these strategies throughout the school year on teacher-created tests and practice events. The goal is for students to see these standardized testing events as an extension of what they have done in the classroom throughout the year.

Area #2: Reading Strategies Instruction (for Standardized Tests)

Many of the skills for success on standardized tests are the same skills students need to be literate and already very much the focus of this book. Concerned educators should keep in mind that nothing can substitute for good literacy instruction. Through direct instruction in reading strategies, teachers address the single most influential factor for improving student test performance (Feuer, Holland, Green, Bertenthal, & Hemphill, 1999). Preparing students for high-stakes tests through test format practice can be a highly effective activity, especially for students with little experience or familiarity with such tests. However, if test format practice is conducted for extended periods of time and to the exclusion of other instruction and content, students will score poorly (Guthrie, 2002). If done in isolation, test format practice provides students with few long-term gains. It is not in itself a well-rounded classroom practice.

> Knowing how to answer questions but not knowing the content is ultimately insufficient.

An effective way to avoid the pitfalls of isolated test practice is to heed Langer's (2001) findings about "beating the odds schools." These high-achieving schools chose to emphasize curriculum improvement over separate and distinct test prep. Like Langer, our experience suggests that when secondary schools adopt a set of instructional practices that work well across content areas, test scores increase (Fisher, 2001). When teachers across the campus begin to apply common literacy strategies in order to boost learning in their classroom, they are also employing an integrated approach to curriculum and testing. In other words, students learn to transport a set of strategies to new and novel situations.

Reviewing Various Types of Questions.   In thinking about the test format suggestion, "Read Questions Carefully. . . " we can conclude that a great deal of instruction and practice must occur for students to be successful with this skill. Simply reading or reviewing the test format suggestions may bring about some awareness. However, reviewing is not sufficient. Students must be provided practice, familiarity and application of the suggestions if they are to use them on test days. Student practice with questions about their readings, identifying the type of questions and corresponding answers, and constructing their own questions, will likely improve student test performance. After all, a test is itself a compilation of questions.

> See chapter 4.

Engaging Students.   Anticipatory activities can help students make use of their prior knowledge during test taking. By prereading, students can gather information about the text and quickly identify features that stand out such as charts, pictures and subtitles. Regular use of the KWL process (Ogle, 1986) is particularly helpful because it creates some habits of mind useful for approaching unfamiliar text. We are not advocating that students construct a KWL chart to answer test questions. We are suggesting that these anticipatory activities engage students in the metacognitive experience of assessing what one knows and what one wants to know. It is especially useful for answering timed test questions. Anticipatory activities also keep students focused on the content so that their performance later is enhanced.

See chapter 2.

Building Knowledge and Fluency.   The chapter on read-alouds and shared reading may not seem connected to test taking at first glance, but consider the teaching that takes place during one of these events. During read-alouds or shared readings, a teacher can model the fluent expression signaled by the content and the punctuation. Read-alouds and shared reading can also build background knowledge and provide students with explicit instruction in the self-monitoring that goes on in the mind of a reader. Faced with an unfamiliar piece of text on a standardized test, a student exposed to these teaching events can apply the same strategies to better answer the questions associated with the passage.

See chapter 3.

Focusing Thinking and Recall.   The notetaking and note making chapter can help teachers provide their students with skills to glean and prioritize main ideas quickly from the text. Notetaking enhances students' thinking by developing thought processes that eliminate extraneous details and instead focuses upon essential points. Note making skills are also helpful when taking standardized tests because students learn to glean information quickly from long text passages.

See chapter 5.

Representing Knowledge.   Teaching students various ways to categorize information using graphic organizers can help them understand the graphs and charts that are frequently found on science and social studies tests. Through the use of graphic organizers, students become familiar with different types of text structures. Using graphic organizers will help students complete the test on time.

See chapter 6.

Understanding the Words on the Test.   Comprehensive vocabulary instruction allows teachers to enrich their students' vocabulary, an essential and directly tested component of many standardized tests. Strategies for successful vocabulary instruction include transportable vocabulary skills such as prefixes and suffixes, semantic features of words, and multiple meaning words. Each of these areas of focus, as well as many others in the chapter, will pay dividends on accountability tests.

See chapter 7.

Assessing Content Knowledge.   Writing to learn provides teachers with a way to check for student understanding of content. In addition, writing to learn helps students think about what they learned, how they learn, why the content is important, and what they still don't know. Regular writing to learn activities also provide students practice in analyzing the tests and the questions on the test for their underlying query.

See chapter 8.

Comprehension Strategy Practice.   Finally, reciprocal teaching helps students perform better on tests because they have learned to read texts critically. Reciprocal teaching provides students with experience in comprehension skills as they discuss the parts of the text they know about, make predictions about the text, and ask questions of the text. In other words, reciprocal teaching provides students with the skills to tackle reading passages in confidence and with effectiveness.

See chapter 9.

In sum, the use of a set of schoolwide literacy strategies can serve the dual functions of good teaching and effective preparation for standardized tests. The ways of thinking inherent in these comprehension strategies are necessary to perform well on the test. Further, when students have multiple opportunities to apply these strategies across the course of their academic day, they become a part of their learning repertoire. Once internalized, they are able to utilize these strategies in testing situations.

Area #3: Student Engagement in Reading

If students are to become better test takers, they must read more (Guthrie, Wigfield, Metsala, & Cox, 1999). Indeed, many tests exist to ensure students are developing literacy. Reading for knowledge, information and pleasure are the essential endeavors of successful and contributing members of a literate society. To ensure that students do become fluent readers, teachers must encourage reading in every subject matter and classroom, as well as outside the classroom.

Engaging students in reading and addressing the challenges of high-stakes standardized tests is, for the school, a team effort. Test format awareness and employment of literacy strategies are good first steps. But, the work does not stop here. The use and enjoyment of reading as part of a life-long learning does not stop at the classroom door.

Consider your reading habits. How much time do you spend reading for information? For enjoyment?

The successful dissemination and use of effective literacy strategies is an ongoing endeavor both for students and their teachers.

Student enjoyment of reading can be fostered through a Silent Sustained Reading program (Pilgreen, 2000). In such a program, the school sets apart a period of time each day devoted to reading. Everyone in the school from the principal to the ninth grade student is provided time to read from books or other texts of their own choosing. As students watch their teacher model reading, they learn directly of the activity's pleasure and importance. When students are allowed to choose their own reading, the inherent interest in the material itself fosters better reading habits and ability. With students spending more time reading, they become better readers and better readers become better test-takers.

Using Results

By examining the test results and reviewing the wide variety of demographic and other data that accompany the results, many conclusions can be drawn about the school's successes or failures. Data-based decisions will allow the school to directly confront the issues that matter (e.g., Chen, Salahuddin, Horsch, & Wagner, 2000). If low scores point to a weakness in specific content or a need for a change in instruction, steps can be taken to provide training in that area. If certain groups of students consistently score poorly, then steps can be taken to provide them with additional intervention and support. Without an awareness of what the tests indicate, the school will not likely address the needs of its faculty or students (Schmoker, 1996, 2001). For example, a group of faculty may meet to discuss test results. Their analysis may lead to an understanding that vocabulary was the most depressed area on the test. Upon further analysis, they may learn that multiple meaning words was the lowest score within the vocabulary domain. This finding could lead to changes in the curriculum across the school. The results from the next assessment could be used to determine if the curriculum change was effective.

The recursive process of collecting data by the teacher in order to improve instructional practice is referred to as "action research."

A criticism of standardized tests is that by the time the results are posted six months later, the students have advanced to the next grade level and are no longer on the administering teacher's roster. This is true and standardized tests are likely to be a poor source for obtaining meaningful information for designing next Monday's lesson. However, standardized test results can be viewed as a snapshot of the entire student body. A photograph of all the students in the school is unlikely to be useful in pinpointing the attributes of single student, but it can create a group portrait of the school at large. Similarly, close analysis of the results can illuminate areas of concern and strength.

This is often a subcommittee of the school's site governance team.

Of course having a forum for discussing such concerns can diffuse defensive responses while assisting schools in getting down to the business of curriculum improvement. One such structure is a Total Quality Review committee, based on the Total Quality Management work of Edward Deming (2001). A TQR committee usually serves in an advisory capacity to the school's governance and is charged with analyzing data and making recommendations based on these results. The committee is typically comprised of representatives of all stakeholders, including noninstructional staff, parents, students and community members, as well as teachers and administrators. By establishing such work groups, schools can make data-driven decisions without engaging in the "blame games" that sink many school reform efforts (Detert, Louis, & Schroeder, 2001).

See *Understanding by Design* by McTighe and Wiggins (2000) for more information on backward planning.

A coordinated series of discussions to align curriculum to tested standards might also take place. The goal of such curriculum discussions would be to better prepare students for high-stakes tests and to allow teachers a reflective process to discern success. Learning about the content of tests will help to ensure that it is covered in core subject matters. Reading across the curriculum is encouraged when test-relevant reading content is shared with teachers from different subjects. In such a process, effective strategies can be linked to important reading content, appropriate test format practice provided and essential test vocabulary disseminated. A Curriculum Discussions Cycle might take the following steps:

1. **Standards Review:** course content alignment to test.
2. **Curriculum Construction:** activities and tasks, scaffolding, materials and assessment events development, rubrics, integration of test questions, vocabulary and strategies suggestions.
3. **Curriculum Delivery:** timelines for delivery, dates for key pieces (trigger events), schedules for test practice, development of common deliveries and common student work submissions.
4. **Examination of Student Work and Test Scores:** reflective conversations regarding student work and tests results, group discussions of expected student performance, review of curriculum delivery.

Conclusion

In this chapter, we have learned of the importance of test format practice, especially for students who are not familiar with the standardized test genre. Achievement on these tests does not stop with test format practice. Test format practice must be integrated into effective literacy instruction. By implementing good literacy strategies, many test format suggestions are provided with a rational basis, relevant and meaningful practice is given to students, and relevant subject matter is explored using the techniques of life-long learners (e.g., Calkins, Montgomery, Santman, & Falk, 1998). Finally, this chapter concluded with ways in which the entire school could increase student engagement in reading. If students are to read more, the school must find innovative ways to present students with text. Providing important and relevant reading content might take place through a sustained silent reading program that allows student self-selections. Ongoing faculty dialogue around literacy and literacy strategies is essential if text is to be found important. Such faculty conversation can take many forms including staff development discussions, teacher literacy demonstrations, collegial coaching activities and curriculum discussion cycles.

References

Calkins, L., Montgomery, K., Santman, D., & Falk, B. (1998). *A teacher's guide to standardized reading tests: Knowledge is power.* Portsmouth, NH: Heinemann.

Chen, J., Salahuddin, R., Horsch, P., & Wagner, S. L. (2000). Turning standardized test scores into a tool for improving teaching and learning: An assessment-based approach. *Urban Education, 5,* 356–384.

Deming, W. E. (2001). *Out of the crisis.* Boston: MIT Press.

Detert, J. R., Louis, K. S., & Schroeder, R. G. (2001). A culture framework for education: Defining quality values and their impact in U.S. high schools. *School Effectiveness and School Improvement, 12,* 183–212.

Duke, N. K., & Ritchart, R. (1997). No pain, high gain standardized test preparation. *Instructor, 107*(3), 89–92, 119.

Feuer, M. J., Holland, P. W., Green, B. F., Bertenthal, M. W., & Hemphill, F. C. (1999). *Uncommon measures: Equivalence and language among educational tests.* Washington, DC: National Academy Press.

Fisher, D. (2001). "We're moving on up:" Creating a schoolwide literacy effort in an urban high school. *Journal of Adolescent & Adult Literacy, 45,* 92–101.

Goals 2000: Educate America Act. (1994). Washington DC: United States Congress Act.

Guthrie, J. T. (2002). Preparing students for high stakes test taking in reading. In A. E. Farstrup & S. J. Samuels (Eds.), *What research has to say about reading instruction* (pp. 370–391). Newark, DE: International Reading Association.

Guthrie, J. T., Wigfield, A., Metsala, J. L., & Cox, K. E. (1999). Motivational and cognitive predictors of text comprehension and reading amount. *Scientific Studies of Reading, 3,* 231–256.

Kohn, A. (2000). *The case against standardized testing: Raising the scores, ruining the schools.* Portsmouth, NH: Heinemann.

Langer, J. A. (2001). Beating the odds: Teaching middle and high school students to read and write well. *American Educational Research Journal, 38,* 837–880.

Lapp, D., Fisher, D., Flood, J., & Cabello, A. (2001). An integrated approach to the teaching and assessment of language arts. In S. R. Hurley & J. V. Tinajero (Eds.), *Literacy assessment of second language learners* (pp. 1-26). Boston: Allyn & Bacon.

McTighe, J., & Wiggins, G. P. (2000). *Understanding by design.* Upper Saddle River, NJ: Prentice Hall.

Meier, D., Kozol, J., & Cohen, J. (2000). *Can standards save public education?* Boston: Beacon.

No Child Left Behind Act of 2001. (2002). Washington DC: United States Congress Act.

Ohanian, S. (1999). *One size fits few: The folly of educational standards.* Portsmouth, NH: Heinemann.

Ogle, D. M. (1986). K-W-L: A teaching model that develops active reading of expository text. *The Reading Teacher, 39,* 564–570.

Pilgreen, J. (2000). *The SSR handbook: How to organize and manage a silent sustained reading program.* Portsmouth, NH: Boynton/Cook.

Popham, W. J. (2001) Teaching to the test? *Educational Leadership, 58*(6), 16–20.

Santman, D. (2002). Teaching to the test? Test preparation in the reading workshop. *Language Arts, 79,* 203–211.

Schmoker, M. (1996). *Results: The key to continuous school improvement.* Alexandria, VA: Association for Supervision and Curriculum Development.

Schmoker, M. (2001). *The results handbook: Practical strategies from dramatically improved schools.* Alexandria, VA: Association for Supervision and Curriculum Development.

Wong, H. K. (1992). *The first days of school.* Mountain View, CA: Harry K. Wong Publications.

Index